MENTAL STATE DEFENCES IN CRIMINAL LAW

For Lily, Dorothea, and Antigone

ουνεχ' υπ' αζαλεου θερεος μεγα κεκμηωτα
παυσαν, ορεξασαι χερσι μελιχρον υδωρ.
ΑΝΥΤΗΣ

Because when he was exhausted by the summer heat, they
refreshed him, holding out sweet water in their hands.
Anyte,
Greek Anthology XVI.291

Mental State Defences in Criminal Law

STEVEN YANNOULIDIS
Monash University, Australia

Routledge
Taylor & Francis Group
LONDON AND NEW YORK

First published 2012 by Ashgate Publishing

Published 2016 by Routledge
2 Park Square, Milton Park, Abingdon, Oxfordshire OX14 4RN
711 Third Avenue, New York, NY 10017, USA

First issued in paperback 2016

Routledge is an imprint of the Taylor & Francis Group, an informa business

British Library Cataloguing in Publication Data
Yannoulidis, Steven.
Mental state defences in criminal law.
1. Insanity defense. 2. Criminal liability. 3. Criminal law--Interpretation and construction. 4. Offenders with mental disabilities--Legal status, laws, etc. 5. Drug abusers--Legal status, laws, etc.
I. Title
345'.04-dc23

Library of Congress Cataloging-in-Publication Data
Yannoulidis, Steven.
Mental state defences in criminal law / by Steven Yannoulidis.
p. cm.
Includes bibliographical references and index.
ISBN 978-1-4094-4645-3 (hardback)
1. Insanity defense--Australia. I. Title.

KU3884.Y36 2012
345.94'04--dc23

2012021242

ISBN 13: 978-1-138-27179-1 (pbk)
ISBN 13: 978-1-4094-4645-3 (hbk)

Contents

List of Figures and Tables

Acknowledgments

Some of the material in this book has appeared in articles in academic journals. These include: 'Causation in the Law of Negligence' (2001) 27 *Monash University Law Review* 319; 'Negotiating "Dangerousness": Charting a Course between Psychiatry and Law' (2002) 9 *Psychiatry, Psychology and Law* 151; 'Mental Illness, Rationality and Criminal Responsibility (Tropes of Insanity and Related Defences)' (2003) 25 *Sydney Law Review* 189; 'Excusing Fleeting Mental States: Provocation, Involuntariness and Normative Practice' (2005) 12 *Psychiatry, Psychology and Law* 23; 'Drug Use and the Defence of Mental Impairment: Some Conceptual and Explanatory Issues' (2006) 18 *Bond Law Review* 165; (with A. Carroll, B. McSherry and D. Wood) 'Drug-Associated Psychoses and Criminal Responsibility' (2008) 26 *Behavioural Sciences and the Law* 633.

I am grateful to Dale Smith for his clarity of mind, to Bernadette McSherry for her work over the years, to which this book is a response, and to all those students whose intellectual curiosity has increased my own.

Table of Cases

Table of Legislation

Australia

Commonwealth of Australia

Australian Capital Territory

Queensland

South Australia

Tasmania

Western Australia

Ireland

New Zealand

South Africa

United Kingdom

Chapter 1
Introduction: General Themes, Reform, Chapter Outlines

General themes

This book is concerned with the operation of the common-law defence of insanity and the related doctrine of automatism. In particular the book will focus on providing a consistent and principled approach to the reform of the insanity defence and the doctrine of automatism. In order to achieve this, the book will explore the appropriate boundaries of each of these in turn.

The defence of insanity and the doctrine of automatism each raise concerns reflecting their individual spheres of operation and development. The first part of this Introduction will outline several of the concerns relating to the defence of insanity and automatism individually. The second part of the Introduction will then indicate the broad issues to be considered, as well as the competing demands which must be balanced, by any reform proposal. The final part of the Introduction will provide an outline of the scope of each chapter in respect to both the general themes addressed and the options for reform discussed.

It will be argued that by including a volitional limb in the common-law defence of insanity, by using a refined notion of meta-responsibility in relation to drug-associated psychosis, and by introducing a new defence of impaired consciousness, a more consistent and principled approach to mental state defences may be achieved.

Insanity

Chapter 2 outlines the elements of the common-law defence of insanity which arose from the rules established in M'Naghten's case in 1843.[1] In brief, for an accused to be afforded a defence, he or she must have experienced a 'defect of reason' arising from a 'disease of the mind' which affected his or her ability to know the nature and quality of the criminal act or that it was wrong. Some Australian jurisdictions now also include an added component of the effect of a disease of the mind on the ability or capacity to control the accused's conduct.

The expressions 'disease of the mind', 'mental disease' or some other statutory variant are used to describe those internal conditions recognized by the law which, when resulting in a relevant incapacity, will give rise to the defence of insanity.

1 *R v M'Naghten* (1843) 10 Cl and Fin 200, 210.

Hence, a preliminary question which arises in the context of the defence of insanity concerns clarifying which states of mental malfunctioning will constitute a disease of the mind. One aspect of this question involves determining the degree to which a disease of the mind should reflect the medical notion of mental disorder. As will be outlined in Chapter 3, two approaches have been adopted in respect of this issue. Some jurisdictions have interpreted the expression consistently with clinical conceptions of mental disorder, thereby giving prominence to expert psychiatric evidence. Other jurisdictions however have chosen to incorporate judicial pronouncements into their definition, thereby asserting the normative and policy-driven nature of the enquiry.

A second question which arises in the context of the insanity defence concerns determining what types of incapacity should be allowed to ground the defence. On current formulations of the defence at common law a disease of the mind must give rise to a 'defect of reason' in order for the defence to be established. Such a 'defect of reason' is conventionally understood as a defect in an individual's capacity for rational thought. As a result of such an interpretation, volitional defects which are not symptomatic of a state of cognitive defect will not be recognized as sufficiently incapacitating for the purposes of the defence. As will be discussed in Chapter 2, the 'cognitive bias' on the part of the common law has come to be viewed as overly restrictive in failing to take into account a variety of mental disorders. Chapter 5 will argue in support of the inclusion of an independent volitional limb to operate alongside the M'Naghten rules. Such a defence of 'volitional insanity' will operate to exempt an individual from criminal responsibility where he or she cannot control his or her conduct, even where he or she knows the nature, quality and wrongness of his or her conduct.

Automatism

As will be discussed in Chapter 2, the doctrine of automatism has come to be understood as involving those mental conditions that cause an individual to act in an involuntary fashion. A distinction is drawn between those states which go to the question of an accused's involuntariness ('sane' automatism) and those states of involuntariness which are due to the effects of a disease of the mind ('insane' automatism). While sane automatism will result in an outright acquittal, insane automatism will generally result in the accused being detained in a secure hospital and subjected to a therapeutic regime.

Given the different outcomes there is a strong incentive for an accused to raise evidence of sane automatism. However, in the absence of a reliable means of identifying the precise cause of an accused's state of mental malfunction, a principal concern with states of automatism is their susceptibility to abuse. Such a concern is particularly acute in the context of 'psychological-blow' automatism involving severe psychological trauma leading to a dissociative state.

One particular feature of cases where psychological-blow automatism has been pleaded is that the conduct in such cases has been characterized by motivated, goal-directed behaviour. Expert evidence is divided in respect of whether or not such behaviour may be characterized as involuntary. Consequently, in such cases there is a concern that there will be a failure to convict where appropriate and not acquit where such acquittals are warranted. In order to foreclose such an outcome, Chapter 6 will argue for the introduction of a new defence of 'impaired consciousness'. The new defence of impaired consciousness will require individuals who claim to have experienced a state of dissociation arising from a psychological blow to satisfy certain normative conditions before they are excused.

Options for reform

In considering reform proposals in respect of the defence of insanity and the doctrine of automatism, several competing factors must be taken into account. One such factor involves ensuring that the scope of the defence of insanity and automatism is not drawn too broadly so as to exempt from responsibility those individuals who, while rational, choose to engage in criminal conduct. As such individuals are able to distinguish between right and wrong and able to control their conduct, they are fit subjects of the criminal law. Chapter 4 will consider the operation of this expectation in the context of drug use and the defence of insanity.

Another factor to be considered in any reform proposal is ensuring that those conditions which are recognized as exempting an individual from responsibility are not overly restrictive in their range. As will be outlined, not all instances of psychiatrically recognized states of mental disorder have been acknowledged as instances of diseases of the mind. However, where a recognized state of mental disorder precludes an individual from acting in either a rational or voluntary manner, such a state should, subject to various other aspects of the disease of the mind enquiry being satisfied, be allowed to ground an insanity defence. Chapter 5 will consider the introduction of a volitional limb to the current common law formulation of the insanity defence.

Another competing consideration which options for reform must balance is the requirement that there exist a consistent set of rules which will allow triers of fact to determine the appropriate verdict for an individual. Chapter 6 will formulate a new substantive partial defence of impaired consciousness in order to ensure that such a set of rules may be applied in instances of sane automatism.

This book is thus concerned with developing a principled approach to the boundaries of the defence of insanity and the doctrine of automatism.

Chapter outlines

This section will provide an outline of the scope of the chapters in this book outlining both the general themes which each chapter addresses and the options for reform discussed.

Chapter 2 provides an overview of both the defence of insanity and the doctrine of automatism while highlighting certain points of tension to be resolved in the following chapters. In particular, Chapter 2 considers the question of how to assess the criminal responsibility of those individuals who raise the defence of insanity or who have claimed to have acted in an involuntary fashion. Further, the chapter highlights a perceived lacuna in the common-law formulation of the insanity defence and calls for the recognition of instances of volitional impairment independent of cognitive defect as sufficient to ground the defence.

Chapter 2 will outline the substantive criminal law in relation to both the defence of insanity and the doctrine of automatism. The discussion of the defence of insanity focuses on the elements of the common-law formulation as found in the M'Naghten rules. The major portion of this discussion focuses on clarifying the 'object' and 'nature' of the knowledge which an accused must lack if he or she is to raise the second limb of the defence: whether the accused knew that what he or she was doing was wrong. After noting these aspects of the defence, the defence's 'knowledge' requirement is then applied to a paradigmatic case of severe mental disorder. This case study will provide a means of examining both the operation of the defence across several jurisdictions as well as revealing the various ways in which an accused may fail to think rationally. The chapter will finish with a comment on the cognitive bias of the M'Naghten rules when compared with the treatment of volitional defects across the various Australian jurisdictions.

The second substantive matter to be discussed in Chapter 2 will concern the doctrine of automatism. A distinction will be drawn between those states of automatism going to involuntariness (sane automatism) and those states subsumed under the defence of mental impairment (insane automatism). The chapter will remark on the difficulties attendant upon distinguishing sane from insane automatism with particular reference to instances of psychological-blow automatism. It will be suggested that such a difficulty has the potential to lead to inconsistent outcomes as a result of ad hoc decision-making by triers of fact. It will be argued that it is the failure at common law, but not under the code jurisdictions of Queensland and Western Australia which are based on the Griffith Code, of automatism claims to be conceived in terms of a structured normative framework akin to criminal-law excuses which is why such ad hoc decision-making occurs. This in turn may result in instances of injustice.

Chapter 3 will analyse the meaning of the legal expression 'disease of the mind' as found in the M'Naghten rules and variant statutory formulations. It will be argued that 'disease of the mind' is a general term under which the courts and legislatures balance three distinct factors: a judgment of responsibility, clinical evidence and community interest. The judgment of responsibility will be seen to articulate the moral intuition that an accused whose mental condition precludes him or her from not choosing to engage in criminally proscribed conduct or to exercise his or her ability to control such conduct should not be held criminally liable. It will be set out how clinical evidence enables a diagnosis of an accused's condition to be made in respect of his or her current condition and future therapeutic prospects. The community-interest aspect of the disease of the mind enquiry will be shown as concerned with the issue of societal protection in the light of the likelihood that a mentally impaired individual's state of mental impairment may recur. The chapter will note that these three factors present differing issues and demands which may give rise to various tensions. One such tension which will be discussed arises in the context of ensuring individual justice in the light of the judgment of responsibility, while maintaining societal protection in keeping with the imperative of community interest. It will be argued that the law manages to reconcile this tension by acknowledging the conceptually distinct nature of each of these respective concerns.

Chapter 4 will focus on those individuals who bring about a state of mental impairment through voluntary drug use. The treatment of this subject will seek to incorporate the analysis of disease of the mind undertaken in Chapter 3 in order to establish a principled response to this issue.

The issue which this chapter will seek to address is whether a state of 'drug-induced psychosis' arising from voluntary drug use should be recognized as a disease of the mind. It will be noted that there are three explanatory/heuristic approaches recognized in dealing with the issue of drug-induced psychosis: causal irrelevance, settled insanity and meta-responsibility. Causal irrelevance is an approach which has been advocated by the Victorian Law Reform Commission (VLRC), and it amounts to the view that the causal antecedents of an accused's state of incapacity are irrelevant in determining whether he or she should be found non-responsible. As will be noted, settled insanity is an approach favoured by American courts. This approach relies on the general 'scientific principle' that a fixed stable state of insanity after drug use or evidence of a predisposition to psychosis prior to drug use will be sufficient to establish that an accused has experienced a state of settled insanity independent of drug use. The third approach which will be analysed is that of meta-responsibility. This approach examines the issue of drug-induced psychosis from the perspective of an accused's prior fault in consuming drugs.

Chapter 4 supports the notion that an accused should be held responsible for his or her prior conduct in bringing about a state of non-responsibility. After noting several concerns with the formulation put forward by certain advocates of meta-responsibility, the chapter will turn to consider several cases arising at common law. As a result of this examination of common-law cases and in light of the weakness inherent in the alternative views, the chapter will formulate a principled response to the question of when an accused individual should be held responsible for having voluntarily consumed drugs which have resulted in a state of non-responsibility.

The principal theme of Chapter 5 will be which types of mental disorder should be recognized as giving rise to the insanity defence. This will require discussing the current cognitive bias of the M'Naghten rules, in addition to considering the various aspects which inform the disease of the mind enquiry.

While code jurisdictions have been prepared to recognize an independent volitional limb, the common law has either refused to characterize volitional impairment as a disease of the mind or refused to acknowledge states of volitional impairment as sufficiently incapacitating for the purpose of the defence of insanity. This chapter will argue for the recognition of an independent volitional limb to be recognized at common law and operate alongside the M'Naghten rules. The chapter will begin by noting that an involuntary act caused by a disease of the mind will not lead to an acquittal but to the 'special verdict'. While such an outcome is the result of the law's concern with societal protection, it will be shown to run counter to criminal-law principles. Further, in order to establish the special verdict, an accused must satisfy the traditional cognitive requirements of the M'Naghten rules. Where an accused fails to satisfy the M'Naghten rules' cognitive bias, he or she will be criminally sanctioned. However, as will be argued, if there are instances where an accused's cognitive (in)capacity does not track his or her volitional (in)capacity, there is a danger that an individual who cannot control his or her conduct will not be able to raise the defence.

However, as the chapter will argue, there are psychiatrically recognized diagnostic categories which are characterized by an individual's inability to control his or her conduct without any cognitive impairment. The chapter will use, by way of example, one such category, namely, pyromania. The diagnostic characteristics of pyromania indicate that an individual may engage in repeated acts of fire-setting without motivation and without loss to his or her cognitive functioning. It will be argued that the best explanation of such a lack of motivation is a state of involuntariness arising from mental disorder.

In order to ensure that individuals suffering from pyromania, who may reveal no cognitive defect, are provided with a defence, it will be suggested that it is incumbent on the criminal law to expand the insanity defence so as to accommodate an independent volitional limb. Alternatively, if it is found that there are no extant instances of pyromania, the provision of such a limb will merely prove redundant. For this reason it will be argued that the common law should play it safe and recognize states of volitional insanity.

Chapter 6 will be concerned with developing a set of rules with which the criminal responsibility of an accused who claims to have acted in a state of sane automatism may be determined. The reform options which motivate this discussion include ensuring certainty in the law by providing a consistent set of rules so as to ensure that people who can control conduct do not raise bogus claims of involuntariness.

Chapter 6 will pick up the concerns expressed in Chapter 2 in respect of distinguishing those states of automatism resulting from physical or psychological trauma and those states of involuntariness indicative of insanity. By advocating for the recognition of a state of volitional insanity, Chapter 5 seeks to accommodate those latter instances of involuntariness arising from a disease of the mind. However, this does not address any of the concerns related to those states of involuntariness which are not the product of a disease of the mind but arise as a result of a state of impaired consciousness. Chapter 6 will formulate a defence of 'impaired consciousness' in order to accommodate those instances of volitional impairment arising from a state of impaired consciousness falling short of insanity.

The chapter will begin by recognizing that not all instances of volitional impairment necessarily amount to states of involuntariness. However, as will be argued, even though such states do not amount to a denial of the physical element of the offence, they are not subject to a necessary condition that is commonly imposed on excusatory defences, namely, the requirement that an accused's impairment satisfy the normative standard of the ordinary person. In order to ensure that not all claims of volitional impairment will amount to a denial of responsibility, it is proposed that the new partial defence of impaired consciousness will require an accused to meet a normative standard. The proposed defence will be framed in terms of a comparison between the degree of difficulty an accused experienced in controlling his or her conduct and that which would be experienced by an ordinary person in similar circumstances. Additionally, the degree of (dis)similarity between the partial defence of diminished responsibility operative in several jurisdictions and the proposed new partial defence of impaired consciousness will be remarked on in this chapter.

Chapter 7, as the concluding chapter of the book, will seek to tie together the themes of the book and suggest avenues for future research. In particular, the conclusion will indicate how by focusing on some of the doctrinal, evidentiary, and substantive problems which the reform proposals raise further research might take the work forward.

Chapter 2
Mental-State Defences: Insanity and Automatism

This chapter will set out the substantive criminal law in relation to the mental-state defence of insanity and the doctrine of automatism. The first part of the chapter will consider the role played by 'knowledge' in both the common-law and statutory formulations of the defence of insanity. The latter part of the chapter will consider the role played by 'volition' in the context of automatism, both as it relates to the criminal law's voluntariness requirement and when it is subsumed under the insanity defence.

The defence of insanity

The M'Naghten rules

The common-law defence of insanity is governed by the so-called M'Naghten rules.[1] The M'Naghten rules form the basis for common-law and most statutory formulations of the insanity defence in Australia.[2] The M'Naghten rules arose in the context of judicial comment following the acquittal, on the grounds of insanity, of Daniel M'Naghten. M'Naghten had been charged with the murder of Prime Minister Peel's secretary Edward Drummond, whom he had mistaken for the prime minister. M'Naghten was under the insane delusion that the Tory party was persecuting him and that he was in danger of being killed. In the light of the public outcry at the acquittal, the matter was debated in the House of Lords. In an attempt to elucidate the scope of the insanity defence the House in its legislative capacity subsequently put to the Law Lords certain questions. One particular question put to the Law Lords was the following: 'In what terms ought the question be left to the jury as to the prisoner's state of mind at the time when the act was committed?' The answer provided by the judges to this

1 *R v M'Naghten* (1843) 10 Cl and Fin 200; 8 ER 718.

2 Every Australian jurisdiction except for New South Wales provides for a statutory formulation of the defence: *Criminal Code* (Cth), s 7.3(1); *Criminal Code* (ACT), s 28; *Criminal Code* (NT), s 43C; *Criminal Code* (Qld), s 27; *Criminal Code* (Tas), s 16; *Criminal Code* (WA), s 27. While terminology differs from jurisdiction to jurisdiction the common-law term 'insanity' will be used as a general term to encompass these differences.

particular question forms the basis of the defence of insanity in the common law world. In particular, the answer provided to this question stipulates that a person is not responsible for his or her crimes on the grounds of insanity if it is

> clearly proved that, at the time of the committing of the act, the party accused was labouring under such a defect of reason, from disease of the mind, as not to know the nature and quality of the act he [or she] was doing; or, if he [or she] did know it, that he [or she] did not know what he [or she] was doing was wrong.[3]

An example of a modern statutory formulation of the insanity defence is that provided for by the Victorian legislation:

> 20. Defence of Mental Impairment
>
> (1) The defence of mental impairment is established for a person charged with an offence if, at the time of engaging in conduct constituting the offence, the person was suffering from a mental impairment that had the effect that –
>
> (a) he or she did not know the nature and quality of the conduct; or
>
> (b) he or she did not know that the conduct was wrong (that is, he or she could not reason with a moderate degree of sense and composure about whether the conduct, as perceived by reasonable people was wrong).
>
> (2) If the defence of mental impairment is established the person must be found not guilty because of mental impairment.[4]

As stated, the M'Naghten rules and the Victorian statutory formulation of this provide for two possible lines of defence. Where it is shown that there was a condition considered to be a disease of the mind, or mental impairment, it is then necessary to show that it had one of two incapacitating effects. An accused may be held non-responsible where, because of a disease of the mind, he or she did not know the nature and quality of the act, or, if he or she did know the nature and quality of the act, he or she did not know it was 'wrong'. Under either limb it has to be shown that the failure of knowledge arose from a defect of reason

---

3 *R v M'Naghten* (1843) 10 Cl and Fin 200, 210 per Tindal CJ.

4 *Crimes (Mental Impairment and Unfitness to be Tried) Act 1997* s 20. The Victorian statute has been held to be declarative of the common law (see *R v Sebalj* [2003] VSC 181 (Unreported, SC Vic, Smith J, 5 June 2003)).

ensuing from a disease of the mind. Each of these matters will be considered below.[5]

Disease of the mind

According to the M'Naghten rules, it must be established that the defect of reason is caused by a disease of the mind. The mere fact that an accused suffers from a defect of reason in the relevant sense will not be sufficient for a finding that the person was not criminally responsible. A causal link between this and an underlying disease must also be established. The meaning of the term 'disease of the mind' is a legal rather than a psychiatric question.[6] Whether a particular type of condition is to be characterized as a disease of the mind is a question of law. That is, the judge will direct the jury as to the meaning of 'disease of the mind'. For example, a judge will rule on whether drug-induced psychosis is a disease of the mind for the purposes of the defence.[7] The jury will decide the question of whether or not the accused was insane at the time of committing the criminal act. That is, the jury will determine on the basis of the evidence led whether the defendant was suffering from a disease of the mind, at the time of the offence, which resulted in the requisite incapacities. For example, the jury will decide whether the defendant's behaviour is consistent with the condition known as schizophrenia, where such a condition satisfies the disease of the mind enquiry.

The requirement that a disease of the mind cause the defect of reason links the defect to an internal cause, an 'underlying pathological infirmity of the mind … which can properly be termed mental illness, as distinct from the reaction of a healthy mind to extraordinary stimuli'.[8] Consequently those 'conditions of intense passion and other transient states attributable to the fault or to the nature of man' will be excluded from the concept.[9] For example, the defence will not be satisfied where the accused's mental faculties have been impaired by an 'external' factor such as voluntary drug use. What is required is an internal infirmity or illness which affects an individual's rational thought processes. There need be no actual

5 The subject of fitness to stand trial is for present purposes treated as beyond the scope of this book and so will not be commented on in the ensuing discussion. For a comprehensive discussion across several jurisdictions of both the legal and clinical issues in respect of the procedural formalities of adjudicative competence, see W. Brookbanks and J. Skipworth, 'Fitness to Plead' in *Psychiatry and the Law: Clinical and Legal Issues*, ed. W. Brookbanks and S. Simpson (Wellington, 2007) 157.

6 *R v Radford* (1985) 42 SASR 266 per King CJ, approved *R v Falconer* (1990) 171 CLR 30.

7 *R v Sebalj* [2003] VSC 181 (Unreported, Supreme Court of Victoria, Smith J, 5 June 2003).

8 *R v Radford* (1985) 42 SASR 266, 274 per King CJ, approved *R v Falconer* (1990) 171 CLR 30, 53–4, 78, 85.

9 O. Dixon, 'A Legacy of Hadfield, McNaghten and Maclean' (1957) 31 *Australian Law Journal* 255, 260.

disease in the sense of an organic disintegration of brain structure. 'Mind' is distinct from 'brain' and refers to the faculties of reason, memory and understanding.[10] Ultimately, 'the condition of the brain is irrelevant as is the question of whether the condition of the mind is curable or incurable, transitory or permanent'.[11] It will be sufficient to satisfy the requirement that the 'functions of the understanding are through some cause, whether understandable or not, thrown into derangement or disorder'.[12] Stanley Yeo has remarked that the literal meaning of the word 'disease' does not cover those cases of mental deficiency which arise from a state of either arrested or incomplete mental development.[13] As a result courts have broadly interpreted 'disease of the mind' so as to incorporate all cases resulting in cognitive deficiency satisfying the requirements of the M'Naghten rules whether due to disease or some other aetiology.[14]

Not all conditions which are clinically recognized as mental disorders will be covered by the expression 'disease of the mind'. This will be regardless of whether or not such disorders have an organic basis.[15] Even, purely physical diseases of only peripheral psychiatric interest, such as arteriosclerosis, epilepsy and diabetes, may satisfy the requirements of the term.[16] The defence of insanity is not concerned with the classification of psychiatric dysfunction but with whether the legal question has been answered, namely, whether such a dysfunction is to be characterized as a disease of the mind. For example, in terms of psychiatric nosology, the symptoms of drug-induced psychosis constitute psychiatric dysfunction. However, such symptoms are not viewed as a disease of the mind for the purposes of the criminal law.[17] Consequently, dysfunction arising from the voluntary use of drugs will not give rise to the operation of the defence of insanity. The issue of drug-induced psychosis and the defence of insanity will be discussed in more detail in Chapter 4.

Legislative formulations of the insanity defence may be distinguished as following one of two approaches in their treatment of the notion of disease of the mind: either by defining 'disease of the mind' according to a list of conditions or by employing terms which are broadly expressed.[18] Where a list of conditions is

---

10 *R v Sullivan* [1984] 1 AC 156, 172 approved *R v Falconer* (1990) 171 CLR 30, 50.

11 *R v Kemp* [1957] 1 QB 399, 407.

12 *R v Porter* (1933) 55 CLR 182, 189.

13 S. Yeo, 'The Insanity Defence in the Criminal Laws of the Commonwealth of Nations' [2008] *Singapore Journal of Legal Studies*, 241, 245.

14 Ibid.

15 Dixon, 'A Legacy of Hadfield, McNaghten and Maclean' (n. 9) 260.

16 While highly contentious such conditions find support in the following cases: *R v Kemp* [1957] QB 399, arteriosclerosis; *Bratty v A-G (Northern Ireland)* [1963] AC 386, epilepsy; *R v Quick* [1973] QB 910, diabetes.

17 *R v Sebalj* [2003] VSC 181 (Unreported, Supreme Court of Victoria, Smith J, 5 June 2003).

18 For a comprehensive account of the various Australian jurisdictions, see S. Bronitt and B. McSherry, *Principles of Criminal Law* (3rd edn, Pyrmont, NSW, 2010) 240–1,

provided, it will usually include 'senility, intellectual disability, mental illness, brain damage and severe personality disorder'.[19] The common-law concept of disease of the mind is incorporated into these formulations by their defining of the expression 'mental illness' so as to excuse only those mental states arising from some internal rather than external cause. For example, the West Australian provision defines 'mental illness' as follows: 'Mental Illness means an underlying pathological infirmity of the mind, whether of short or long duration and whether permanent or temporary, but does not include a condition that results from the reaction of a healthy mind to extraordinary stimuli'.[20] Examples of 'extraordinary stimuli' in the definition above would include instances of trauma or substance abuse.

In contrast to the provision of a list of conditions, other jurisdictions use broadly expressed terms to clarify the common-law concept of disease of the mind which they do not further define.[21] For example, the Victorian statute employs the expression 'mental impairment' which is left undefined.[22] Stanley Yeo has suggested that these expressions have been left intentionally undefined in order to allow courts to interpret and apply them to the particular case in issue.[23]

Chapter 3 will discuss in more detail the relevant factors to be considered in determining whether a particular condition satisfies the disease of the mind enquiry.

Defect of reason

As noted above, the M'Naghten rules will be satisfied where a disease of the mind causes a defect of reason. According to the M'Naghten rules, a defect of reason may result in an accused either not knowing the nature and quality of his or her

---

'Table 1: Elements of the Defence of Mental Impairment'.

19 See *Criminal Code* (Cth) s 7.3(8),(9); *Criminal Code* (ACT) s 27(1),(2); *Criminal Code* (WA) s 1(1)(2), not including 'severe personality disorder'; *Criminal Code* (NT) s 43A, not including 'severe personality disorder'; *Criminal Law Consolidation Act 1935* (SA) s 269A, 269C, not including 'brain damage' or 'severe personality disorder'.

20 *Criminal Code* (WA) s 8, interpreting the term 'mental illness' appearing in s 27 the insanity provision as amended following *R v Falconer* (1990) 171 CLR 30; cp. *Criminal Code* (Cth) s 7.3(9).

21 *Criminal Code* (Qld) s 27, 'state of mental disease or natural mental infirmity'; *Criminal Code* (Tas) s 16, 'mental disease' defined narrowly as 'natural mental imbecility'; *Crimes (Mental Impairment and Unfitness to be Tried) Act 1997* (Vic) s 20, 'mental impairment'.

22 *Crimes (Mental Impairment and Unfitness to be Tried) Act 1997* (Vic) s 20, the defence of mental impairment has been held to be unavailable in the absence of a 'disease of the mind': *R v Sebalj* [2003] VSC 181 per Smth J (SC), referred to in *R v Sebalj* [2004] VSC 212; see *R v R* [2003] VSC 187 per Teague J; *R v Martin* [2005] VSC 497 per Bongiorno J.

23 Yeo, 'The Insanity Defence in the Criminal Laws of the Commonwealth of Nations' (n. 13) 246.

act or not knowing that it is wrong. As commonly understood, the requirement of a defect of reason in the M'Naghten rules has been viewed as delimiting the scope of the defence within very narrow constraints.[24] In particular, 'defect of reason' has been held to refer only to the purely cognitive aspects of an accused's behaviour.[25] It is a defect in the capacity for rational thought which is the primary focus of the expression. As a result of this interpretation, significant emotional or volitional deficiencies will not, in themselves, constitute a defect of reason.[26] However, as will be discussed later, such deficiencies may be the product of a relevant cognitive incapacity which will ground the defence. Consequently, on a strict application of the M'Naghten rules for the purposes of the insanity defence only states of cognitive disorder will be viewed as determinative.

This book will seek to determine whether those states of mental malfunctioning captured by the expression 'defect of reason' are too narrow to delineate adequately the range of incapacitating states of mental malfunction attendant upon a state of insanity. Consequently, a question this book will set out to answer is whether or not there are other effects besides cognitive incapacity arising from a disease of the mind to which the law should have regard. In particular, this book examines whether an accused's inability to control his or her conduct arising from a state of mental disorder characterized as a disease of the mind should be recognized as sufficient to give rise to the insanity defence. This question will be considered in Chapter 5.

Nature and quality

An accused may be held non-responsible where, because of a disease of the mind, he or she is precluded from knowing the 'nature and quality' of his or her act.

The Court of Appeal in *R v Codere*[27] held that the 'nature and quality' phrase denoted the 'physical character' of an action as distinct from its moral aspects. A failure to know the physical character of an act has been held to mean that the defendant did 'not know what he [or she] is doing'.[28] Similarly, the High Court of Australia has held that the phrase 'nature and quality' means 'the capacity to comprehend the significance of the act of killing and of the acts by means of which it was done'.[29] Paradigmatic cases include the husband who in the belief that he is

24 H. Fingarette, *The Meaning of Criminal Insanity* (Berkeley, 1972) 144; F. McAuley, *Insanity, Psychiatry and Criminal Responsibility* (Dublin, 1993) 23.

25 *R v Porter* (1933) 55 CLR 182; *R v S* [1979] 2 NSWLR 1, 42.

26 *Sodeman v R* (1936) 55 CLR 192, 214–5 per Dixon J, affirmed *Brown v A-G for South Australia* [1959] ALR 808, 814.

27 (1916) 12 Cr App R 21.

28 *Weeks* (1993) 66 A Crim R 466, 482 per Nash J, citing *Codere* (1916) 12 Cr App R 21; *Willgloss* (1960) 105 CLR 295, 300.

29 *Sodeman v R* (1936) 55 CLR 192, 215 per Dixon J.

squeezing a lemon in fact strangles his wife.[30] Equally, a lack of knowledge may result in an individual believing that he or she is cutting a loaf of bread when in fact he or she is cutting another person's arm.[31] Such a defendant fails to understand the 'nature and quality of his [or her] act' in the sense that he or she does not know what he or she is doing.

However, the expression 'nature and quality' signifies something more than merely the surface features of the accused's conduct. As expressed by the Canadian Supreme Court, 'an accused may be aware of the physical character of his action (i.e. choking) without necessarily having the capacity to appreciate that, in nature and quality, the act will result in the death of a human being'.[32] The expression 'appreciate' in place of 'know' has been interpreted as implying that a 'deeper level of cognition' on the part of an accused is required.[33] Such a 'deeper level of cognition' has been understood as including not only knowledge of the surface features of the act but also the consequences of such an act.

Instances may be imagined where the accused may know the surface features of his or her act, yet, as a result of a state of mental disorder, not know the consequences of the act. For example, an individual may be aware that he or she is choking another person without realizing that in so doing, he or she will bring about the death of a human being.[34] *In R v Porter*,[35] the common-law requirement of an accused's lack of knowledge of the nature and quality of an act has been interpreted as consisting of both a lack of knowledge of the surface features of the act and its harmful consequences. In that case the High Court held that an accused is entitled to the defence of insanity where his or her mental disorder 'was such as that he could not appreciate the physical thing he was doing *and* its consequences'.[36]

Situations where an accused's mind is so disturbed that he or she does not know the nature and quality of the act are rarely encountered in practice. As will be discussed in more detail in Chapter 3 when clinical accounts of mental disorder are considered, severe cases of mental disorder rarely preclude an individual from appreciating the character of his or her conduct. The problem in most cases of severe mental illness will not involve an individual's lack of knowledge of the nature and quality of his or her act but rather the way in which such knowledge is

---

30 See *R v Porter* (1933) 55 CLR 182, 188 per Dixon J, for other instances.

31 *R v Codere* (1916) 12 Cr App R 21; *R v Landry* (1991) 62 CCC (3d) 117.

32 *R v Cooper* (1979) 51 CCC (2d) 129, 147 per Dickson J.

33 Yeo, 'The Insanity Defence in the Criminal Laws of the Commonwealth of Nations' (n. 13) 250, arguing that terms such as 'appreciates' and 'understands' should be used in formulations of the defence of insanity in place of 'knows' when describing the accused's perception of the nature and quality of his or her act in order to better convey the notion of a 'deeper level of cognition'.

34 *R v Cooper* (1979) 51 CCC (2d) 129, 147 per Dickson J.

35 (1933) 55 CLR 182.

36 Ibid. 189 per Dixon J (emphasis added).

processed.[37] Hence, in most instances it will not be an accused's lack of knowledge of the nature and quality of his or her act that will ground a defence of insanity. Rather, it will be the way in which he or she processes such knowledge which will give rise to the defence. The central issue is generally whether in the context of his or her delusional thinking he or she knows that the paradigmatic act of killing another person is wrong. Consequently, that aspect of the rules concerned with an accused's knowledge of the nature and quality of the act will not be commented on further in the course of the present work. Rather, this book will focus on that limb of the rules in respect of a defendant's knowledge of the wrongness of his or her act.

A number of distinctions may be drawn in respect of an accused's knowledge of the wrongness of his or her act. In particular, a distinction may be drawn between, on the one hand, that which may be known, the 'object' of knowledge, and, on the other, the cognitive processes constitutive of an agent knowing, the 'nature' of such knowledge. The following two sections will consider the object and nature of an accused's knowledge of the wrongness of his or her act respectively.

The object of knowledge: moral or legal?

At common law, an accused must lack knowledge of the wrongness of his or her particular act for the defence of insanity to be established. The courts have differed in England and Australia as to whether or not the object of the accused's knowledge means legally or morally wrong. In *R v M'Naghten*,[38] Lord Tindal CJ stated:

> If the accused was conscious that the act was one which he ought not to do, and if that act was at the same time contrary to the law of the land, he is punishable; and the usual course therefore has been to leave the question to the jury, whether the party accused has a sufficient degree of reason to know that he was doing an act that was wrong.[39]

In *R v Codere*,[40] Lord Reading CJ for the Court of Criminal Appeal sought to clarify the ambiguity of the above formulation by holding that:

> Once it is clear that the appellant knew that the act was wrong in law, then he was doing an act which he was conscious he ought not to do, and as it was against the law, it was punishable by law; ... The difficulty no doubt arises over the words 'conscious that the act was one which he ought not to do', but, looking

37 See B. Hannan, 'Depression, Responsibility and Criminal Defences' (2005) 28 *International Journal of Law and Psychiatry* 321.

38 (1843) 10 Cl and Fin 200; 8 ER 718.

39 Ibid. 722.

40 (1916) 12 Cr App R 21.

> at all the answers in *M'Naghten*'s case, it seems that if it is punishable by law it is an act which he ought not to do, and that is the meaning in which the phrase is used in that case.[41]

Subsequently in *R v Windle*,[42] Lord Goddard CJ for the English Court of Appeal held that in respect of the law in England 'wrong' meant 'contrary to law':

> Courts of law can only distinguish between that which is in accordance with law and that which is contrary to law. … The law cannot embark on the question, and it would be an unfortunate thing if it were left to juries to consider, whether some particular act was morally right or wrong. The test must be whether it is contrary to law.[43]

So, the position in England is that what is meant by the object of knowledge in the M'Naghten rules is that the act is *legally* wrong.[44]

However, the position differs with respect to Australian common law. The High Court in *Stapleton v R*[45] refused to apply *Windle* and held that 'wrong' was not to be defined narrowly as a legal wrong, the question instead being whether the accused 'could not think rationally of the reasons which to ordinary people make that act right or wrong'.[46] Hence, in respect of an accused's knowledge of the wrongness of his or her act, Australian courts have favoured a test of knowledge of *moral* rather than *legal* wrongness.[47] As expressed by Dixon J, in order to determine whether an accused lacks the requisite knowledge,

> the question is whether he was able to appreciate the wrongness of the particular act he was doing. … If through a disease or defect or disorder of the mind he could not think rationally of the reasons which to ordinary people make that act right or wrong. If through the disordered condition of the mind he could not reason about the matter with a moderate degree of sense and composure it may be said that he could not know that what he was doing was wrong.[48]

---

41 Ibid. 28.

42 [1952] 2 QB 826.

43 Ibid. 833.

44 While it is clear that in English law the test is not one of *moral* wrongness, it is not entirely uncontroversial to say that it is for this reason a test of *legal* wrongness. The issue is discussed in relation to the required understanding in the case of children in G. Williams, *Criminal Law-General Part* (London, 1961), 817 ff and, T. Crofts, *The Criminal Responsibility of Children in Germany and England* (Aldershot, 2002) 42 ff.

45 (1952) 86 CLR 358.

46 Ibid. 367, citing *R v Porter* (1933) 55 CLR 182, 189.

47 *R v Porter* (1933) 55 CLR 182, 189 per Dixon J; *Stapleton v R* (1952) 86 CLR 358.

48 *R v Porter* (1933) 55 CLR 182, 189–90 per Dixon J.

That is, in Australia, at common law, the accused is exempted from responsibility where, as a result of a disease of the mind, he or she could not 'think rationally' about whether his or her act was morally wrong. Where an accused is suffering from a disease of the mind making it impossible for him or her to reason with a 'moderate degree of sense and composure' about the normative implications of his or her action he or she will be taken not to know that the conduct as perceived by reasonable people was wrong.[49] This gloss on the phrase 'could not know that what he [or she] was doing was wrong' has been adopted in the formulation of several Australian jurisdictions.[50]

In contrast, the relevant part of the Queensland, Western Australian and Tasmanian formulations of the defence reads that an accused will be held non-responsible for his or her conduct if due to mental disorder he or she was deprived of 'the *capacity* to know that [he or she] ought not to do the act or make the omission'.[51] The High Court has interpreted this clause as raising the issue of whether the accused lacked the capacity to know that his or her conduct 'was wrong according to the ordinary standards adopted by reasonable men'.[52] The distinction between an accused's 'capacity' for knowledge as distinct from his or her 'lack' of knowledge will be discussed further in the following section.

What of the individual who believes that his or her acts are not wrong? Such an individual's view of morality is not to be substituted for that of society. The issue will be decided according to whether or not, as a result of a disease of the mind, he or she knows that society regards his or her act as wrong. A person who knows that reasonable people would consider such conduct to be wrong will be taken to know that it is wrong, regardless of his or her own view of the morality of such conduct.[53] Even where an individual believes that his or her conduct is not morally wrong, the defence will not be available if he or she knows that such conduct is wrong according to the standard of reasonable people.[54] Alternatively,

---

49 *Sodeman v R* (1936) 55 CLR 192, 215; *Willgoss v R* (1960) 105 CLR 295, 310; *R v S* [1979] 2 NSWLR 1.

50 *Criminal Code* (Cth) s 7.3(1) (b); *Criminal Code* (ACT) s 28(2); *Criminal Code* (NT) s 43 C (1)(b); *Crimes (Mental Impairment and Unfitness to be Tried) Act 1997* (Vic) s 20(1)(b).

51 *Criminal Code* (Qld) s 27(1) (emphasis added); cp. *Criminal Code* (WA) s 27; *Criminal Code* (Tas) s 16(1), 'incapable of knowing that the act or omission was one that he or she ought not to do or make'.

52 *Stapleton v R* (1952) 86 CLR 358, 375 per Dixon CJ, Webb, Kitto JJ; cp. 23(2) (b) of the New Zealand *Crimes Act 1961*, 'incapable of knowing that the act or omission was morally wrong, having regard to the commonly accepted standards of right and wrong'.

53 See I.D. Leader-Elliott, *The Commonwealth Criminal Code: A Guide for Practitioners* (Canberra, 2002) 129.

54 Contrast the position in New Zealand where, notwithstanding the contrary wording of the statute, the statutory test for insanity has been interpreted by courts as requiring a subjective moral standard, the question being whether the accused did not regard the act as wrong for him or her to do, even if he or she knew it was contrary to public standards

someone who believed that they were acting under divine command may know that what they are doing is legally wrong yet not be able to appreciate that it would be morally condemned. Such an individual lacks the capacity to understand the normative judgments of the community.[55]

In summary, the English view is that an accused who seeks to raise the defence must be shown not to know that his or her act is a legal wrong. In contrast, the position in Australia is that 'wrong' is not to be interpreted according to the accused's personal standards, but rather according to the standards of ordinary people. Nevertheless, the High Court in *Stapleton* noted that there would be little difference whether an accused's understanding of what was wrong was measured in terms of knowing that his or her act was wrong in terms of contrary to law or wrong according to ordinary standards.[56] In most instances acts that are contrary to the law will also be contrary to morality. However, as the court noted, there are cases where an accused may know that an act is punishable by law yet not know that such an act is morally wrong according to ordinary standards.[57] An instance of such a case will be presented below.

The nature of knowledge: actual or capacity?

This section examines what is meant by the 'nature' of an accused's knowledge of the wrongness of his or her particular act. The nature of an accused's knowledge refers to the cognitive processes required on the part of an agent in order for him or her to know that an act is wrong. As put in *R v Porter*:[58]

> The question is whether he was able to appreciate the wrongness of the particular act he was doing. … If through a disease or defect or disorder of the mind he could not think rationally of the reasons which to ordinary people make that act right or wrong.
>
> If through the disordered condition of the mind he could not reason about the matter with a moderate degree of sense and composure it may be said he could not know that what he was doing was wrong.[59]

---

of morality (*R v Macmillan* [1966] NZLR 616, 622). For a defence of this approach, see W. Brookbanks, 'Insanity' in *Psychiatry and the Law*, ed. W. Brookbanks and S. Simpson (n. 5) 141.

55 *Stapleton v R* (1952) 86 CLR 358. Several criticisms have been levelled at the objective moral standard requirement in this formulation (see Brookbanks, 'Insanity' (n. 54) 141; Yeo, 'The Insanity Defence in the Criminal Laws of the Commonwealth of Nations' (n. 13) 251).

56 (1952) 86 CLR 358, 375 per Dixon CJ, Webb, Kitto JJ.

57 Ibid.

58 (1933) 55 CLR 182.

59 Ibid. 189–90 per Dixon J.

For an accused to 'know that what he was doing was wrong' is for him or her to 'appreciate the wrongness of the particular act he was doing'. To 'appreciate' is to 'think rationally' which will require the defendant to 'reason with a moderate degree of sense and composure'.

In respect of the cognitive processes required on the part of an accused in order for him or her to 'reason with a moderate degree of sense and composure', a further distinction may be drawn between the accused's *actual* knowledge and his or her *capacity* for such knowledge. Actual knowledge requires an individual to appreciate the extant reasons that to most people make the act right or wrong. That is, actual knowledge is concerned with those things people 'affirmatively believe', for example, an affirmatively held belief that, '$100 is too high a price to pay for a ticket to a football match'. In the context of the M'Naghten rules, actual knowledge will require an individual to affirmatively believe that his or her actions were legally (England) or morally (Australia) wrong.

A capacity for knowledge, on the other hand, is the capacity people have to reason about things, that is 'affirm reasons for their belief'. For example, an individual will fail to evince such a capacity where, all things being equal, he or she holds the belief that '$100 is too high a price to pay for a ticket to a football match, though $200 is not'. In the context of the M'Naghten rules, a capacity for knowledge will be evinced by an individual who is able to 'reason about the matter with a moderate degree of sense and composure'. There is no direction in either case law or legislation as to the meaning of what it is 'to reason with a moderate degree of sense and composure'. However, in keeping with the purpose of the defence, an accused's capacity for knowledge will amount to his or her capacity to reason and reach rational decisions. On such a reading, the question raised by the defence is whether a disease of the mind so obstructed the thought processes of the accused as to render him or her incapable of knowing that his or her act was morally wrong according to ordinary standards.

There are competing interpretations in Australian jurisdictions as to whether it is actual knowledge or a capacity for knowledge that is required. At common law, the M'Naghten rules require an examination of an accused's actual knowledge of the wrongfulness of his or her act, namely, whether or not the crime which he or she committed was morally wrong.[60] In the language of the M'Naghten rules, 'the party accused was labouring under such a defect of reason, from disease of the mind … that he did not know he was doing what was wrong'.[61]

Similarly, the *Crimes (Mental Impairment and Unfitness to be Tried) Act 1997* (Vic) section 20(1)(b) refers to an accused who 'did not know that the conduct was wrong (that is, he or she could not reason with a moderate degree of sense and composure about whether the conduct, as perceived by reasonable people, was

60 *Stapleton* (1952) 86 CLR 358.

61 *R v M'Naghten* (1843) 10 CL and Fin 200, 210 per Lord Tyndal CJ.

wrong)'.[62] The Victorian Act has been held to be declarative of the common law.[63] Similarly the Northern Territory Code requires that the accused 'did not know that the conduct was wrong'.[64] Further, the Commonwealth Code,[65] the ACT Code[66] and the South Australian Act[67] all require, for the defence to be established, that the defendant lack actual knowledge of the wrongness of his or her act at the time of the offence. Section 7.3(1)(b) of the Commonwealth Criminal Code reads:

> A person is not criminally responsible for an offence if ... (b) the person did not know that the conduct was wrong (that is, the person could not reason with a moderate degree of sense and composure about whether the conduct, as perceived by reasonable people was wrong).

The language employed by the Commonwealth Code is identical to that employed in the Victorian Act: 'did not know that the conduct was wrong'. Equally, the code borrows from Dixon J's judgment in *Porter* in requiring a person to 'reason with a moderate degree of sense and composure'.[68] Both the commentary to section 302 'Mental Impairment' of the Commonwealth Code[69] and the published *Guide for Practitioners*[70] make it clear that this formulation 'moves away from the existing Griffith Code concepts based on capacity in favour of tests phrased in terms of what D actually knew'.[71] That is, the Commonwealth Code requires actual knowledge, rather than a capacity for knowledge, on the part of a defendant.

In contrast, an approach calling for a capacity-based interpretation of the knowledge requirement is to be found in the Griffith Code jurisdictions. In those jurisdictions it must be shown that the accused lacked the 'capacity to know that the person ought not to do the act or make the omission'.[72] Analogously, the Tasmanian Code requires that the accused was 'incapable of knowing that the act or omission was one that he or she ought not to do or make'.[73] It has been suggested that a test of incapacity restricts the defence of insanity to a greater degree than a test of lack

62 S 20(1)(b).

63 *Sebalj* [2003] VSC 181 (Unreported, Supreme Court of Victoria, Smith J, 5 June, 2003).

64 *Criminal Code* (NT) s 43C(1)(b).

65 *Criminal Code* (Cth) s 7.3(1)(b).

66 The *Criminal Code* (ACT) commenced on 1 Jan. 2006. Section 320(1)(b) of the former *Crimes Act 1900* (ACT) provided that an element of the defence was satisfied where an accused was 'incapable of understanding that what he or she was doing was wrong'.

67 *Criminal Law Consolidation Act 1935* (SA) s 269C(b).

68 (1933) 55 CLR 182, 189.

69 Criminal Law Officer's Committee, *Model Criminal Code – Chapter 2: General Principles of Criminal Responsibility: Final Report* (Canberra, 1993), 37.

70 Leader-Elliott, *The Commonwealth Criminal Code* (n. 53) 129.

71 Criminal Law Officer's Committee, *Model Criminal Code – Chapter 2* (n. 69) 37.

72 *Criminal Code* (Qld) s 27(1); *Criminal Code* (WA) s 27, 'he or she'.

73 *Criminal Code* (Tas) s 16 (1)(a)(ii).

of actual knowledge: a person may possess the capacity to know the wrongness of his or her act yet not be able to exercise it at the time of the offence.[74] While the expression 'capacity' is used in several jurisdictions it is argued that it is only because courts have ignored the restrictive narrowness of a capacity-based approach to the insanity defence that the defence has not been restricted even further than it currently is.[75]

Another issue raised by the nature of an accused's knowledge is the degree of impairment required to an accused's mental functioning before the defence of insanity will be established. Stanley Yeo has suggested that in order to support the defence of insanity a 'very high degree of mental impairment is required to sufficiently eliminate these capacities'.[76] It is because the defence results in a state of non-responsibility or total exemption from criminal responsibility, that a very high degree of mental impairment will be required in order to establish the defence.[77] It will only be where such a level of impairment results that it would be unwarranted to attribute any blame to an accused for failing to act according to the law. A lesser degree of incapacity should result in a finding of diminished responsibility rather than one of non-responsibility.[78]

It is submitted that similar observations should apply in respect of the nature of an accused's inability to control his or her conduct as a result of a state of volitional impairment characterized as a disease of the mind.[79] That is, a lack of control rather than incapacity to control conduct should be sufficient to raise the defence. Further, a very high degree rather than some lesser degree of impairment should be required on the part of an accused before he or she will be permitted to raise the defence. I will return to this issue in the context of the formulated defence of impaired consciousness in Chapter 6.

The next section will consider the implications of the above analysis of the object and nature of an accused's knowledge of the wrongness of his or her acts.

---

74 S. Yeo, 'Commonwealth and International Perspectives on the Insanity Defence' (2008) 32 *Criminal Law Journal* 11; though contrast the New South Wales Law Reform Commission (NSWLRC), *People with Cognitive and Mental Health Impairments in the Criminal Justice System: Criminal Responsibility and Consequences*, Consultation Paper 6 (Sydney, 2010) 3.61, claiming that a capacity-based approach may result in a broader formulation than that found at common law.

75 Yeo, 'The Insanity Defence in the Criminal Laws of the Commonwealth of Nations' (n. 13) 248.

76 Ibid.

77 G. Ferguson, 'A Critique of Proposals to Reform the Insanity Defence' (1989) 14 *Queen's Law Journal* 135, 141.

78 Ibid. Though, as will be discussed in Chapter 6, not all jurisdictions recognize a defence of diminished responsibility.

79 Yeo, 'The Insanity Defence in the Criminal Laws of the Commonwealth of Nations' (n. 13) 248.

Clarifying 'knowledge'

This section will begin by outlining the various possibilities generated by combining the distinctions drawn above in respect of the object and nature of 'knowledge'. This will be followed by an application of these various combinations to the facts of a paradigmatic case of mental disorder in order to better clarify the operation of the knowledge requirement of the M'Naghten rules.

Matrix of possibilities

The respective distinctions between the object and nature of knowledge generate the following set of possibilities:

1. Actual knowledge of legal wrong: the accused did affirmatively believe that the act was not a legal wrong: *Windle*,[80] *Codere*,[81] 'once it is clear that the appellant knew that the act was wrong in law, then he was doing an act which he was conscious he ought not to do, and as it was against the law, it was punishable by law'.[82]
2. Actual knowledge of moral wrong: the accused did affirmatively believe that the act was not a moral wrong: Cth Code: 'the person did not know that the conduct was wrong',[83] ACT Code,[84] NT Code,[85] SA Act,[86] Vic Act,[87] *Porter*,[88] *Stapleton*.[89]
3. Capacity for knowledge of legal wrong: the accused could not reason about the matter, that is, whether the act was a legal wrong, with a moderate degree of sense and composure: hypothetical example: 'Murder is not a criminal offence, as my mother told me so'. In mistaking his or her mother's advice for legal authority the accused reveals his or her incapacity to reason about the legal wrongness of the act.

80 [1952] 2 QB 826.
81 (1916) 12 Cr App R 21.
82 Ibid. 28.
83 *Criminal Code* (Cth), s 7.3(1)(b).
84 *Criminal Code* (ACT), s 28.
85 *Criminal Code* (NT), s 43C (1)(b).
86 *Criminal Law Consolidation Act 1935*, ss 269C, 269E.
87 *Crimes (Mental Impairment and Unfitness to be Tried) Act 1997*, s 20.
88 (1933) 55 CLR 182.
89 (1952) 86 CLR 358.

4. Capacity for knowledge of moral wrong: the accused could not reason about the matter, that is, whether the act was a moral wrong, with a moderate degree of sense and composure: Griffith Codes,[90] Tas Code.[91]

Arranged schematically the above analysis reveals the following combinations:

Table 2.1 Matrix of possibilities 1: object and nature of knowledge

Object	Legal	Moral
Nature		
Actual	English position: *Codere, Windle*	Cth, ACT, NT, SA, Vic, *Porter, Stapleton*
Capacity	(hypothetical)	Griffith Code, Tas.

The following section will seek to apply the above analysis to a particular case of mental disorder in order to better understand what might constitute the 'legal standard of disorder of the mind sufficient to afford a ground of irresponsibility for a crime'.[92]

Case study: R v Hadfield

In providing jury directions in *Porter*, Dixon J sought to explain how an accused may fail to

> appreciate the wrongness of the particular act he was doing ... if through a disease or defect or disorder of the mind he could not think rationally of the reasons which to ordinary people make that act right or wrong. If through the disordered condition of the mind he could not reason about the matter with a

90 *Criminal Code* (Qld), s 27; *Criminal Code* (WA), s 27. While the Griffith Code does not specify what sort of understanding is required the better view is to hold that in those code jurisdictions, such as Queensland and Western Australia, which adopt the Griffith Code the defence will be available to someone who while knowing the legal status of his or her conduct does not appreciate that it would not be morally condemned: *Stapleton v R* (1952) 86 CLR 358. In support of this position see E. Colvin, and J. McKechnie, *Criminal Law in Queensland and Western Australia* (5th edn. Chatswood, NSW, 2008) 17.28.

91 *Criminal Code* (Tas), s 16.

92 *R v Porter* (1933) 55 CLR 182, 189 per Dixon J.

> moderate degree of sense and composure it may be said that what he was doing was wrong.[93]

While to 'appreciate' was held to mean 'think rationally', and this was further defined as to 'reason with a moderate degree of sense and composure',[94] Dixon J failed to enunciate the senses in which an individual may be said to think rationally. In particular, the expression 'think rationally' fails to articulate a distinction that may be drawn between the *admission* of relevant considerations, on the one hand, and the *weighing* of such considerations, on the other.

For the purposes of the present discussion, I will take 'relevant considerations' to mean premises which are not delusionally flawed, that is, premises that are not the result of delusions arising from a state of mental disorder.[95] Hence, an accused may think rationally in either of the following senses: admitting relevant considerations, that is, non-delusionally flawed premises, or reasoning soundly with or weighing correctly a given set of premises notwithstanding the nature of such premises.

As a result of the above analysis the 'legal standard of disorder' appealed to by Dixon J in *Porter* may refer to the standard of lucid reasoning, in the sense of practical reason, or the standard of admitting only non-delusionally flawed premises or both. The significance of this distinction becomes apparent where an accused acts on a delusionally flawed premise in a means–end rational fashion. To suggest that such an accused is rational is to ignore one particular aspect of what it means to 'think rationally', namely, that the reasons for action which an individual admits for consideration are not delusionally flawed. The case of *R v Hadfield* is illustrative of this distinction.[96]

Hadfield held the delusional belief that he was under divine instruction to die in order to save the world. As he considered the act of suicide a mortal sin, he decided to shoot at King George III and in this way bring about his own death for the capital offence of regicide. Lord Kenyon CJ held that Hadfield was insane at the time he did the act and ordered the jury to bring a verdict of not guilty subject to detention in custody given his dangerousness.[97] The case is important as it seems to provide the earliest instance of a reported case involving an acquittal of a defendant

---

93 Ibid.

94 Ibid.

95 A delusion is defined as 'a false belief based on incorrect inference about external reality ... [in the face of] incontrovertible proof or evidence to the contrary' (American Psychiatric Association, *Diagnostic and Statistical Manual of Mental Disorders* (4th edn, text revision, Washington, DC, 2000) 297 (DSM-IV-TR)).

96 (1800) 27 St Tr 1281.

97 *Hadfield* is the first case where a verdict of not guilty results in a qualified acquittal on the basis of an accused's perceived dangerousness. Legal authority for detention in custody, following a finding of insanity, was passed by statute only subsequent to Lord Kenyon's ruling (39 & 40 Geo 3 c 94) and authorized Hadfield's continued detention.

suffering from a diagnosable form of schizophrenia. Equally *Hadfield* provides a clear indication that it was no longer a requirement that only those totally deprived of understanding, or 'wild beasts', were subject to the defence.[98] In *Hadfield*, the fact that the accused was able to discern that suicide was a sin indicated that he had not lost all understanding of the difference between right and wrong.[99]

Hadfield failed to think rationally and was eligible for the defence given his admission of a delusionally flawed premise, namely, the messianic delusion that by bringing about his own execution he would save the world. Once such an irrelevant consideration was admitted, it was a premise in his practical reasoning leading to his decision to shoot the king. While Hadfield's thinking reflected means–end rationality, the delusionally flawed premise on which it was based was not a consideration which a rational person would have admitted as part of his or her thinking.

This is not to suggest that before an individual may be said not to think rationally his or her reasons for action must fail to reveal a recognizable pattern of coherence with other extant reasons. While a lack of a recognizable pattern of coherence may constitute a sufficient condition of severe mental illness, it is not a necessary condition of such illness. For example, certain varieties of severe mental illness such as paranoid schizophrenia may give rise to an encapsulated delusional belief system that reveals a great degree of inner coherence.[100] In such cases the delusional beliefs may even be supported by the 'evidence' of accompanying hallucinations.[101]

Hadfield is an instance of that class of case remarked on by the High Court in *Stapleton*, where

> [while] the insane motives of the defendant arise from [a] complete incapacity to reason as to what is right or wrong (his insane judgment even treating the act as one of inexorable obligation or inescapable necessity) he may yet have at the back of his mind an awareness that the act he proposes to do is punishable by law.[102]

---

98 For the 'wild beast' notion of insanity, see 1 Hale *Pleas of the Crown*, 31–2, the insane are 'not as reasonable creatures, their actions [being] in effect in the condition of brutes', cited in F. McAuley and J.P. McCutcheon, *Criminal Liability: A Grammar* (Dublin, 2000) 645; cp. *R v Arnold* (1723) 16 How St Tr 695, 766, to be found insane 'a man must be totally deprived of his understanding and memory so as not to know what he is doing, no more than an infant, brute or wild beast'.

99 McAuley and McCutcheon, *Criminal Liability* (n. 98) 645–6.

100 DSM-IV-TR (n. 95) 821.

101 A hallucination is defined as 'a sensory perception that has the compelling sense of reality of a true perception but that occurs without external stimulation of the relevant sensory organ' (DSM-IV-TR (n. 95) 823; see J. Radden, *Madness and Reason* (London, 1985) 68–9).

102 (1952) 86 CLR 358, 375 per Dixon CJ, Webb and Kitto JJ.

It was Hadfield's knowledge of the illegality of his action which prompted him to shoot at King George. Hadfield shot at the king precisely because he knew that it was illegal and that it would result in his own death for the capital offence of treason. However, given his delusional belief that he was acting under divine providence, Hadfield did not know that his act was morally wrong according to ordinary standards. Believing that he had been commanded by a higher authority to kill the king in order to fulfil a messianic belief, Hadfield lacked knowledge of the moral wrongness of his act. The case of *Hadfield* demonstrates that the ability to tell legal right from legal wrong is not necessarily excluded by insanity but that this ability often co-exists with serious mental disorder.[103]

So how is Dixon J's reference to the 'legal standard of disorder of the mind which is sufficient to afford a ground of irresponsibility for a crime' to be understood?[104] As detailed above, a person will be said to think rationally not only where his or her reason admits relevant considerations, that is, non-delusionally flawed premises, but also where he or she reasons soundly with such a given set of premises. Consequently, the case of *Hadfield* provides an apposite opportunity to assess the ability of each of the different jurisdictional formulations of the defence to accommodate a paradigmatic instance of severe mental disorder.[105]

As applied to the case of *Hadfield* the matrix of possibilities outlined above detailing the various combinations of the object and nature of knowledge produces the following results:

1. Actual knowledge of legal wrong: Hadfield had actual knowledge that his act was legally wrong, consequently, he would not have a defence under English law as per *Codere* and *Windle*.
2. Actual knowledge of moral wrong: as Hadfield believed that his act was in response to the higher authority of divine providence Hadfield lacked actual knowledge that it was morally wrong. However, it remains an open question whether Hadfield knew that reasonable people would consider the conduct to be wrong. If he knew that reasonable people would consider his conduct to be wrong, he would be taken to know that it is wrong. Consequently, Hadfield may have a defence under the Commonwealth Code, ACT Code, NT Code, SA Act, Vic Act and the M'Naghten rules.
3. Capacity for knowledge of legal wrong: the fact that Hadfield actually knew it was illegal to shoot the king does not necessarily mean that he had the capacity for knowledge of legal wrong. Nevertheless, Hadfield would probably have no defence under the hypothetical defence calling for a lack of capacity for knowledge of legal wrong, as he was able to reason with a moderate degree of sense and composure in relation to such legal wrong.

---

103 See McAuley and McCutcheon, *Criminal Liability* (n. 98) 645–9.

104 *R v Porter* (1933) 55 CLR 182, 189.

105 While *Hadfield* is cited by the High Court in *Stapleton* the case is not mentioned in this regard; nevertheless, the facts of the case lend themselves to such analysis.

4. Capacity for knowledge of moral wrong: if the admission of a delusionally flawed premise in a defendant's reasoning is sufficient to preclude him or her from thinking rationally Hadfield lacked the capacity for knowledge of moral wrong. Hence, Hadfield may have had a defence under the Griffith Code and Tasmanian Code.

Arranged schematically, the above analysis reveals the following outcomes in respect of the facts of *Hadfield*:

Table 2.2 Matrix of possibilities 2: *R v Hadfield*

Object	Legal	Moral
Nature		
Actual	No defence	Probably a defence
Capacity	Probably no defence	Probably a defence

What is shown by the above analysis is that a defendant such as Hadfield who knows that his or her act is legally wrong yet who believes that it is morally correct, will have a defence in all Australian jurisdictions. That is, regardless as to whether the nature of such knowledge is actual knowledge or the capacity for such knowledge, where the object of knowledge is understood as a moral wrong an accused such as Hadfield will have a defence.[106]

However, notwithstanding the ability of the common law to accommodate a paradigmatic case such as *Hadfield*, it has been remarked that the focus of the M'Naghten rules on an accused's absence of knowledge is unduly narrow.[107] In particular, both volitional and emotional defects will fail to be recognized as sufficient to give rise to the insanity defence at common law.[108] The following

106 See P.A. Fairall and S. Yeo, *Criminal Defences in Australia* (4th edn, Chatswood, NSW, 2005) 251.

107 Ibid. 258; McAuley and McCutcheon, *Criminal Liability* (n. 98) 65–6; Western Australian Law Reform Commission, *The Criminal Process and Persons Suffering from Mental Disorder*, Discussion Paper (Fremantle, 1987), 3.9. This view has not been shared by the Victorian Law Reform Commission (VLRC), who recommended against the introduction of a volitional limb to the defence arguing that the Victorian statutory formulation of the defence which is declarative of the common law was sufficiently flexible to accommodate cases where the accused could not control his or her actions (Victorian Law Reform Commission, *Defences to Homicide: Final Report*, Report No 94 (Melbourne, 2004) 5.27–33).

108 *Sodeman v R* (1936) 55 CLR 192; *A-G (SA) v Brown* [1960] AC 432 (PC); *Bratty v A-G (Northern Ireland)* [1963] AC 386; contrast, *Doyle v Wicklow County Council* [1974]

section will turn to a consideration of what will be referred to as the 'cognitive bias' of the M'Naghten rules.

Knowledge in the M'Naghten rules: cognitive bias

Pursuant to the M'Naghten rules, if an accused is unable to control his or her conduct yet knows the nature and quality of his or her act and knows that the act is wrong, the defence of insanity is not available.[109] However, if, because of an inability to control his or her conduct, an accused does not know the nature and quality of his or her act or know that it is wrong, then the defence of insanity will be available.[110] As stated by Dixon J in *Sodeman*:[111]

> It is important to bear steadily in mind that if through disorder of the faculties a prisoner is incapable of controlling his relevant acts, this may afford the strongest reason for supposing that he is incapable of forming a judgment that they are wrong, and in some cases even of understanding their nature.[112]

Sodeman's case was affirmed by the High Court in *Brown v A-G (SA)*.[113] In *Brown* the accused appealed to the High Court against his conviction on the basis of the trial judge's direction to the jury that 'uncontrollable impulse' was no defence in law. The High Court held that the judge had erred in directing the jury that the accused's uncontrollable impulse was a reason for rejecting the defence. As stated by the court: 'On the contrary [uncontrollable impulse] may afford strong ground for the inference that a prisoner was labouring under such a defect of reason from disease of the mind as not to know that he was doing what was wrong'.[114] On appeal by the prosecution, the decision in *Brown* was overturned by the Privy Council who held that the above statement by the High Court implied that, as a matter of law, uncontrollable impulse was recognized as a symptom of insanity as defined by the M'Naghten rules. The Privy Council accepted that irresistible impulse could be symptomatic of insanity as defined by the M'Naghten rules.[115] However, in order for the defence of insanity to be available medical evidence would be required showing that the irresistible impulse was the result of mental disease, and that such disease caused the requisite incapacity. As expressed by Lord Tucker for the Privy Council:

IR 55, 71 (SC) affirmed *People (DPP) v O'Mahoney* [1985] IR 517.

109 *Sodeman v R* (1936) 55 CLR 192; *A-G (SA) v Brown* [1960] AC 432 (PC).

110 *Sodeman v R* (1936) 55 CLR 192; *A-G (SA) v Brown* [1960] AC 432 (PC).

111 (1936) 55 CLR 192.

112 Ibid. 214–15.

113 [1959] ALR 808.

114 Ibid. 814.

115 *A-G (SA) v Brown* [1960] AC 432 (PC).

> Their Lordships must not, of course, be understood to suggest that in a case where evidence has been given (and it is difficult to imagine a case where such evidence would be other than medical evidence) that irresistible impulse is a symptom of the particular disease of the mind from which a prisoner is said to be suffering and as to its effect on his ability to know the nature and quality of his act or that his act is wrong it would not be the duty of the judge to deal with the matter in the same way as any other relevant evidence given at the trial.[116]

Consequently, it would be necessary to establish on the basis of clinical evidence whether the impulse was symptomatic of the disease of the mind from which the accused suffered. Additionally, it would need to be established that the disease of the mind caused the accused not to know the nature and quality of his or her act or that it was wrong.

All jurisdictions, apart from Victoria and New South Wales, depart from the M'Naghten rules in recognizing an accused's incapacity, or inability, to control his or her conduct as an independent limb of the defence.[117] For example section 27 of the Griffith Code states:

> (1) A person is not criminally responsible for an act or omission if at the time of doing the act or making the omission the person is in such a state of mental disease or natural mental infirmity as to deprive the person of capacity to understand what the person is doing, or of capacity to control the person's actions, or of capacity to know that the person ought not to do the act or make the omission.[118]

An accused raising evidence of a volitional defect in Victoria and New South Wales will not be able to rely on an independent volitional limb to the defence of insanity. Such an accused will be required, pursuant to the M'Naghten rules, to establish the relevant cognitive incapacities. For example in *Sodeman v R*,[119] the appellant sought to appeal to the High Court from the Victorian Court of Criminal Appeal decision dismissing his appeal against a conviction for murder. The appellant argued that due to a mental disease from which he was suffering he was deprived of the capacity of controlling his actions and so was not responsible for the murder. The High Court reaffirmed that the M'Naghten rules do not recognize a volitional defect as an independent ground for the defence

116 Ibid. 449–50.

117 *Criminal Code* (Cth) s 7.3(1) (c); *Criminal Code* (ACT) s 28(1) (c); *Criminal Code* (NT) s 43 C (1)(c); *Criminal Code* (Qld) s 27(1); *Criminal Law Consolidation Act 1935* (SA) s 269C(c); 16(1)(b); *Criminal Code* (WA) s 27; *Criminal Code* (Tas) s.16(1)(b), holding that the act or omission was done under 'an impulse which, by reason of mental disease, he was in substance deprived of any power to resist'.

118 *Criminal Code* (Qld) s 27; *Criminal Code* (WA) s 27.

119 (1936) 55 CLR 192.

of insanity. Dixon J held that 'if [the accused] is able to understand the nature of his act and to know that it is wrong, an incapacity through disease of the mind to control his actions affords no excuse and leaves the prisoner criminally responsible'.[120]

Similarly, in New South Wales an accused cannot ground an insanity defence on the basis of incapacity to control his or her conduct.[121] For example, in *R v Heatley*,[122] a remand prisoner killed another inmate in his cell. Medical evidence tendered for the defence indicated that as a result of a mental illness Heatley was experiencing homicidal urges at the time of the offence.[123] Nevertheless, the court held that while the illness impaired the defendant's ability to control his urges, as he knew both the nature and wrongness of his act, the insanity defence was not available.[124] The accused was ultimately convicted of manslaughter on the basis of the partial defence of substantial impairment. Hence, in both New South Wales and Victoria where an accused cannot control his or her conduct yet knows the nature, quality and wrongness of his or her act the insanity defence is not available.

In contrast, Chapter 5 will argue, subject to certain conditions being met, for the recognition of such states as instances of volitional insanity. In particular, Chapter 5 will outline the diagnostic criteria of a psychiatrically recognized mental disorder which indicates that an individual suffering from such a disorder may know the nature and wrongness of his or her act and yet not be able to control his or her conduct. Pursuant to the analysis of the notion of disease of the mind to be undertaken in Chapter 3 it will be argued that such a mental disorder should be characterized as a disease of the mind. On the basis of such a characterization Chapter 5 will argue for the recognition of such a disorder as an instance of volitional insanity. The defence of volitional insanity would operate to exempt an individual who cannot control his or her conduct at common law, even where he or she knows the nature, quality and wrongness of his or her conduct.

The remainder of this chapter will consider the role played by the volitional element in the doctrine of automatism.

---

120 Ibid. 214–15, reaffirmed by the High Court in *Brown v A-G (SA)* [1959] ALR 808, 814. More recently the VLRC decided against introducing a volitional element to the defence (Victorian Law Reform Commission, *Defences to Homicide: Final Report* (n. 107) 5.27–33).

121 Though such an accused may, subject to the elements of the defence being established, raise a partial defence of 'substantial impairment' (*Crimes Act 1900* (NSW) s 23 A).

122 *R v Heatley* [2006] NSWSC 1199, cited in New South Wales Law Reform Commission (NSWLRC), *Consultation Paper 6: People with Cognitive and Mental Health Impairments in the Criminal Justice System* (n. 74) 3.41; cp. *Veen (No 1)* (1979) 143 CLR 458; *Veen (No 2)* (1988) 164 CLR 465; *Adams* [2001] NSWSC 773.

123 *Heatley* [2006] NSWSC 1199 para [46]–[62].

124 Ibid. para [75].

Volition and automatism

The first section will outline the nature of the common-law doctrine of automatism. This in turn will be followed by the drawing of a distinction between instances of automatism going to voluntariness and those instances which are subsumed by the insanity defence. The final section will highlight several difficulties faced by the criminal law in respect of the correct characterization of states of automatism.

Lack of volition

Automatism refers to an individual's lack of control of his or her conduct resulting in him or her acting in an unwilled fashion.[125] It is an individual's lack of volition which gives rise to automatism. Cases that have been recognized as giving rise to a lack of voluntariness include instances of concussion caused from a blow to the head,[126] somnambulism,[127] extreme stress,[128] epilepsy[129] and certain physiological states.[130] Certain cases and commentators have suggested that it is an accused's lack or altered state of consciousness which is the defining feature of automatism.[131] This focus on an accused's consciousness has in turn led to calls for automatism to be subsumed, along with the defence of insanity, within a general defence of mental disorder.[132] For now I simply note this view and will return to it in Chapter 6.

In both Australia and Canada, another line of authority indicates that it is the absence of volition, rather than consciousness, which is the defining feature of automatism.[133] Lord Denning, in the House of Lords decision of *Bratty v A-G*

---

125 S. Yeo, 'Clarifying Automatism' (2002) 25 *International Journal of Law and Psychiatry*, 445; the first use of the term in its modern form is to be found in *R v Harrison-Owen* (1951) 35 Cr App R 108, 111–12.

126 *Low* (1991) 57 A Crim R 8; *Wogandt* (1988) 33 A Crim R 31.

127 *Parks* (1992) 75 CCC (3d) 287.

128 *Falconer* (1990) 171 CLR 30; *Radford* (1985) 42 SASR 266; *Rabey* (1977) 37 CCC (2d) 461.

129 *Youssef* (1990) 50 A Crim R 1; *Bratty v A-G (Northern-Ireland)* [1963] AC 386; *Sullivan* [1984] 1 AC 156.

130 *Hall* (1988) 36 A Crim R 368, cerebral oedema; *Hennesy* [1989] 2 All ER 9, diabetes; *Kemp* [1957] 1 QB 399, arteriosclerosis.

131 *Joyce* [1970] SASR 184; *Burr* [1969] NZLR 736; *DPP v Leonboyer* (1999) 109 A Crim R 168; *Broome v Perkins* (1986) 85 Cr App R 321; *Isitt* (1978) 67 Cr App R 44; *Haynes v MOT* (1988) 3 CRNZ 587; B. McSherry, 'Defining What is a "Disease of the Mind": The Untenability of Current Legal Interpretations' (1993) 1 *Journal of Law and Medicine* 76, 78.

132 B. McSherry, 'Voluntariness, Intention and the Defence of Mental Disorder: Toward a Rational Approach' (2003) 21 *Behavioural Sciences and the Law* 581.

133 *Ryan v R* (1967) 121 CLR 205, 214 per Barwick CJ; *R v Pantelic* (1973) 21 FLR 253 per Fox J; *R v Dodd* (1974) 7 SASR 151; *Jeffs v Graham* (1987) 8 NSWLR 292; *Barker*

(Northern Ireland),[134] held that 'automatism [means] an act which is done by the muscles without any control by the mind, such as a spasm, a reflex action or a convulsion'.[135] Barwick CJ in *Ryan v R*[136] noting Lord Denning's remarks in *Bratty*[137] approvingly, held that the term 'automatism' was merely a 'convenient expression ... to comprehend involuntary deeds where the lack of concomitant or controlling will to act is due to diverse causes'.[138] His Honour held that the real issue in regard to automatism is whether an exercise of will is absent, not whether there is a lack of consciousness on the part of the accused. In the words of the judgment: 'It is of course the absence of the will to act or, perhaps, more precisely, of its exercise rather than lack of knowledge or consciousness which ... decides criminal liability'.[139] Similarly, the Canadian Supreme Court has held that 'voluntariness, rather than consciousness, is the key legal element of automatistic behaviour since the defence of automatism amounts to a denial of the voluntariness component of the *actus reus*'.[140] Courts in these jurisdictions have been prepared to accept that a degree of consciousness, or awareness, will not preclude a finding of automatism.[141]

The issue of an accused's voluntariness will rarely arise as in most instances it will be assumed that the acts of the accused were performed voluntarily.[142] In particular, there is a presumption that the act of a person who is conscious is voluntary. However, such a presumption of voluntariness is not the same as the legal presumption of sanity operating at common law.[143] As expressed by Mason CJ, Brennan and McHugh JJ in *Falconer*:[144]

> Because we assume that a person who is apparently conscious has the capacity to control his actions, we draw an inference that the act is done by choice. ... The presumption that the acts of a person, apparently conscious, are willed or voluntary is an inference of fact, and, as a matter of fact, there must be good

---

v Burke [1970] VR 884, 891; *Stone* (1999) 134 CCC (3d) 353, 421 per L'Hereux-Dube, Gonthier, Cory and McLachlin JJ concurring.

134 [1963] AC 386.

135 Ibid. 409; cp. *Criminal Code* (Cth) s 4.2(3) (b), noting 'an act performed during sleep or unconsciousness' as an example of conduct that is involuntary.

136 (1967) 121 CLR 205.

137 [1963] AC 386, 409.

138 (1967) 121 CLR 205, 214.

139 Ibid.

140 *R v Stone* (1999) 134 CCC (3d) 353, 421 per L'Hereux-Dube, Gonthier, Cory and McLachlin JJ concurring.

141 *Rabey* (1981) 54 CCC (2d) 1; *Parks* (1992) 75 CCC (3d) 287; *R v Radford* (1985) 42 SASR 266, 275-6 per King CJ; *Burr v R* [1969] NZLR 736, 745 per Turner J.

142 *Ryan v R* (1967) 121 CLR 205, 213 per Barwick CJ.

143 *Middleton* (2000) 114 A Crim R 258, 272 per Anderson J, cited in Fairall and Yeo, *Criminal Defences in Australia* (n. 106) 295.

144 *R v Falconer* (1990) 171 CLR 30.

> grounds for refusing to draw the inference. Generally speaking, grounds for refusing to draw the inference appear only when there are grounds for believing that the actor is unable to control his actions.[145]

While sometimes referred to as a 'defence', the doctrine of automatism merely requires the accused to raise evidence of involuntariness. In order for the issue of voluntariness to arise, the defence carries the evidential burden of raising automatism.[146] Evidence presented during the course of the trial will seek to rebut the presumption of voluntariness.[147] Where, generally by means of clinical evidence, a 'proper foundation' has been raised by the accused that his or her conduct was involuntary the evidential burden will be satisfied.[148] The prosecution then carries the burden of establishing voluntariness by negating automatism beyond a reasonable doubt.[149] At common law as voluntariness is treated as an element of the *actus reus*, or physical element, of each offence, a failure to establish voluntariness will result in an acquittal.[150] As expressed by Deane and Dawson JJ in *Falconer*:[151]

> The important thing is ... that an accused is entitled to an acquittal if the prosecution fails to prove that his acts were voluntary. ... If on the evidence an accused's acts may have been involuntary as a result of the operation of events upon a sound mind – as a result of automatism – then a reasonable doubt about the voluntariness of those acts will be sufficient to entitle him to [an] acquittal. In such a case there will be a reasonable hypothesis consistent with both innocence and a sane mind and we do not conceive it to be the policy of the law that in that

---

145 Ibid. 41–2 per Mason CJ, Brennan and McHugh JJ, approving *R v Radford* (1985) 42 SASR 266.

146 *Youssef* (1990) 50 A Crim R 1, 4 per Hunt J; *DPP v Olcer* (2003) 143 A Crim R 337; cp. *R v Stone* (1999) 134 CCC (3d) 353, where the Canadian Supreme Court held that the legal burden is on the defence to prove involuntariness on the balance of probabilities.

147 *Ryan v R* (1967) 121 CLR 205, 215–6 per Barwick CJ; *Bratty v A-G (Northern Ireland)* [1963] AC 386, 406 per Viscount Kilmuir.

148 *Bratty v A-G (Northern Ireland)* [1963] AC 386, 413 per Denning J; *Youssef* (1990) 50 A Crim R 1, 4 per Hunt J; *DPP v Olcer* (2003) 143 A Crim R 337.

149 Contrast *R v Falconer* (1990) 171 CLR 30, 56 per Mason CJ, Brennan and McHugh JJ, calling for the burden of proof relating to automatism as it goes to voluntariness to be placed on the accused on the balance of probabilities; cp. the majority judgment in *Stone* (1999) 134 CCC (3d) 353 (SC) to like effect.

150 The Criminal Codes of Queensland and Western Australia take a different approach to that of the common law. Unlike the common law the Criminal Codes based on the Griffith Code do not use the concept of *actus reus* (physical element) or *mens rea* (fault element). In these code states lack of will operates as a defence and is found in Chapter 5 'Criminal Responsibility', ss 22, 23, 24 *Criminal Code* (Qld), and Chapter V 'Criminal Responsibility' ss 22, 23, 23A, 23B, 24 *Criminal Code* (WA).

151 *R v Falconer* (1990) 171 CLR 30.

> event there should be either a conviction or indefinite committal to an institution for the criminally insane.[152]

However, not all states of automatism go to the question of voluntariness. A distinction must be drawn between two recognized varieties of automatism: sane (non-insane) and insane automatism.[153] The remainder of this chapter will outline this distinction and note several tests judicially developed in order to distinguish sane from insane automatism.

Sane and insane automatism

The High Court in the leading case of *R v Falconer* has distinguished automatism as it relates to involuntariness from automatism as it relates to the defence of insanity.[154] In that case the High Court considered the relation between section 23 and section 27 of the Western Australian Criminal Code.[155]

At that time Section 23 provided that 'a person is not criminally responsible for an act or omission which occurs independently of his [or her] will'. The section asserts voluntariness as a fundamental requirement of criminal responsibility. Section 27 of the code sets out the insanity defence:

> A person is not criminally responsible for an act or omission on account of unsoundness of mind if at the time of doing the act or making the omission he [or she] is in such a state of mental impairment as to deprive him [or her] of capacity to understand what he [or she] is doing, or capacity to control his [or her] actions, or of capacity to know that he [or she] ought not to do the act or make the omission.

All members of the High Court held that section 27 encompasses involuntary action where such involuntariness arises from a state of 'mental impairment'. Section 27(1) defines 'mental impairment' as meaning 'intellectual disability, mental illness, brain damage or senility'. Where the accused's involuntary acts are

---

152 Ibid. 63 per Deane and Dawson JJ.

153 Warren Brookbanks calls for the expressions 'external cause' and 'internal cause' to be adopted in place of 'sane' and 'insane' automatism ('Insanity' (n. 54) 144); while the suggestion provides for greater analytic transparency this book will employ the more conventional expressions 'sane' and 'insane' on the grounds of familiarity.

154 (1990) 171 CLR 30.

155 *Criminal Code* (WA); s 23 of the *Criminal Code* (WA) was divided into 3 sections (ss 23, 23A, 23B) in 2008 these latter sections being inserted by section 4 of the *Criminal Law Amendment (Homicide) Act 2008* which was in turn amended by section 7 of the *Arson Legislation Amendment Act 2009*. The High Court reference to s 23 is restated as s 23A as a result of these recent amendments. See, in general, T. Crofts and K. Burton, *The Criminal Codes: Commentary and Materials* (6th edn, Pyrmont, NSW, 2009), [9.160], [10.270], [10.450].

the result of mental impairment, as defined, he or she must plead insanity. In such a case the accused is entitled to a qualified acquittal. Where, however, the accused's involuntary acts are not the product of mental impairment, as defined, but arise from some other mental condition, which causes the involuntary action, the accused will be entitled to an outright acquittal. Hence, the distinction between automatism as subsumed within the defence of mental impairment and automatism as it relates to involuntariness will turn on whether the state of automatism proceeds from a state of mental impairment.

The scope of automatism is the same at common law as it is under the code jurisdictions.[156] At common law whether automatism is understood as restricted to the defence of insanity or as relating to involuntariness will be determined by whether or not the mental condition which caused the involuntary action is characterized as a disease of the mind.[157] If automatism does not proceed from a disease of the mind the ensuing state is one of involuntariness. Where however automatism is due to a disease of the mind, the only defence available to an accused is that of insanity or insane automatism.[158] As expressed by King CJ in *Radford*:[159]

> If the conduct which would otherwise be criminal is involuntary, the accused is entitled to acquittal unless the involuntariness results from disease of the mind. If it results from disease of the mind, the accused is guilty unless the evidence proves on a balance of probabilities that the conduct resulted from a defect of reason caused by the disease of the mind in consequence of which the accused did not understand the nature and quality of his actions or did not know that they were wrong.[160]

Consequently, in order for insane automatism to be established it must be shown that due to a disease of the mind the accused did not know the nature, quality or wrongness of his or her conduct.[161] This will result in a qualified acquittal, with the defendant most likely subject to detention in a secure psychiatric facility. If, on the other hand, automatism does not proceed from a disease of the mind, the state of involuntariness will be characterized as one of 'sane' automatism and result in an unconditional acquittal. The scope of automatism may be arranged schematically as follows:

---

156 *R v Falconer* (1990) 171 CLR 30; this is however subject to the exception of automatism arising in the context of self-induced intoxication (*O'Connor* (1980) 146 CLR 64; *R v Kusu* [1981] Qd R 136).

157 *Rabey v R* (1981) 54 CCC (2d) 1; *R v Cottle* [1958] NZLR 999; *R v Falconer* (1990) 171 CLR 30.

158 *Bratty v A-G (Northern Ireland)* [1963] AC 386.

159 *R v Radford* (1985) 42 SASR 266.

160 Ibid. 273.

161 *R v Rabey* (1977) 37 CCC (2d) 461; Fairall and Yeo, *Criminal Defences in Australia* (n. 106) 284; Yeo, 'Clarifying Automatism' (n. 125) 445.

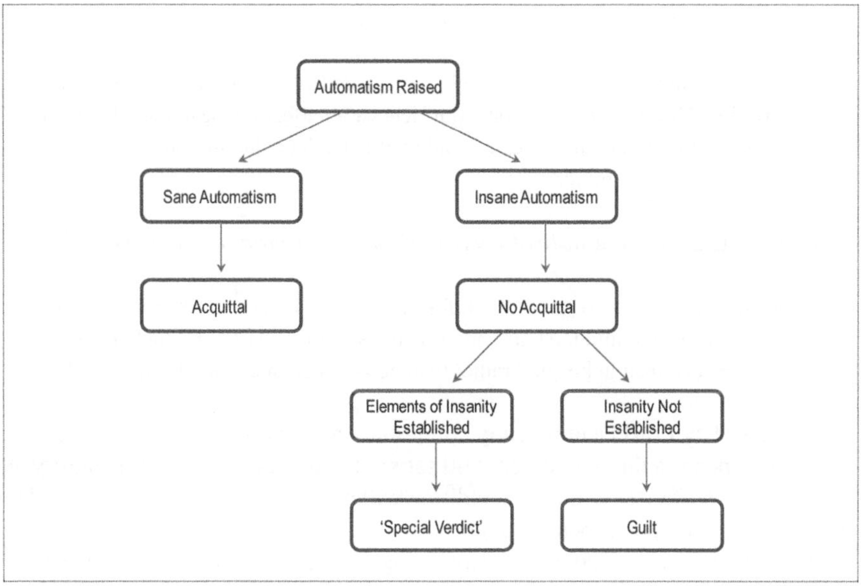

Figure 2.1 Scope of automatism

The following section will outline the way in which the criminal law distinguishes between those states of automatism going to voluntariness (sane automatism) and those states of automatism subsumed under the mental impairment defence (insane automatism).

Distinguishing sane and insane automatism

Three tests have been judicially developed in order to define which mental conditions may be characterized as a disease of the mind: the recurrence or 'continuing-danger' test, the 'internal–external' test and the 'sound–unsound mind' test, the latter having been developed in the context of psychological-blow automatism.[162] Where such a test is satisfied, the state of automatism will result in a finding of insane automatism and may lead to detention under a therapeutic regime. Where the state of automatism does not satisfy any of these tests it will be characterized as sane automatism and may lead to outright acquittal of the accused. Each of these tests will be considered in turn.

162 See B McSherry, 'Defining What is a "Disease of the Mind"', (n. 131) 82.

The continuing-danger test In *R v Meddings*,[163] it was held that:

> The potentiality of repetition … might be regarded as a discrimen between cases of irrational behaviour due to some transient cause affecting the mind, other than disease of the mind, and cases of irrational behaviour due to defective reason from disease of the mind.[164]

Similarly, Lord Denning in *Bratty v A-G (Northern Ireland)*,[165] remarked that:

> Any mental disorder which has manifested itself in violence and is prone to recur is a disease of the mind. At any rate it is the sort of disease for which a person should be detained in hospital rather than be given an unqualified acquittal.[166]

As expressed by Lord Denning, any condition which has the potential to recur and in so doing poses a threat to others will satisfy the disease of the mind enquiry. An accused who suffers from such a condition will not be unconditionally released but will be subject to a therapeutic regime.

Several criticisms have been made against the use of the recurrence or continuing-danger test as a means of distinguishing sane from insane automatism. First, the prediction of dangerousness is unreliable and may result in what have been described as false positives, or instances of over-prediction.[167] Secondly, there is no necessary connection between the recurrence of a condition and the danger posed by an accused suffering from such a condition. There are a range of conditions that have the potential to recur yet which are controllable through medication or appropriate health management. For example, diabetes,[168] epilepsy[169] and sleepwalking[170] are all conditions, the occurrence of which may be controlled through medical intervention. To detain an individual in a secure psychiatric facility for a condition that may be readily managed on the basis that if left untreated it may recur is unfair.[171] Thirdly, and conversely, if recurrence

163 [1966] VR 306.

164 Ibid. 309 per Sholl J.

165 [1963] AC 386.

166 Ibid. 412.

167 See H.J. Steadman, 'From Dangerousness to Risk Assessment of Community Violence: Taking Stock at the Turn of the Century' (2000) 28 *Journal of the American Academy of Psychiatry and Law* 265.

168 *Hennessy* [1989] 2 All ER 9.

169 *Sullivan* [1984] 1 AC 156.

170 In respect of the controversy surrounding the correct characterization of 'somnambulism', see Brookbanks 'Insanity' (n. 54) 146: *Burgess* [1991] 2 QB 92, sleepwalking constitutes a disease of the mind and therefore not relevant to issue of voluntariness; contra, *Parks* (1992) 75 CCC (3d), sleepwalking is a sleep disorder and not a disease of the mind and consequently relevant to the issue of voluntariness.

171 McSherry, 'Defining What is a "Disease of the Mind"', (n. 131) 83.

is the test adopted to decide whether a condition will be characterized as sane or insane automatism even a serious mental condition that is not likely to recur will fail the test.[172] The fact that a condition such as for example mental disorder resulting from cerebral oedema, is not likely to recur, is not sufficient to preclude its characterization as a disease of the mind.[173] Consequently, the potential for recurrence, or continuing danger, will not provide a sufficient condition by which to distinguish sane from insane automatism.

Internal–external test The internal–external test draws a distinction between those states of automatism that have been produced by external causes and those that arise from internal causes.[174] As expressed by the Canadian Court of Appeal:

> In general, the distinction to be drawn is between the malfunctioning of the mind arising from some cause that is primarily internal to the accused, having its source in his [or her] psychological or emotional make-up, or in some organic pathology, as opposed to a malfunctioning of the mind which is the transient effect produced by some specific external factor such as, for example, concussion.[175]

Where an accused's state of automatism has been produced by an external cause, such as for example, a physical blow,[176] the resultant state will be consistent with sane automatism. The accused's automatism in such an instance will go to the issue of the voluntariness of his or her action. In contrast, where an accused's state of automatism has been produced by an internal cause, such as epilepsy[177] or a neurological disorder[178] such a state will be subsumed under the test of insanity. The rationale for the internal–external test is the view that, where the cause of automatism is internal to the accused, actions arising from the state of automatism will be more likely to recur. In the light of such recurrence, the accused is considered to be inherently dangerous and should not be accorded a full acquittal

---

172 *Rabey* (1981) 54 CCC (2d) 1, 17 per Dickson J; *Parks* (1992) 75 CCC (3d) 287, 309–10 per La Forest J.

173 *Hall* (1988) 36 A Crim R 368; see, *Stone* (1999) 134 CCC (3d) 353, 438 per Bastarache J; *R v Kemp* [1957] 1 QB 399, 407.

174 The distinction draws on the common law formulation used by King CJ to determine instances of insanity: *R v Radford* (1985) 42 SASR 266, 274; cp. *Criminal Code* (WA) s 8; *Criminal Code* (Cth) s 7.3(9).

175 *R v Rabey* (1977) 37 CCC (2d) 461, 477, affirmed Supreme Court of Canada *Rabey v R* (1981) 54 CCC1.

176 *Cooper v McKenna; Ex parte Cooper* [1960] Qd R 406; *Wogandt* (1988) 33 A Crim R 31.

177 *R v Cottle* [1958] NZLR 999; *Bratty v A-G (Northern Ireland)* [1963] AC 386; *R v Sullivan* [1984] 1 AC 156; *Youssef* (1990) A Crim R 1.

178 *Police v Bannin* [1991] 2 NZLR 237; *Hughes* (1989) 42 A Crim R 270.

but should be detained in a secure psychiatric facility. The policy considerations underpinning the test find full expression in *Bratty v A-G (Northern Ireland)*.[179]

However, the internal–external test has been criticized as a basis on which to distinguish sane from insane automatism. Toohey J in *R v Falconer*[180] noted that 'the application of the "external factor" test is artificial and pays insufficient regard to the subtleties surrounding the notion of mental disease'.[181] While the internal–external test is reliant on identifying an underlying pathological state, certain medical conditions are by their nature complex and blur the distinction between internal and external causes.[182] Consequently, the identification of an underlying pathological state will, in certain instances, be arbitrary. In particular, the artificial nature of the internal–external test has resulted in rulings in, for example, cases of sleep-walking and diabetes that are difficult to reconcile. For example, notwithstanding the view that sleep-walking results from an internal condition, it has traditionally been held to be relevant to the issue of an accused's voluntariness.[183] In *R v Parks*,[184] the Canadian Supreme Court held that the accused's sleep-walking was not a disease of the mind but a sleep disorder relevant to the question of his voluntariness. Yet, in *Burgess v R*,[185] it was held that, as sleep-walking is an internal condition likely to recur, it is a disease of the mind and relevant to the issue of the accused's sanity.

Similarly, the application of the internal–external test has led to arbitrary results in the case of diabetes. In *R v Quick*,[186] the accused was a diabetic and was suffering from hypoglycaemia (deficiency in blood sugar) at the time of the offence. At his trial the accused's defence of involuntariness on the basis of automatism was rejected, the trial judge ruling that the only defence available on the evidence was that of insanity. On appeal, the Court of Appeal held that the hypoglycaemic episode was not the direct result of the accused's diabetes. Rather, it was the accused's intake of insulin which gave rise to his condition. Applying the internal–external test, the Court of Appeal held that the cause of the automatic state was an external factor and not a mental malfunction caused by a disease of the mind. The court noted that if an external factor such as a drug is applied to an accused and results in a transient state of automatism, such a state cannot be said

179 *Bratty v A-G (Northern Ireland)* [1963] AC 386, 409–11 per Lord Denning.

180 (1990) 171 CLR 30.

181 Ibid. 75–6.

182 See *Stone* (1999) 134 CCC (3d) 353, 434 per Bastarache J, citing La Forest J in *Parks* (1992) 75 CCC (3d) 287, 309–10.

183 *R v Tolson* (1889) 23 QBD 168; *Bratty v A-G (Northern Ireland)* [1963] AC 386, 403 per Lord Denning; *Falconer* 171 CLR 30, 75–6 per Toohey J.

184 (1992) 75 CCC (3d) 287; see McSherry, 'Defining What is a "Disease of the Mind"' (n 131) for an analysis of the sleepwalking cases.

185 [1991] 2 QB 92.

186 [1973] QB 910.

to have been produced by a disease of the mind.[187] Consequently, on the facts, the accused's state of automatism gave rise to an issue of involuntariness.

However, in *Hennessy v R*,[188] evidence was tendered indicating that the accused's state of automatism was caused by hyperglycaemia (an excess of blood sugar). The hyperglycaemia, in turn, was the direct result of the accused's failure to take insulin. At trial, it was ruled that the accused's condition was due to a disease of the mind and could only give rise to the defence of insanity. On appeal, the Court of Appeal upheld the trial judge's ruling that the accused's condition was not the product of an external factor. Lord Lane CJ noted that the condition arose from an inherent defect, namely, diabetes, and, for that reason, was the result of a disease of the mind.[189] Yet, notwithstanding the above, there is no principled reason to distinguish an accused who fails to take insulin from one who takes an excessive amount.

It was noted above that the rationale for the internal–external test is the view that, where the cause of the automatism is internal to the accused, actions arising from the automatism will be more likely to recur. Given such recurrence the accused is considered to be dangerous and not accorded a full acquittal. However, the internal–external test fails to provide means by which to distinguish those accused who pose a danger from those who do not. For example, there is no reason to believe that an accused suffering from hypoglycaemia is any less dangerous than an accused that has experienced hyperglycaemia.

Notwithstanding the above difficulties most common-law jurisdictions, notably England and Canada, continue to use the internal–external test. However, in the leading Australian case of *R v Falconer*,[190] the High Court held that evidence of dissociation arising from severe emotional shock should not be treated as irrelevant to the issue of voluntariness merely because it is not caused by an external physical event.[191] In that case the High Court proceeded to refine the test for distinguishing between sane and insane automatism by focusing on the cause of the automatism.

Sound–unsound mind test Cases involving psychological-blow automatism are characterized by the accused entering a state of 'dissociation'.[192] Most instances of dissociation occur in the context of traumatic events involving physical or

187 [1973] QB 910, 920.

188 [1989] 2 All ER 9.

189 Ibid. 293.

190 *R v Falconer* (1990) 171 CLR 30.

191 Ibid. 76 per Toohey J (Deane, Dawson and Gaudron JJ agreeing), citing *Radford* (1985) 42 SASR 266, 276 per King CJ.

192 See DSM-IV-TR (n. 95) 447, 'a disruption in the usually integrated functions of consciousness, memory, identity, or perception of the environment'; M. Steinberg, *Handbook for the Assessment of Dissociation: A Clinical Guide* (Washington, DC, 1995) 8–13, recognizes five core symptoms of dissociation: 'amnesia, depersonalisation, derealization, identity confusion and identity alteration'.

sexual abuse. It is the psychologically shocking nature (the psychological blow) of such events which may result in an accused entering a state of automatism. Early case law indicated that evidence of anxiety, depression and stress is not capable of giving rise to a state of automatism going to the issue of voluntariness.[193] However, the High Court case of *R v Falconer*[194] held that dissociation caused by anxiety, depression and stress may give rise to a state of automatism relevant to voluntariness. Where the state of dissociation is not the result of a disease of the mind, then the accused's state of automatism may result in an outright acquittal. Where, however, the state of dissociation has arisen as a result of a disease of the mind, only a qualified acquittal will be available to the accused. Consequently, the issue in such cases is whether the resulting dissociative state may be characterized as a disease of the mind. The sound–unsound mind test is a refinement of the internal–external test, developed in the context of dissociation arising as a result of extreme psychological shock. The sound–unsound mind test provides guidance in determining whether an accused has an underlying pathological infirmity of mind, or 'unsound mind', and whether he or she poses a future danger.

The test for determining whether a dissociative state should fall within automatism subsumed under the defence of insanity, or give rise to the issue of the accused's voluntariness, was developed by King CJ in *R v Radford*.[195] In that case it was held that 'the significant distinction is between the reaction of an unsound mind to its own delusions or to external stimuli on the one hand and the reaction of a sound mind to external stimuli, including stress producing factors, on the other hand'.[196] As a result of this formulation two questions assume critical importance in determining the appropriate characterization of an accused's state of automatism in the context of psychological blow automatism:[197]

1. How is it to be determined whether the mind of the accused is sound or unsound?
2. What will amount to a 'stress producing' factor for the purpose of assessing the external stimuli that may cause a sound mind to react?

In respect of the first question, the High Court in *R v Falconer* applied King CJ's distinction and held that a psychological blow resulting from an external event may result in non-insane automatism.[198] Further, in order to establish whether an

193 *Tsigos* [1964–5] NSWR 1607; *Joyce* [1970] SASR 184; *Sullivan* [1984] 1 AC 156; *Hennessy* [1989] 2 All ER 9.

194 *R v Falconer* (1990) 171 CLR 30, 55 per Mason CJ, Brennan, McHugh JJ.

195 (1985) 42 SASR 266.

196 Ibid. 276.

197 See Fairall and Yeo, *Criminal Defences in Australia* (n. 106) 284 for a comparable approach.

198 (1990) 171 CLR 30, 76 per Toohey, Mason CJ, Brennan and McHugh JJ.

accused's mind was sound or unsound, the court placed an objective gloss on the sound–unsound mind test. The court held that:

> The law must postulate a standard of mental strength which, in the face of a given level of psychological trauma, is capable of protecting the mind from malfunction to the extent prescribed in the respective definitions of insanity. That standard must be the standard of the ordinary person: if the mind's strength is below that standard, the mind is infirm; if it is of or above that standard, the mind is sound or sane. This is an objective standard which corresponds with the objective standard imported for the purpose of provocation.[199]

Moreover, the High Court held that:

> If the psychological trauma causes a sound mind, possessed of the requisite standard of strength, to malfunction only transiently so as to produce the effects mentioned in the M'Naghten Rules … the malfunction cannot be attributed to mental infirmity but to the 'nature of the man': that is to say, a malfunction which is transient and not prone to recur and to which the mind of the ordinary person would be subject if exposed to the same psychological trauma is neither a mental disease nor a natural mental infirmity. It is [not] … an instance of insanity at common law.[200]

Consequently, an accused's state of dissociation will be held to amount to non-insane automatism where the dissociative state is (1) transient, (2) caused by trauma, whether physical or psychological, which the mind of an ordinary person would be likely not to have withstood and (3) not prone to recur. A state of mind which does not satisfy these exempting qualifications will amount to a disease of the mind.[201]

In respect of the second question the High Court in *Falconer* failed to articulate what the 'given level of psychological trauma' must be, that an accused should withstand, in order to satisfy the objective test. However, in *R v Radford (No 2)*,[202] King CJ held that:

---

199 Ibid. 55 per Mason CJ, Brennan and McHugh JJ; Gaudron J, to like effect, postulated a state of mind 'experienced by or encountered in normal persons' (85).

200 Ibid. 61 per Mason CJ, Brennan and McHugh JJ.

201 The 'ordinary-person' test has not met with universal approval, with several commentators remarking on problems associated with appeals to an objective standard (see Fairall and Yeo, *Criminal Defences in Australia* (n. 106) 290–1; Bronitt and McSherry, *Principles of Criminal Law* (n. 18) 264-5; however, as the latter authors acknowledge, similar difficulties confront the 'ordinary person' test in the context of provocation and self-defence.

202 (1987) 11 Crim LJ 231.

> Feelings of jealousy and resentment over the breakdown of matrimonial and other sexual relationships and hatred of a rival lover are commonplace human emotions. The law must firmly repress any tendency for people harbouring such dark emotions to give in to them by way of murderous violence.[203]

Similarly, in *R v Rabey*,[204] it was held that:

> The ordinary stresses and disappointments of life which are the common lot of mankind do not constitute an external cause constituting an explanation for the malfunctioning of the mind which takes it out of the category of a disease of the mind.[205]

In that case the Court of Appeal held that where a state of dissociation results from an ordinary event, the source of the dissociation must be the accused's psychological or emotional, state. The Court of Appeal did however accept that 'extraordinary external events', such as being attacked with a knife, or seeing a family member murdered or seriously injured, may affect the ordinary person.[206] Consequently, for the purpose of assessing the external stimuli which may cause a sound mind to react, that which will amount to a 'stress producing' factor must be something more than an ordinary event. What will be required is an event involving an extraordinary degree of stress.

Notwithstanding the refinements introduced by the sound–unsound mind formulation to the internal–external test, all of the tests have been viewed as 'failing to distinguish between sane from insane automatism with any clarity, and in some cases caus[ing] even greater confusion about the distinction'.[207] Similarly, the Supreme Court of Canada in *R v Stone*[208] held that the continuing-danger test 'must be qualified to recognize that while a continuing danger suggests a disease of the mind, a finding of no continuing danger does not preclude a finding of a disease of the mind'.[209] Further, the Supreme Court noted that the internal–external test was not 'a universal classificatory scheme for "disease of the mind" [given that in certain cases] the dichotomy between internal and external causes becomes blurred'.[210]

---

203 Ibid. 232; see further B. McSherry, 'Men Behaving Badly: Current Issues in Provocation, Automatism, Mental Impairment and Criminal Responsibility' (2005) 12 *Psychiatry, Psychology and Law* 13.

204 (1977) 37 CCC (2d) 461.

205 Ibid. 477 per Martin J (CA), approved *Rabey v R* [1980] 2 SCR 513 D (SC).

206 Ibid.; cp. *R v Tsigos* [1964–5] NSWR 1607; *R v Joyce* [1970] SASR 184.

207 Victorian Law Reform Commission, *Defences to Homicide: Final Report* (n. 107) 5.139.

208 [1999] 134 CCC (3d) 353.

209 Ibid. 438 per Bastarache J.

210 Ibid. 434 per Bastarache J.

In the light of these reservations, the Supreme Court of Canada proceeded to elucidate both the purpose of the tests and the way in which they are to be applied. In *Stone*, the Supreme Court held that both the continuing-danger and internal–external test are to be treated merely as analytic tools, or factors, rather than as mutually exclusive methods in determining the characterization of an accused's automatism. As expressed in the judgment:

> The continuing danger factor should not be viewed as an alternative or mutually exclusive approach to the internal cause factor. Although different, both of these approaches are relevant factors in the disease of the mind inquiry. As such, in any given case, a trial judge may find one, the other or both of these approaches of assistance. To reflect this unified, holistic approach to the disease of the mind question, it is therefore more appropriate to refer to the internal cause factor and the continuing danger factor, rather than the internal cause theory and the continuing danger theory.[211]

Moreover, as the *Stone* Court noted, other factors will also be of relevance in establishing whether an accused has suffered from a disease of the mind:

> In determining this issue, policy concerns [will] assist trial judges in answering the fundamental question of mixed law and fact which is at the centre of the disease of the mind inquiry: whether society requires protection from the accused and, consequently, whether the accused should be subject to evaluation under the regime contained in Part XX.1 of the Code.[212]

Similarly, the High Court in *Falconer* noted that both the continuing danger and the internal–external test were artificial and not to be rigidly followed. Rather, both these tests were to be used merely as guides in determining whether a state of automatism was to be characterized as a state of sane or insane automatism.[213] When rigidly followed the tests provide 'artificial' means of deciding which accused will be acquitted outright and which accused will be restrained in a secure psychiatric facility.[214] As analytic tools the tests provide guidance rather than conclusive proof of whether an accused's state of automatism is to be characterized as a disease of the mind. However, as outlined above, the fact that instances of sane and insane automatism reveal 'overlaps and blurred borderlines' leads to difficulty in distinguishing instances of automatism as they relate to involuntariness

211 Ibid. per Bastarache J.

212 [1999] 134 CCC (3d) 353, 440–1.

213 *R v Falconer* (1990) 171 CLR 30, 50–1 per Mason CJ, Brennan and McHugh JJ, 77 per Toohey J, 84 per Gaudron J.

214 McSherry, 'Defining What is a "Disease of the Mind" ' (n. 131) 89.

and when subsumed under the defence of mental impairment.[215] The next section will consider the problems faced by the criminal law in the light of the current uncertainty surrounding the correct characterization of states of automatism.

A deeper problem: injustice

A recent South Australian case, *R v Singh*,[216] is illustrative of the difficulties of characterizing certain states of automatism as instances of sane automatism. Singh was estranged from his wife, the mother of his 2-year-old daughter. After an acrimonious separation, Singh's wife obtained a domestic violence order against Singh in regards to entering her premises, assaulting, harassing or threatening her. As a result of the order pre-determined times were set aside for contact visits between Singh and his daughter. During the course of one such visit the daughter began screaming as Singh tried to put her in his car. Evidence was tendered at the trial that at this point Singh was abused and struck by his wife. Immediately thereafter Singh removed a rifle from his vehicle and shot his estranged wife dead with four shots fired at close range. He was found the following day in a motel room in Sydney where he had driven with his daughter after having replaced the South Australian number plates of his vehicle with New South Wales ones. He claimed to have no recollection of any of the events subsequent to being struck by his wife the preceding day. At his trial for murder, Singh was convicted and sentenced to prison for a 24-year non-parole period. On appeal to the Supreme Court of South Australia, it was held the trial judge had misdirected the jury in respect of the burden of proof and a re-trial was ordered.[217] At his re-trial psychiatric evidence tendered by Singh raised automatism ('dissociative amnesia') caused by external stress as having resulted in a state of involuntariness at the time of the offence. The jury returned a majority verdict acquitting Singh.

It has been remarked that cases such as *Singh* highlight the difficulties associated with pleas of sane automatism.[218] In particular, the extension of the doctrine of automatism to cases of dissociation arising from a psychological blow has been viewed as problematic in several respects.[219] As noted earlier, where

---

215 E. Lederman, 'Non-Insane and Insane Automatism: Reducing the Significance of a Problematic Distinction' (1985) 34 *International Criminal Law Quarterly* 820; cp M. Goode, 'On Subjectivity and Objectivity in Denial of Criminal Responsibility' (1987) 11 *Criminal Law Journal* 131, 151–2.

216 (2003) 86 SASR 473 (SC SA); See, McSherry, 'Men Behaving Badly' (n. 203) 17–19.

217 Ibid.

218 See *R v Szymusiak* [1972] 3 OR 602, 608 per Shroeder JA describing evidence of psychological-blow automatism as 'the last refuge of a scoundrel'; contrast VLRC's view that the law relating to automatism should not be changed (Victorian Law Reform Commission, *Defences to Homicide: Final Report* (n. 107) 5.160).

219 See B. McSherry, 'Getting Away with Murder? Dissociative States and Criminal Responsibility' (1998) 21 *International Journal of Law and Psychiatry* 163; McSherry 'Men

evidence of involuntariness is raised it is incumbent on the prosecution to rebut such evidence beyond a reasonable doubt. Where a jury has a reasonable doubt as to whether an accused did in fact suffer from a state of dissociation at the time of the offence he or she must be acquitted. However, as the VLRC has pointed out, 'there is no reliable way of verifying whether a particular trauma was the cause of the unconscious or unwilled state'.[220] Yet, in the absence of a clear causal connection between a psychological blow and a claimed state of dissociation, it will always be difficult to establish whether the dissociative state has been caused by the psychological blow or whether in fact the accused was suffering from such a state.[221] In such cases it may prove to be extremely difficult for the prosecution to rebut a claim of involuntariness. Further, instances of sane automatism will often be accompanied by claims of amnesia on the part of the accused in respect of the offence.[222] Yet, there is no way of medically determining whether the amnesia was the result of the psychological blow or whether it was in response to the, paradigmatic, act of killing.[223] Research indicates that in such instances the act of killing may prove so traumatic that it will result in the offender blocking it from his or her memory in order to protect him- or herself.[224] Finally, several cases of psychological-blow automatism have occurred in circumstances in which the accused may have had a reason, or motive, to kill his or her victim.[225] It has been suggested that as such cases involve behaviour which is purposeful and goal-directed it provides 'an insufficient basis for an automatism argument'.[226]

As voluntariness is a threshold condition of criminal conduct, a lack of voluntariness will exculpate in all cases. However, unless the circumstances in which evidence of automatism may be raised are limited, there is a potential for bogus claims of involuntariness being raised by accused. Yet, a failure of courts to convict where appropriate and acquit where deserved will result in a denial of justice. In order to safeguard against such injustice eventuating Chapter 6 will

---

Behaving Badly' (n. 203); Victorian Law Reform Commission, *Defences to Homicide: Final Report* (n. 107) 5.160.

220 Victorian Law Reform Commission, *Defences to Homicide: Final Report* (n. 107) 5.140.

221 Ibid.

222 See S. Porter et al., 'Memory for Murder: A Psychological Perspective on Dissociative Amnesia in Legal Contexts' (2001) 24 *International Journal of Law and Psychiatry* 24, citing research indicating that up to 65% of accused involved in cases of murder or attempted murder report amnesia; cp. *Leonboyer* [2001] VSCA 149, para 49.

223 Victorian Law Reform Commission, *Defences to Homicide: Final Report* (n. 107) 5.142.

224 Ibid., citing *Leonboyer* [2001] VSCA 149, para 49, psychiatric evidence tendered by Professor Mullen.

225 *Falconer* (1990) 171 CLR 30; *Leonboyer* [2001] VSCA 149; *Hawkins v R* (1994) 179 CLR 500.

226 Victorian Law Reform Commission, *Defences to Homicide: Final Report* (n. 107) 5.143, citing 'some of the psychiatrists consulted by the Commission'.

argue for the explicit recognition of a defence of impaired consciousness. As a result of such a defence, when an accused seeks to be acquitted on the basis of evidence of automatism, there will be a requirement that such evidence satisfy the necessary conditions of an excuse. The defence will seek to ensure that claims of sane automatism are circumscribed within a normatively structured framework. It will be argued in Chapter 6 that unless claims of automatism are restricted within such a normatively structured framework decisions may result in acquittals which are not deserved, as well as failures to excuse where appropriate.

Conclusion

This chapter has outlined the substantive criminal law in relation to the mental state defence of insanity and the doctrine of automatism. The chapter began by noting the key elements of the M'Naghten rules and proceeded to analyse these in turn. The major portion of the discussion of the M'Naghten rules concerned the object and nature of the knowledge requirement as expressed in the second limb of the defence: whether the accused knew that what he or she was doing was wrong. The analytic thrust of this portion aimed to clarify both the object and nature of the knowledge which the accused must lack if he or she is to raise the defence. Australian courts and legislatures have viewed the object of knowledge which the accused must lack as knowledge of the moral wrongness of his or her act. In respect of the nature of the knowledge the accused must lack, Australian jurisdictions are divided as to whether it is actual knowledge or a capacity for knowledge of the wrongness of his or her act which an accused must lack.

As a characteristic example of serious mental disorder *Hadfield* provided an apposite case study of the operation of the insanity defence across several actual and hypothetical jurisdictions. The analysis of *Hadfield*'s case revealed the various ways in which an accused may fail to think rationally and so be accorded the insanity defence. In particular, *Hadfield*'s case revealed the way in which serious mental disorder may co-exist with the ability to tell legal right from wrong. Further, the analysis revealed that the current operation of the insanity defence in both the common-law and code jurisdictions would acquit an accused such as Hadfield regardless of whether actual knowledge or a capacity for knowledge is required. This part of the chapter concluded with a comment on the cognitive bias of the M'Naghten rules and the way in which states of volitional impairment are treated across the various Australian jurisdictions.

The second substantive matter analysed in this chapter concerned the operation of the doctrine of automatism. It was shown that as conventionally understood a lack of voluntariness is the defining feature of automatism. Further, case law reveals two varieties of automatism: sane and insane. Sane automatism is related to the criminal law's requirement that all criminal conduct must be voluntary. An absence of voluntariness that is not the result of a disease of the mind will lead to an acquittal. Where, however the absence of voluntariness is due to a disease of the mind, automatism is subsumed under the defence of insanity. The M'Naghten rules apply to a state of automatism that is caused by a disease of the mind. Consequently, in order for insane automatism to be established it must be shown that, due to a disease of the mind, the accused did not know the nature of the conduct or its wrongness. A state of insane automatism will lead to a qualified acquittal with the accused most likely being subjected to a therapeutic regime. Having outlined the tests and commented on their respective shortcomings, it was noted that the tests had come to be judicially viewed as merely factors to be considered in determining whether an accused is to be released unconditionally.

The final part of this chapter considered an issue to be taken up in more detail in Chapter 6 below, namely, the problem of injustice arising from the difficulty of verifying instances of sane automatism. It was noted in this part that the extension of the doctrine of automatism to problematic cases such as psychological-blow automatism rendered the doctrine subject to abuse. It was contended that it is a failure to restrict the circumstances in which automatism is raised that gives rise to the potential for bogus claims of involuntariness. In particular, the absence of a structured framework, akin to that found in modern criminal-law excuses, has the potential to lead to a degree of ad hoc decision-making by courts and juries. Moreover, it was noted that such ad hoc decision-making may result in instances of injustice with the acquittal of accused who do not deserve to be acquitted on the basis of involuntariness.

The next chapter will explore those factors which assist the court in determining whether a disease of the mind has been established. The exploration of these factors will take place in the context of the question of whether it is possible to justify the disposition of a mentally impaired acquittee on the basis of 'social defence' considerations.

Chapter 3

Disease of the Mind: Individual Justice and Societal Protection

Introduction: competing demands

The M'Naghten rules[1] require a defect of reason to arise from a disease of the mind. This chapter will consider both the meaning of the latter expression and the various factors which inform this meaning in the context of both the common law and statute. It will be argued that the expression 'disease of the mind' is a general term under which courts and legislatures balance three factors: clinical evidence, a judgment of responsibility and community interest.

The first factor, clinical evidence, refers to the provision of expert psychiatric and forensic psychological evidence. An aspect of such clinical evidence will involve the classification of an accused's behaviour in terms of a diagnostic category. The classification of an accused's behaviour allows an expert witness to provide the trier of fact with a greater understanding of what the symptoms of a particular condition are. Such an understanding will allow the trier of fact to determine whether the accused was suffering from such a condition at the time of the offence. Additionally, clinical evidence will assist the court in determining the legal issue of whether a particular condition amounts to a disease of the mind. That is, evidence of the symptoms, nature and causes of an accused's condition will be relevant to the court in determining whether a particular condition is capable of constituting a disease of the mind. The clinical expertise with which psychiatry applies discrete diagnostic categories to individuals is an aspect of psychiatry's therapeutic rationale. Such clinical expertise permits expert psychiatric and forensic psychological evidence to be used in diagnosing an individual's treatability and, moreover, evaluating his or her (future) risk to others. This will be relevant to the question of such an individual's treatment and disposition.

The second factor which is encompassed by the disease of the mind enquiry is a judgment of responsibility. The judgment of responsibility addresses the question of an agent's moral and legal responsibility. The question of responsibility concerns whether an individual has the requisite capacities to be held morally responsible and so be potentially liable for the imposition of any sanctions thought appropriate by the law. A responsible agent is an agent who will be considered to

---

1 *R v M'Naghten* (1843) 10 Cl and Fin 200; 8 ER 718.

be a fit subject of our responsibility practices.[2] One such responsibility practice involves the larger normative exercise undertaken by the criminal law in according categories of liability to the rational and autonomous conduct of individuals. The judgment of responsibility is important as it articulates the intuition that it is wrong to punish an individual whose mental condition precludes him or her from either knowing the nature and quality or wrongness of his or her act or who lacks the capacity to control his or her conduct.

The third factor informing the disease of the mind enquiry is community interest. Community-interest considerations encompass the societal interest in being protected from the threat of harm posed by those considered to be at risk of harming others. There is a community interest in ensuring that such individuals are properly managed and treated justly by being provided with the requisite resources and facilities. While the disease of the mind is a distinct aspect of the defence of insanity to that of the disposition of the accused, both are informed by concerns with societal protection. In particular, the community-interest aspect of the defence will be of relevance to the issue of the correct characterization of an accused's state of mind, in addition to the question of his or her disposition. The way in which a concern with societal protection informs the disease of the mind enquiry and the disposition of a mentally impaired acquittee will be discussed below.

While there is a great deal of overlap between these factors each factor accounts for a discrete area of enquiry involving different issues and methodologies. As a result of these differing issues and methodologies, tensions and competing demands arise when these same factors are used in order to determine the disease of the mind enquiry. Consequently, an investigation of the concept of disease of the mind offers an opportunity to view the operation of several competing demands and the way in which these competing demands are treated by the criminal law. For example, clinical evidence will be of relevance in determining both the meaning of disease of the mind and whether the evidence is capable of establishing that the accused was suffering from such a disease of the mind. However, as will be argued below clinical evidence alone cannot be determinative of the enquiry. The degree to which psychiatric evidence will be allowed to inform the disease of the mind enquiry will depend on the extent to which it has an impact on the judgment of responsibility and social-defence considerations.[3]

Methodologically, the approach followed in this chapter begins from a similar starting point to that adopted by Nicola Lacey and Alan Norrie in the area of criminal law and philosophy.[4] According to these theorists, the law is confronted

2 For an account of the nature of such responsibility practices, see P. Cane, *Responsibility in Law and Morality* (Oxford, 2002).

3 See D. Greig, *Neither Bad nor Mad: The Competing Discourses of Psychiatry, Law and Politics* (London, 2002).

4 See N. Lacey, 'Contingency, Coherence, and Conceptualism' in *Philosophy and the Criminal Law*, ed. A. Duff (Cambridge, 1998) 9; A. Norrie, 'Simulacra of Morality?

with a series of complex claims arising from various communal, moral and professional imperatives. For these theorists, any conflicting demands arising from these imperatives represent irreconcilable contradictions. One such contradiction concerns the issue of individual justice and societal protection.[5]

According to Nicola Lacey, social practices within and around the arena of criminal justice are part of a delicately balanced equilibrium depending on 'holding tensions at bay by exploiting logically contradictory discourses but disguising the fact by moving between different levels of, and spheres for, analysis'.[6] While at one level contradictory, at another level such an approach represents 'part of a complex strategy which allows the criminal law to keep various balls of different shapes and colours in the air at once'.[7] For Lacey and Norrie, the criminal law consists of a number of contradictions which, instead of being genuinely reconciled are by means of a sleight of hand ('complex strategy') made to seem reconciled. Any tensions arising in the law from these contradictions are socio-historical in nature and dynamic, sensitive to historical change and traceable to changes in social institutions.[8]

In contrast to the above account this chapter will argue that in the context of the defence of insanity the law does genuinely reconcile claims arising from communal, moral and professional imperatives. While there is complexity in the law as a result of the various demands arising from these imperatives, any attendant tensions have been resolved in a historically stable fashion.[9] The precise manner in which the law negotiates such a resolution will be discussed in the final substantive section of this chapter.

The chapter will begin with an overview of the disease of the mind enquiry as understood pursuant to the M'Naghten rules[10] and modern statutory enactments. This will then be followed by an account of how each of the various factors informs the disease of the mind enquiry. The first factor to be considered will be expert evidence and in particular the way in which clinical accounts of 'mental disorder' differ from the legal conception 'disease of the mind'. This will then be followed by an analysis of the judgment of responsibility and the various factors which are operative in distinguishing between those internal states for which an accused will be held responsible and those for which he or she will not. The third factor which

Beyond the Ideal/Actual Antinomies of Criminal Justice' in *Philosophy and the Criminal Law*, ed. A. Duff (Cambridge, 1998), 101.

5 See A. Norrie, *Crime, Reason and History: A Critical Introduction to Criminal Law* (2nd edn, London, 2001).

6 N. Lacey, 'A Clear Conception of Intention: Elusive or Illusory?' (1993) 56 *Modern Law Review* 621, 636.

7 Ibid. 641.

8 N. Lacey, 'Responsibility and Modernity in Criminal Law' (2001) 9 *Journal of Political Philosophy*, 249; N. Lacey, 'In Search of the Responsible Subject: History, Philosophy and Criminal Law Theory' (2001) 64 *Modern Law Review* 350.

9 See V. Tadros, *Criminal Responsibility* (Oxford, 2005) 3.

10 *R v M'Naghten* (1843) 10 Cl and Fin 200; 8 ER 718.

will be considered is the question of community interest. The community-interest aspect of the disease of the mind enquiry will be seen to be concerned with the issue of societal protection in the light of the likelihood that a mentally impaired individual's state of mental impairment may recur. The analysis of this aspect of the disease of the mind enquiry will also comment on the degree to which social-defence concerns underpin the issue of the disposition of an individual found to be mentally impaired. The final substantive section will outline the way in which these three factors are reconciled by the criminal law in the context of the disease of the mind enquiry. This section will also respond to objections of both a practical and principled nature raised against the criminal law's use of social-defence considerations in order to determine the disposition of an individual found non-responsible due to a disease of the mind. The final section will provide an overview of the analysis undertaken and conclusions reached.

Disease of the mind: two conceptions

While all Australian jurisdictions have statutory formulations of the defence, only some are declarative of the M'Naghten rules.[11] I will begin with the common-law defence of insanity before considering the various statutory formulations.

An influential statement defining disease of the mind at common law is that of King CJ in *R v Radford*:[12]

> The expression 'disease of the mind' is synonymous, in my view with 'mental illness'. The essential notion appears to be that in order to constitute insanity in the eyes of the law, the malfunction of the mental faculties called 'defect of reason' in the *M'Naghten rules*, must result from an underlying pathological infirmity of the mind, be it of long or short duration and be it permanent or temporary, which can be properly termed mental illness, as distinct from the reaction of a healthy mind to extraordinary external stimuli.[13]

King CJ's comment suggests that the expression 'disease of the mind' is to be given the same meaning as 'mental illness'. Equally, in *Radford*, it was held that the expression 'mental disease' is synonymous in meaning with 'disease of the mind'.[14] Consequently, at common law it is recognized that the expressions 'disease of the mind', 'mental disease' and 'mental illness' are synonymous.

---

11 A statutory formulation declarative of the common law is the *Crimes (Mental Impairment and Unfitness to be Tried) Act 1997* (Vic); see *R v Sebalj* [2003] VSC 181 (Unreported, SC Vic, Smith J, 5 June 2003).

12 (1985) 42 SASR 266.

13 Ibid. 274.

14 *Radford* (1985) 42 SASR 266, 274 per King CJ, approved *Falconer* (1990) 171 CLR 30, 49 per Mason CJ, Brennan, McHugh JJ.

This view has been accepted by the High Court as an accurate statement of law.[15] The distinction drawn by King CJ is that between a disease of the mind as 'an underlying pathological infirmity of the mind', on the one hand, and 'the reaction of a healthy mind to extraordinary external stimuli', on the other. According to this analysis a distinction may be drawn between those states of malfunction which have their source in an internal factor and those states of mental malfunction which have their source in an external factor. Where, the malfunctioning of the mind is caused by an external factor the defence of insanity is not available, and where the malfunction results in the accused's conduct being involuntary, the matter is dealt with as one of sane automatism.

Different expressions are used amongst the various Australian jurisdictions. The expression used under the codes of Queensland and Tasmania is 'mental disease'.[16] More recent statutory expressions are to be found in the Northern Territory, South Australia and Victoria. In each of these jurisdictions the expression used is 'mental impairment'.[17] Similarly, in the Commonwealth, ACT and Western Australian codes, the requisite disorder of mind is referred to as 'mental impairment', which is further defined as including various mental states.[18]

While statutory interpretations of 'disease of the mind' differ amongst the various jurisdictions, two distinct approaches have been recognized by commentators.[19] Some statutory formulations have sought to incorporate judicial pronouncements on the M'Naghten rules.[20] Other legislative enactments have sought to adopt refinements in clinical accounts of mental malfunction thereby bringing the definition of 'disease of the mind' more into line with those states of malfunctioning which correspond to the clinical notion of mental disorder.[21] An example of a statute that seeks to encompass judicial developments of the concept

15 *R v Falconer* (1990) 171 CLR 30, 53 per Mason CJ, Brennan and McHugh JJ, 60 per Deane and Dawson JJ, 85 per Gaudron J.

16 *Criminal Code* (Qld) s 27(1), 'or natural mental infirmity'; *Criminal Code* (Tas) s 16.

17 *Criminal Code* (NT) s 43; *Criminal Law Consolidation Act 1935* (SA) s 269C, 269E; *Crimes (Mental Impairment and Unfitness to be Tried) Act 1997* (Vic) s 20, not defined.

18 *Criminal Code* (Cth) s 7.3(1); *Criminal Code* (ACT) s 28; *Criminal Code* (WA) s 27. For the purposes of this chapter all such legislative expressions will be referred to as 'disease of the mind' without it necessarily being implied thereby that no differences of meaning exist between such statutory expressions and the common law expression.

19 P.A. Fairall and S. Yeo, *Criminal Defences in Australia* (4th edn, Chatswood, NSW, 2005) 254; S. Bronitt and B. McSherry, *Principles of Criminal Law* (3rd edn, Pyrmont, NSW, 2010), 242–3; Victorian Law Reform Commission, *Defences to Homicide: Options Paper* (Melbourne, 2003), 5.86.

20 *Criminal Code* (Cth) s 7.3(1); *Criminal Code* (ACT) s 28.

21 *Crimes Act 1900* (ACT) s 428B, replaced by the *Criminal Code* (ACT) s 28.

of disease of the mind is to be found in the Commonwealth Criminal Code.[22] The code defines 'mental impairment' as including 'senility, intellectual disability, mental illness, brain damage, and severe personality disorder'.[23] The code further defines 'mental illness' as:

> An underlying pathological infirmity of the mind, whether of long or short duration and whether permanent or temporary, but does not include a condition that results from the reaction of a healthy mind to extraordinary external stimuli. However, such a condition may be evidence of a mental illness if it involves some abnormality and is prone to recur.[24]

In particular, the code's definition of mental illness adopts the common-law formula derived from the judgment of King CJ in *Radford*.[25] Another statutory enactment that has sought to accommodate judicial developments of the insanity defence in its formulation is the Victorian Act. The Victorian Act, the *Crimes (Mental Impairment and Unfitness to be Tried) Act 1977* (Vic), has abrogated the McNaghten defence of insanity.[26] In place of the defence of insanity a new 'Defence of Mental Impairment' has been introduced requiring an accused to suffer from a mental impairment causing him or her to either not understand the nature and quality of his or her conduct or know that it is wrong.[27] While the Victorian Act employs the expression 'mental impairment' no definition of this is offered.[28] However, it has been held that the Victorian Act's formulation is a legislative restatement of the common law.[29] As a result, under the Victorian Act the expression 'mental impairment' bears the same meaning as the expression 'disease of the mind' found in the common-law defence of insanity.[30]

An example of a statutory enactment that seeks to accord with modern clinical conceptions of mental disorder is to be found in the *Crimes Act 1900* of the Australian Capital Territory, which has now been superseded by the *Criminal Code* (ACT).[31] The *Crimes Act 1900* uses the expression 'mental dysfunction'

---

22 *Criminal Code* (Cth) s 7.3(9); cp. *Criminal Code* (ACT) s 27(2); *Criminal Code* (NT) s 43A; *Criminal Code* (WA) s 1.

23 *Criminal Code* (Cth) s 7.3(8).

24 *Criminal Code* (Cth) s 7.3(9); cp. *Criminal Code* (ACT) s 27(3); *Criminal Code* (NT) s 43A; *Criminal Law Consolidation Act 1935* (SA) s 269A; *Criminal Code* (WA) s 1.

25 (1985) 42 SASR 266, 274; cp. *Criminal Code* (NT) s 43A.

26 *Crimes (Mental Impairment and Unfitness to be Tried) Act 1997* (Vic) s 25.

27 *Crimes (Mental Impairment and Unfitness to be Tried) Act 1997* (Vic) s 20.

28 *Crimes (Mental Impairment and Unfitness to be Tried) Act 1997* (Vic) s 20.

29 *R v R* [2003] VSC 187 (Unreported, SC Vic, Teague J, 5 Mar. 2003); *R v Sebalj* [2003] VSC 181 (Unreported, SC Vic, Smith J, 5 June 2003); *R v Martin* [2005] VSC 497.

30 *R v R* [2003] VSC 187 (Unreported, SC Vic, Teague J, 5 Mar. 2003) para 12; *R v Sebalj* [2003] VSC 181 (Unreported, SC Vic, Smith J, 5 June 2003) para 19.

31 *Criminal Code* (ACT).

for the requisite mental disorder which is defined as 'a disturbance or defect, to a substantially disabling degree, of perceptual interpretation, comprehension, reasoning, learning, judgment, memory, motivation or emotion'.[32] Simon Bronitt and Bernadette McSherry have contended that the benefit of employing a definition which is closer to the clinical conception of mental disorder is that it is 'flexible enough to accord with changing medical conceptions of mental disorders [and] is of more guidance to clinical experts'.[33] In support of this claim it has been further argued that the common-law expression, 'an underlying pathological infirmity of the mind' is 'vague'. It has been suggested that the reason for such vagueness is that in determining which states of mental dysfunction will be candidates in establishing the defence 'courts having been traditionally influenced by policy rather than medical reasons'.[34] Similarly, Paul Fairall and Stanley Yeo have pointed out that it is 'public policy considerations concerning criminal responsibility, and not clinical science, [which] determine the issue of innocence or guilt'.[35] Such public-policy considerations have been said to include, in particular, concerns about the breadth of the defence of insanity and the community interest in controlling and treating mentally disordered individuals.[36]

While there is merit in the views of these authors they are partial in failing to account for all of the various aspects of, and factors informing, the disease of the mind enquiry. The first contention by Bronitt and McSherry in focusing on those states which will give rise to the relevant incapacities gives too much weight to psychiatric evidence. As a result, statutory formulations in line with clinical conceptions of mental disorder fail to focus on what may be referred to as the 'community-interest' aspect of the disease of the mind enquiry. The community-interest aspect of the disease of the mind enquiry will be discussed below. In contrast, the second view by Bronitt and McSherry as well as Fairall and Yeo, in focusing on public-policy issues informing the disposition of an accused fails to take adequate account of what may be referred to as the 'responsibility' aspect of the disease of the mind enquiry. That is, by focusing on public-policy considerations statutory formulations in line with common-law developments fail

---

32 *Crimes Act* (ACT) s 428B; this is no longer in operation having been superseded by s 28 of the *Criminal Code* (ACT) which incorporates a definition of 'mental impairment' and 'mental illness' modelled on the *Criminal Code* (Cth). For another example of a (proposed) statutory amendment in accord with psychiatric conception of mental disorder, see Committee on Mentally Abnormal Offenders (Butler Committee), *Report of the Committee on Mentally Abnormal Offenders* (London, 1975) 188, cited in Victorian Law Reform Commission, *Defences to Homicide: Options Paper* (n. 19) 'Table 17: Statutory Definitions Covering Impaired Mental Functioning'.

33 Bronitt and McSherry, *Principles of Criminal Law* (n. 19) 243.

34 Ibid.

35 Fairall and Yeo, *Criminal Defences in Australia* (n. 19) 255.

36 S. Yeo, 'The Insanity Defence in the Criminal Laws of the Commonwealth of Nations' [2008] *Singapore Journal of Legal Studies*, 241, 247, citing *R v Rabey* (1978) 37 CCC (2d) 461, 473 per Martin JA (Ont. CA).

to reflect the judgment of responsibility which informs the disease of the mind enquiry. This aspect of the disease of the mind enquiry will also be discussed below.

In place of both of these partial views the remainder of this chapter will argue that the disease of the mind enquiry achieves a balance between the judgment of responsibility and the community-interest aspects of the enquiry. Moreover, it will be argued that while there is a lack of congruence between the legal conception of disease of the mind and the clinical conception of mental disorder, clinical evidence will nevertheless inform both the judgment of responsibility and community-interest aspects of the enquiry.[37]

However before considering the way in which the law reconciles the tensions arising from the various aspects of the disease of the mind enquiry the following three sections will analyse each of these aspects in turn. The first of these sections will analyse the nature of, and purposes served by, expert evidence.

Expert evidence and disease of the mind

This section will begin with an account of the clinical conception of 'mental disorder'. This will then be followed by an analysis of the reasons why the clinical concept 'mental disorder' does not accord with the legal concept 'disease of the mind'.

Clinical accounts of mental disorder

An individual's state of mental malfunction may be defined on various levels of abstraction, for example, syndromal pattern, dysfunction or aetiology. While each of these is an indicator of a mental malfunction none is equivalent to the concept of mental disorder itself.[38] Current clinical formulations of an individual's state of mental malfunction recognize the importance of social, psychological and biological factors in the aetiologies of mental malfunction.[39] In so doing such formulations adopt what has been referred to as a bio-psychosocial model of mental disorder.[40] An example of such usage is to be found in the *Diagnostic and Statistical Manual of Mental Disorders* (DSM-IV-TR), which defines the term 'mental disorder' as:

---

37 See Bronitt and McSherry, *Principles of Criminal Law* (n. 19) 243; Victorian Law Reform Commission, *Defences to Homicide: Options Paper* (n.19) 5.15–19.

38 American Psychiatric Association, *Diagnostic and Statistical Manual of Mental Disorders* (4th edn, text revision, Washington, 2000) xxx (DSM-IV-TR).

39 R.D. Miller, 'Hidden Agendas at the Law–Psychiatry Interface' (1990) 20 *Journal of Psychiatry and Law* 35, 51.

40 R.E. Kendell, 'The Concept of Disease and its Implications for Psychiatry' (1975) 127 *British Journal of Psychiatry* 305.

> A clinically significant behavioural or psychological syndrome or pattern that occurs in an individual and that is associated with present distress (for example a painful symptom) or disability (that is, impairment in one or more important areas of functioning) or with a significantly increased risk of suffering death, pain, disability, or an important loss of freedom.[41]

According to the DSM-IV-TR severe conditions of mental disorder are provided with an 'Axis I' classification and are characterized by some form of severe psychological dysfunction.[42] In particular, paradigmatic instances of mental disorder which are provided with an Axis I diagnostic categorization are characterized by a thought disorder such as psychosis.[43] For example, in the instance of the paradigmatic case of schizophrenia, the DSM-IV-TR defines the differential diagnosis of schizophrenia as including psychotic symptoms. Psychosis 'refers to delusions, any prominent hallucinations, disorganized speech, or disorganized or catatonic behavior'.[44] According to the DSM-IV-TR, a 'delusion' is defined as: 'a false belief based on incorrect inference about external reality … [in the face of] incontrovertible proof or evidence to the contrary'.[45] A 'hallucination' is defined as 'a sensory perception that has the compelling sense of reality of a true perception but that occurs without external stimulation of the relevant sensory organ'.[46] Inferences about disorganized thinking are based primarily on the individual's speech which may range from 'loose associations', slipping from one topic to another, to, in severe cases, disorganized 'word salad'.[47] Catatonic symptoms however are non-specific and may occur in other mental disorders.[48]

Axis I psychiatric disorders are characterized by a lack of 'reality testing'.[49] A lack of reality testing is conventionally understood as involving 'a pervasive inability to engage reality'.[50] A failure of reality testing may lead an individual

41 DSM-IV-TR (n. 38) xxxi.

42 Ibid. 28. As expressed in the DSM-IV-TR (n. 38) 27, 'a multi-axial system involves an assessment on several axes, each of which refers to a different domain of information that may help the clinician plan treatment and predict outcome. There are five axes included in the DSM-IV-TR multi-axial classification.'

43 Ibid.

44 Ibid. 821.

45 Ibid.

46 Ibid. 823.

47 Ibid. 300.

48 Ibid. 301. DSM-IV-TR 186 notes that 'catatonia is manifested by any of the following: motoric immobility, excessive motor activity, extreme negativism or mutism, peculiarities of voluntary movement, echolalia [parrot-like, senseless repetition of a word or phrase], echopraxia [repetitive imitation of the movements of another person]'.

49 Ibid. 297. A 'gross impairment of reality testing' was the expression used in previous editions of the DSM; the current manual eschews a definition focused on the severity of functional impairment in favour of a definition based on symptoms.

50 F. McAuley, *Insanity, Psychiatry and Criminal Responsibility* (Dublin, 1993) 35.

to draw erroneous conclusions from accurately perceived objects.[51] Moreover, a person experiencing a severe mental disorder is just as likely to mistake the flux of his or her own consciousness for such evidence. As a result, an individual who lacks the ability to 'engage reality' may come to mistake his or her own idiosyncratic interpretation of the world for an inter-subjective interpretation, or meaning, which most people share of the objective world. The failure to distinguish between an idiosyncratic and inter-subjective variety of meaning has been described as constituting a 'fundamental want of reason'.[52] Consequently, a lack of reality testing should not be understood as confined only to the misinterpretation of reality caused by psychotic symptoms. A lack of reality testing, or the inability to engage reality, will also include failures of 'public agreement' arising from a lack of a shared understanding of the world:

> It is not reality in the sense of some objective standard of truth which fails to be acknowledged; it is rather reality in the sense of the features which are shared between other thinkers and perceivers – the aspects on the basis of which there is public agreement in judgement.[53]

The criterion for rationality relates knowledge not to the *content* of an individual's beliefs but rather to cognitive *processes*. It is the way a belief or consideration is formed and held, not its truth or falsity, which will determine its rationality. The beliefs upon which an individual acts are justified if they are the product of correct cognitive processes.[54] Major disorders of thought processes involve disturbances in three areas: cognitive focus, reasoning and concept formation.[55] Cognitive focus is the failure to effectively select relevant aspects of a stimuli field or to adjust attention in response to changing situations.[56] Disturbed reasoning involves over-generalized thinking, the drawing of conclusions without evidence and combinative thinking, an inappropriate condensation of impressions and ideas into beliefs and conclusions.[57] Concept formation disturbance involves a failure to distinguish between false and veridical perceptual experiences and beliefs.[58]

---

51 J. Radden, *Madness and Reason* (London, 1985) 78.

52 Ibid. 66.

53 Ibid 59. For the use in a civil context of the notion of 'inter-subjective judgment' as a criterion for determining an individual's 'insight' into his or her condition, see K. Diesfeld and S. Sjostrom, 'Interpretive Flexibility: Why Doesn't Insight Incite Controversy in Mental Health Law?' (2007) 25 *Behavioural Sciences and the Law* 85, 89.

54 R. Schopp, *Automatism, Insanity and the Psychology of Criminal Responsibility: A Philosophical Inquiry* (Cambridge, 1991) 183.

55 Ibid. 185.

56 M. Gelder, P. Harrison and D. Cowen, *Shorter Oxford Textbook of Psychiatry* (5th edn, Oxford, 2006) 15–16.

57 Schopp, *Automatism, Insanity and the Psychology of Criminal Responsibility* (n. 54) 186.

58 Radden, *Madness and Reason* (n. 51) 78.

Concept formation disturbance involves 'over-inclusiveness': 'the inability to conserve conceptual boundaries with the result that there is an incorporation of irrelevant ideas'.[59] Consequently, an individual's inability to engage reality denotes a cognitive failure which includes, in addition to purely perceptual errors, major disorders of thought processes leading to faulty reasoning and judgment. Such cognitive failure will result in thought processes which will generate irrelevant beliefs or considerations.

Conditions that are characterized by significant disturbances of psychological functioning are diagnostically distinguished from those conditions that involve a personality disorder.[60] While personality disorders, such as 'antisocial personality disorder' are clinically recognized mental disorders, they do not involve a lack of reality testing and are accorded an 'Axis II' classification by the DSM-IV-TR.[61] When a condition is categorized as an Axis II personality disorder, the relevant condition is said to involve an enduring pattern of feeling, thinking and behaving that is relatively stable over time and which does not occur exclusively during an episode of an Axis I disorder.[62] The diagnosis of an Axis II classification is based on an evaluation, relative to socially conditioned expectations, of such an individual's enduring pattern of feeling, thinking and behaving.

Some commentators have remarked on the failure of the legal concept 'disease of the mind' to accord with the clinical concept 'mental disorder'.[63] The reason why the clinical conception of mental disorder does not accord with legal usage will be the subject of the next section.

Psychiatric conception and legal usage

Lord Devlin remarked on the relationship between medical opinion and the question of whether a condition is a disease of the mind by holding:

> There is no general medical opinion upon what category of diseases are properly to be called diseases of the mind. Doctors' personal views, of course, are not binding upon me. I have to interpret the rules according to the ordinary principles of interpretation, but I derive help from their interpretations inasmuch as they illustrate the nature of the disease and the matters which from the medical point of view have to be considered in determining whether or not it is a disease of the mind.[64]

59 Gelder, Harrison and Cowen, *Shorter Oxford Textbook of Psychiatry* (n. 56) 306.

60 DSM-IV-TR (n. 38) 687.

61 Ibid. 29; 'Diagnostic Category 301.7 Antisocial Personality Disorder',701–6.

62 Ibid. 688.

63 See Bronitt and McSherry, *Principles of Criminal Law* (n. 19) 243; Victorian Law Reform Commission, *Defences to Homicide: Options Paper* (n. 19) 5.15–19.

64 *R v Kemp* [1957] QB 399, 406.

Several points may be made in the light of this remark. First, there is no medically recognized diagnostic category that amounts to a disease of the mind. Second, expert evidence is not determinative of the enquiry whether there is a disease of the mind. However, clinical evidence will assist by revealing the various effects of the condition. This evidence will be 'highly relevant to the judicial determination of whether such a condition is capable of constituting a "disease of the mind"'.[65] Where a condition is characterized as a disease of the mind, clinical evidence as to the symptoms, nature and causes of an accused's condition will also be of assistance to the fact finder in determining the ultimate issue of whether the accused was in fact affected by the particular mental condition. That is, by outlining the precise manifestations of particular types of mental malfunctioning expert evidence will assist the trier of fact in determining the question of whether the behaviour of the accused was attributable to such malfunctioning. Additionally, clinical evidence will assist courts in determining the likelihood of an individual's mental illness recurring in order to establish whether or not he or she should be released. That is, clinical evidence will assist the court in determining the question of an accused's disposition subsequent to a finding of mental impairment.[66] The issue of the likelihood of an individual's mental illness recurring, and the relationship between mental illness and violent behaviour, will be considered in greater detail below.

The characterization of a given mental state as a mental disorder is not a necessary condition for its recognition as a disease of the mind. For example, cases of epilepsy have not been recognized as instances of mental disorder. Nevertheless, such cases have, on occasion, been held to give rise to the defence of insanity.[67] Equally, the fact that a particular mental condition is recognized as a mental disorder will not be sufficient to ensure that it is characterized as an instance of a disease of the mind. For example, while the status of Axis II disorders is distinguished clinically from Axis I disorders for diagnostic purposes, they are nevertheless still recognized as instances of mental disorder. However, the various Australian jurisdictions differ in their characterization of Axis II disorders for the purposes of the insanity defence. While at common law it is well recognized that a personality disorder such as antisocial personality disorder will not be sufficient to ground a defence of insanity,[68] both the *Criminal Code* (Cth) and the *Criminal Code* (ACT) recognize severe personality disorder as mental impairment for the purposes of the defence of mental impairment.[69]

---

65 *R v Rabey* (1977) 37 CCC (2d) 461, 473–4 per Martin JA (Ont. CA).

66 S. Glazebrook, 'Risky Business: Predicting Recidivism' (2010) 17 *Psychiatry, Psychology and Law* 88, 97.

67 *R v Cottle* [1958] NZLR 999; *R v Sullivan* [1984] 1 AC 156; *R v Foy* [1960] Qd R 225 (CA Qld); *Youssef* (1990) 50 A Crim R 1 (CCA NSW).

68 *Willgoss v R* (1960) 105 CLR 295; *Jeffrey v R* [1982] Tas R 199; *Hodges v R* (1985) 19 A Crim R 129.

69 *Criminal Code* (Cth) s 7.3(8); *Criminal Code* (ACT) s 27(1). However, only these codes amongst Australian jurisdictions recognize severe personality disorder as evidence

The differences between the two conceptions, the legal and the clinical, are explicable not only in terms of the terminology used, but also in terms of a further and deeper conceptual divide between the law and psychiatry.[70] The nature of this divide may be understood by considering the purposes served by both psychiatry and law. The difference in the purposes served by these two disciplines is apparent from the reasons provided by the Victorian Law Reform Commission in its decision against providing a revised definition of the expression 'mental impairment' in the Victorian *Crimes (Mental Impairment and Unfitness to be Tried) Act.*[71]

As previously noted, while the Victorian Act does not define 'mental impairment' it has been judicially recognized as a legislative re-statement of the common law.[72] During the course of the VLRC's review of *Defences to Homicide*, submissions were received calling for a revised definition of 'mental impairment' to be implemented in line with medical understandings.[73] However, the commission in its final report decided to leave the expression 'mental impairment' undefined. Two reasons were considered persuasive by the commission in reaching this decision.

First, the use of diagnostic criteria was considered to be an inappropriate basis for defining the legal expression 'mental impairment'.[74] In regards to the use of diagnostic criteria, the commission observed that the DSM-IV-TR explicitly disavows the use of its diagnostic classifications in a legal context.[75] Further, the commission remarked on the mutability of medical knowledge in respect of the extant varieties of mental malfunctioning. The commission correctly observed that such mutability would be a problematic basis for legal decision-making in the context of the criminal law. As has been noted above, the criminal law is dependent on expert evidence in order to assist in the correct characterization of an accused's state of mental disorder and consequent responsibility. However, where such expert evidence is in a state of flux and forms the basis for legal decision-making, there is a possibility that reliance on such evidence will lead to inconsistent results.[76] Yet, given the onerous nature of both criminal sanctions and the dispositional regime attendant upon a finding of insanity, certainty in the law

---

for the purpose of the mental impairment defence (see Bronitt and McSherry, *Principles of Criminal Law* (n. 19) 244–5).

70 See K.W.M. Fulford, 'Value, Action, Mental Illness, and the Law' in *Value and Action in the Criminal Law*, ed. S. Shute, J. Gardner and J. Horder (Oxford, 1993) 279.

71 *Crimes (Mental Impairment and Unfitness to be Tried) Act 1997* (Vic), s 20.

72 *R v R* [2003] VSC 187 (Unreported, SC Vic, Teague J, 5 Mar. 2003); *R v Sebalj* [2003] VSC 181 (Unreported, SC Vic, Smith J, 5 June 2003).

73 Victorian Law Reform Commission, *Defences to Homicide: Final Report*, Report No 94 (Melbourne, 2004) 5.17.

74 Ibid. 5.18.

75 Ibid. 5.19, citing DSM-IV-TR (n. 38) xxxii–xxxiii. The limitations associated with the use of diagnostic manuals in forensic settings will be discussed in Chapter 5 below.

76 Ibid. 5.19; see *Blocker v The United States* (1961) 288 F.2d 853, concerning the reclassification of 'sociopathic personality' as a mental disease by expert witness.

must be established. It is incumbent on the criminal law to ensure that a consistent set of rules determine when people are and are not criminally responsible.

The second reason provided by the commission for deciding to leave the expression 'mental impairment' undefined was the view that 'the lack of formal definition provides the defence with considerable flexibility'.[77] The commission believed that by defining the expression the defence could be restricted unnecessarily.[78]

It was noted above that the clinical account of severe mental disorder is focused on an individual's failure of reality testing as characterized by cognitive failure. Such cognitive failure includes both purely perceptual errors in addition to major disorders of thought processes resulting in faulty reasoning and judgment. In contrast the legal conception 'disease of the mind' includes 'any illness, disorder or abnormal condition which impairs the human mind and its functioning'.[79] The purpose of the legal expression, 'disease of the mind' is to determine, pursuant to a test of moral responsibility, who is a fit subject of our responsibility practices rather than who is suffering from a recognized mental disorder.[80] As a medical discipline, and in keeping with its therapeutic rationale, psychiatry is concerned with the allocation of psychiatric disorders to diagnostic categories in order to facilitate treatment. Hence, for the purposes of forensic psychiatry, the cause of an individual's behaviour is the subject of categorization and treatment. In contrast, the defence of insanity is not a medical diagnosis but a legal excuse. In particular, the defence of insanity exempts an individual from criminal responsibility.[81] While expert evidence may indicate whether an individual is suffering from a mental disorder, such evidence will not be determinative of the legal enquiry, namely, whether he or she should be exempted from criminal responsibility. The issue is whether the accused's mental faculties were impaired by 'disease, disorder or disturbance' not whether he or she was suffering from a recognized mental disorder.[82]

As will be explored below, whether an individual may be held criminally responsible will be determined according to a test of moral responsibility not a medical diagnosis. Whether an individual will be exempted from criminal responsibility will be determined by evaluating the effects of the 'disease, disorder

77 Victorian Law Reform Commission, *Defences to Homicide: Final Report* (n. 73) 5.18.

78 Ibid.

79 *R v Cooper* (1980) 51 CCC (2d) 129, 144 per Dickson J.

80 *United States v Brawner* (1972) 471 F. 2d 969; cp. *Durham v United States* (1954) 214 F.2d 862, 874, where it was held that an accused has a good defence to a criminal charge 'if his unlawful act was the product of mental disease or mental defect'.

81 The significance of the distinction between 'excuses' and 'exemptions' will be discussed in Chapter 6 in the context of the proposed defence of impaired consciousness.

82 *R v Porter* (1933) 55 CLR 182, 188 per Dixon J; cp. *R v Sullivan* [1984] 1 AC 156; *R v Kemp* [1957] 1 QB 399; *R v Quick* [1973] QB 910.

or disturbance' in the light of the moral enquiry. This will result in what will be referred to as a 'judgment of responsibility'. By ensuring that the legal expression is not tied down to diagnostic criteria courts and relevant bodies remain free to facilitate the execution of this normative task undertaken as part of the disease of the mind enquiry.

The following section will outline the nature of the judgment of responsibility in the context of the disease of the mind enquiry.

Responsibility and disease of the mind

This section will begin with an account of the judgment of responsibility. This will be followed by a discussion of the way in which the judgment of responsibility is accommodated within the disease of the mind enquiry.

Judgment of responsibility

The judgment of responsibility aspect of the disease of the mind enquiry addresses the question of an agent's moral and legal responsibility. The judgment of responsibility is important as it articulates the intuition that it is wrong to punish an individual whose mental condition precludes him or her from either knowing the nature and quality or wrongness of his or her act or from controlling his or her act. That is, the judgment of responsibility is concerned with the question of whether an individual has the requisite ability to be held morally responsible and so be potentially liable to the imposition of any sanctions thought appropriate by the law.

The law is underpinned by the assumption that individuals are rational and autonomous and so their criminal conduct is the result of rational choice. As a basic principle of criminal responsibility, individuals are responsible agents who should be punished if they choose to engage in unlawful conduct or for failing to exercise their ability to control such conduct. Where an individual who has the ability to discern right from wrong and the ability to choose right from wrong consciously chooses to commit a wrong then both holding him or her criminally responsible and punishing him or her are morally justified. The defence of insanity provides a criterion by means by which the responsible may be distinguished from those who are exempt from responsibility. The question of whether a particular condition will exempt an individual from criminal responsibility will be determined by assessing whether the individual could know or understand, that what he or she was doing was wrong, or whether he or she could control his or her actions.

In the absence of either the ability to reason or the ability to control his or her conduct an individual is exempt from responsibility and for this reason not a fit subject of criminal law. Consequently, a defence such as insanity, which seeks to distinguish those individuals who are responsible from those who are not, should, as a matter of principle, acknowledge both rational and volitional defects as sufficient to exempt an individual from responsibility. Chapter 5 will argue for the recognition of states of volitional impairment as sufficient to give rise to a defence of volitional insanity at common law.

While the capacity to reason or to control their conduct will differ amongst individuals, where a minimal capacity exists, an individual will be expected to exercise such capacity by not choosing to do wrong or by controlling his or her conduct.

However, not all states of mental malfunction giving rise to incapacity will be recognized as a disease of the mind. The way in which states are distinguished will be the subject of the next section.

Responsibility and fault

As noted above, it has been held that in order for a disease of the mind to be found there must be 'an underlying pathological infirmity of mind, be it of long or short duration and be it permanent or temporary, as distinct from the reaction of a healthy mind to extraordinary external stimuli'.[83] According to this analysis a distinction may be drawn between those states of malfunction caused by some source internal to the accused and those states of malfunction caused by some source that is external to the accused. However, an additional distinction may be drawn in respect of those states of malfunction which have an internal source. In *R v Porter*, it was held in relation to the disease of the mind enquiry that:

> [An accused's] state of mind must be one of disease, disorder or disturbance. Mere excitability of a normal man, passion, even stupidity, obtuseness, lack of self-control, and impulsiveness, are quite different things from what I have attempted to describe as a state of disease or disorder or mental disturbance arising from some infirmity, temporary or of long standing.[84]

The nature of the distinction noted in *Porter* was further commented upon by Sir Owen Dixon who stated that:

> The reason why it is required that the defect of reason should be 'from disease of the mind' seems to me no more than to exclude drunkenness, conditions of intense passion and other transient states attributable either to the fault or to the nature of man.[85]

83 *R v Radford* (1985) 42 SASR 266, 274 per King CJ; cp. *Criminal Code* (Cth) s 7.3(9); *Criminal Code* (ACT) s 27(3); *Criminal Code* (NT) s 43A; *Criminal Law Consolidation Act 1935* (SA) s 269A; *Criminal Code* (WA) s 1.

84 *R v Porter* (1933) 55 CLR 182, 188 per Dixon J.

85 O. Dixon, 'A Legacy of Hadfield, M'Naghten and Maclean' (1957) 31 *Australian Law Journal* 255, 260.

Consequently, a distinction may be drawn amongst those internal states which are due to the 'fault or nature of man' and those internal states which are not due to the 'fault or nature of man'. A state of 'disease, disorder or disturbance' brought about through an internal state due to the fault or nature of man will not be recognized as a disease of the mind. For example, states that are excluded as diseases of the mind are those 'conditions of intense passion attributable to the nature of man'.[86] Similarly, where an accused's state of disease, disorder or disturbance is due to the fault of man, such a state will not be recognized as an instance of a disease of the mind.[87] For example, in the context of substance abuse, where a psychotic state has been brought about by an accused through the voluntary consumption of drugs, the fact that such psychosis is a psychiatrically recognized disorder will not be sufficient for it to be characterized as a disease of the mind.[88] This is because the disorder in such a case is attributable to the fault of man. The question of drug-induced psychosis will be considered in more detail in the following chapter.

Hence, where an accused's malfunction of the mind is due either to the fault or to the nature of man, he or she will be held fully responsible. Conversely, where the state of mental malfunction is due to an internal condition which is not due to the fault or nature of man then the resulting state of disease, disorder or disturbance may be characterized as a disease of the mind. Subject to such a condition giving rise to the relevant incapacities, the accused may be provided with the 'special verdict'.

Arranged schematically the above analysis reveals the following:

Table 3.1 Disease of the mind and responsibility

Source of malfunction	Potential verdict
Internal (not attributable to fault or nature of accused)	'Not guilty because of mental impairment'[a]
Internal (attributable to fault or nature of accused)	Guilty
External	Not guilty[b]

Notes:

[a] This formulation of the special verdict is to be found in the *Crimes (Mental Impairment and Unfitness to be Tried) Act 1997* (Vic) s 20(2).

[b] Where the malfunction results in the accused's conduct being involuntary.

86 *R v Carter* [1959] VR 105, 110 per Sholl J; *Parker v R* (1963) 111 CLR 610, 653 per Windeyer J approved *Green* (1997) 191 CLR 334, 402–3 per Kirby J.

87 *R v Sebalj* [2003] VSC 181 (Unreported, SC Vic, Smith J, 5 June 2003) para 19; *R v Martin* [2005] VSC 497. Though note, where a state of intoxication from the use of licit substances either causes an underlying condition, or exacerbates a pre-existing underlying condition, then the defence may apply (*R v Meddings* [1966] VR 306, 310 per Scholl J, *Re: Bromage* [1991] 1 Qd R 1).

88 *R v Sebalj* [2003] VSC 181 (Unreported, SC Vic, Smith J, 5 June 2003).

However, the fact that an individual is found with the relevant incapacities due to an internal state not attributable to his or her fault or nature will not result in his or her unqualified acquittal. The issue of the disposition of a mentally impaired acquittee will be decided by other factors. In particular, community-interest concerns will be used in order to resolve the issue of a mentally impaired acquittee's disposition.[89] The next section will explain the nature of such 'public policy considerations concerning criminal responsibility'.[90]

Community interest: disease of the mind and disposition

The third aspect of the disease of the mind enquiry, community interest, is concerned with societal protection.[91] Community-interest considerations turn on the protection of the community from the threat posed by those considered to be at risk of harming others. As a result, a question which underlies the legal interpretation of the expression 'disease of the mind' is whether the accused is likely to cause harm to others if not confined? If the accused is at risk of harming others, then, subject to the other factors of the enquiry being satisfied, his or her mental condition will be considered to be a disease of the mind for the purposes of the insanity defence.[92] Hence, an individual's potential risk for violence will be used as a criterion for establishing whether he or she suffers from a disease of the mind.

Underpinning the community-interest aspect of the disease of the mind enquiry is the operative presumption that certain mental illnesses are prone to recur and are associated with violence. This presumption will be seen to operate in the context of the judicially formulated tests aimed at distinguishing sane from insane automatism. Moreover, a concern that an individual's mental illness may result in violence will be seen to underpin the 'ordinary person' test used in this area of law. However, the disease of the mind enquiry is a distinct enquiry to that of the disposition of a mentally impaired acquittee. As a result, the community-interest aspect of the disease of the mind enquiry is only tangentially concerned with the question of an accused's disposition. It is only, once the characterization of an accused's state of mind has been completed that a decision as to his or her disposition will be made. Modern trends relating to the disposition of mentally impaired acquittees reveal the importance of societal protection considerations at this point.

89 I.G. Campbell, *Mental Disorder and Criminal Law in Australia and New Zealand* (Sydney, 1988) 128.

90 Fairall and Yeo, *Criminal Defences in Australia* (n. 19) 255.

91 See G. Ferguson, 'A Critique of Proposals to Reform the Insanity Defence' (1989) 14 *Queen's Law Journal* 135,141.

92 B. McSherry, 'Defining what is a "Disease of the Mind": The Untenability of Current Legal Interpretations' (1993) 1 *Journal of Law and Medicine* 76, 86.

The first part of this section will show how the presumption that certain mental illnesses are prone to recur and are associated with violence operates in the 'disease of the mind' enquiry. The second part of this section will consider as an example of modern trends in disposition the current Victorian legislation.[93]

Recurrence and violence

The community-interest aspect of the disease of the mind enquiry is underpinned by the presumption that certain mental illnesses are prone to recur and are associated with violence. The most obvious means of showing that the presumption of recurrence which underlies concerns with community protection is relevant to the disease of the mind enquiry is by reference to the distinction between sane and insane automatism. As seen in Chapter 2, the tests for distinguishing between sane and insane automatism can be seen as the way in which courts determine whether the accused was suffering from a disease of the mind at the time of the offence. As will be shown below, the tests, in particular, the focus on the possibility of recurrence and the use of an ordinary person standard as part of one such test, clearly reflect concerns with societal protection.

The first test considered in Chapter 2, the continuing-danger, or recurrence, test most clearly reveals the significance which the presumption of recurrence has in determining which mental conditions may be characterized as disease of the mind. In *R v Meddings*,[94] the potential for repetition was considered important and a possible basis for distinguishing between sane and insane automatism:

> Potentiality of repetition might be regarded as a discrimen between cases of irrational behaviour due to some transient cause affecting the mind, other than disease of the mind, and cases of irrational behaviour due to defective reason from disease of the mind.[95]

Similarly, Lord Denning in *Bratty v A-G (Northern Ireland)*[96] remarked that:

> Any mental disorder which has manifested itself in violence and is prone to recur is a disease of the mind. At any rate it is the sort of disease for which a person should be detained in hospital rather than be given an unqualified acquittal.[97]

Another test which reveals the relevance of the presumption that certain mental illness are prone to recur to issues of community protection and in turn the disease of the mind enquiry is the internal–external test. As noted in Chapter 2, where an

93 *Crimes (Mental Impairment and Unfitness to be Tried) Act 1997* (Vic).
94 [1966] VR 306.
95 Ibid. 309 per Sholl J.
96 [1963] AC 386.
97 Ibid. 412.

accused's state of automatism is the result of an external cause, the resultant state will be characterized as sane automatism.[98] However, where an accused's state of automatism has its source in an internal cause, such a state will be characterized as insanity.[99] The rationale for the approach adopted by the internal–external test is the belief that an internal cause is more likely to recur. For example, in *Burgess v R*,[100] it was held that as sleep-walking is an internal condition, and for this reason likely to recur, it should be characterized as a disease of the mind. As there is a risk of recurrence the accused is deemed to be inherently dangerous to the community and for this reason should be placed under a therapeutic regime rather than acquitted outright.

As noted in Chapter 2, a too rigid application of the above tests for the purpose of distinguishing sane from insane automatism may result in inconsistent results. Nevertheless, the Supreme Court of Canada in elucidating the purpose of the tests and how they were to be applied re-asserted the significance of societal protection to the disease of the mind enquiry:

> In determining this issue, policy concerns [will] assist trial judges in answering the fundamental question of mixed law and fact which is at the centre of the disease of the mind inquiry: whether society requires protection from the accused and, consequently, whether the accused should be subject to evaluation under the regime contained in Part XX.1 of the Code.[101]

While the above tests continue to be used in Canada and England, the Australian High Court has sought to distinguish between sane and insane automatism by focusing on the state of mind of the accused. In the context of psychological-blow automatism, the High Court held that the fact that the cause of the accused's state of dissociation was the result of an external cause would not be fatal to his or her plea of sane automatism.[102] In order to determine whether an accused's dissociation was symptomatic of an 'underlying pathological infirmity of mind', or 'unsound mind', or whether it was the response of a 'sound mind' to extreme psychological shock, the High Court stipulated an objective test. The court held that:

> The law must postulate a standard of mental strength which, in the face of a given level of psychological trauma, is capable of protecting the mind from malfunction to the extent prescribed in the respective definitions of insanity. The standard must be the standard of the ordinary person.[103]

98 See *Cooper v McKenna; Ex parte Cooper* [1960] Qd R 406.

99 See *R v Cottle* [1958] NZLR 999; *R v Sullivan* [1984] 1 AC 156; *Youssef* (1990) A Crim R 1.

100 [1991] 2 QB 92.

101 *R v Stone* [1999] 134 CCC (3d) 353, 440–1 per Bastarache J.

102 *R v Falconer* (1990) 171 CLR 30.

103 Ibid. 55 per Mason CJ, Brennan and McHugh JJ.

In outlining the operation of the standard the High Court noted that:

> A malfunction which is transient and not prone to recur and to which the mind of an ordinary person would be subject if exposed to the same psychological trauma is neither a mental disease nor a natural mental infirmity. It is [not]... an instance of insanity at common law.[104]

As a result, an accused's state of dissociation due to psychological trauma will be characterized as sane automatism where the state of dissociation is transient, caused by a level of trauma which the mind of an ordinary person would not have been likely to withstand and is not prone to recur. Where, however, an individual fails to meet the standard of the ordinary person, and his or her mental malfunction is not transient, and is prone to recur, the community-interest aspect of the disease of the mind enquiry holds that such a state should be recognized as a disease of the mind.

While, as remarked in Chapter 2, the objective-person test has not been universally adopted, courts are reluctant to extend the defence of sane automatism to individuals who dissociate due to the 'ordinary stresses and disappointments of life'.[105] This approach by the courts suggests that some form of objective standard continues to be applied in distinguishing sane from insane automatism.[106] An accused who falls outside of the standard of ordinary people and whose mental malfunction is prone to recur because of ordinary life stressors will be considered to be suffering from a disease of the mind.

The use of an ordinary person test in order to distinguish instances of sane from insane automatism is aimed at establishing which of those accused who have acted involuntarily are mentally impaired. There is a presumption that such individuals present a threat to community interests and so should be subject to a therapeutic regime. The need for such a regime is underpinned by the belief that a mentally impaired acquittee's mental illness is likely to recur and pose a threat to the community. Community-interest concerns that an accused's condition will recur are moreover underpinned by an assumption that certain varieties of mental illness cause individuals who suffer from them to become more violent.

It has been claimed in the past that any violence associated with individuals suffering from the paradigmatic case of schizophrenia is not attributable to the

104 Ibid. 61 per Mason CJ, Brennan and McHugh JJ.

105 *R v Rabey* (1977) 37 CCC (2d) 461, 477 per Martin J (CA), approved *Rabey v R* [1980] 2 SCR 513 D (SC).

106 New South Wales Law Reform Commission, *People with Cognitive and Mental Health Impairments in the Criminal Justice System: Criminal Responsibility and Consequences*, Consultation Paper 6 (Sydney, 2010) 3.102, citing *R v Falconer* [1990] 171 CLR 30, 73–4 per Toohey J, 85 per Gaudron J; cp. *R v Radford (No 2)* (1987) 11 Crim LJ 231, 232 per King CJ.

manifestations of the individual's mental state disturbance itself.[107] Manifestations such as delusions, hallucinations, word salad, lack of affect and the like are described as 'mediating' factors of the mental disorder itself. Such mediating factors are to be distinguished from 'confounding' influences, such as substance abuse and personality disorder, which are commonly associated with the mental disorder. On methodological grounds it has been suggested that any attempt to establish a correlation between a schizophrenic disorder and violence will need to remove such confounding influences from the analysis.[108] Past studies have suggested that, when such confounding influences have been removed, while there is an association, there is probably no causal link between schizophrenia's mediating factors and the risk of future violence.[109] As a result of such a finding it has been remarked that 'the most important message for public policy-makers is that although there may be an increased risk of violent behaviour associated with schizophrenia, it is of the same order as the increased risk associated with being young and male'.[110] However, more recent work has taken the view that: 'the relationship between the schizophrenic syndromes and violent and antisocial behaviours is *inherent* to the disorder itself and the effects of the disorder on the sufferer's functioning'.[111] As a result of such research personality factors and/or social conditions have increasingly come to be viewed as mediating criminality in schizophrenia.[112] This has led to the categorical assertion that:

> There is a correlation between having a schizophrenic syndrome and increased rates of antisocial behaviour in general and violence in particular. The evidence for such associations which is not just statistically significant, but points to a clinically and socially significant relationship, is now overwhelming.[113]

---

107 P.E. Mullen, 'Mental Disorder and Dangerousness' (1984) 18 *Australian and New Zealand Journal of Psychiatry* 8.

108 Ibid.; see H. Hafner and W. Boker, *Crimes of Violence by Mentally Abnormal Offenders* (Cambridge, 1982).

109 P. Mullen, 'The Dangerousness of the Mentally Ill and the Clinical Assessment of Risk' in *Psychiatry and Law: Clinical and Legal Issues*, ed. W. Brookbanks (Wellington, 1996) 93, 100; cp. P.E. Mullen, 'Criminality, Dangerousness and Schizophrenia' in *Schizophrenia: An Overview and Practical Handbook* (London, 1992) 145, 154.

110 Mullen, 'The Dangerousness of the Mentally Ill and the Clinical Assessment of Risk' (n. 109) 103.

111 P.E. Mullen, 'Schizophrenic Syndrome, Violent and Other Antisocial Behaviours' in *Psychiatry and the Law*, ed. W. Brookbanks and S. Simpson (Wellington, 2007) 293, 296 (emphasis added).

112 Ibid. 298 (citations omitted).

113 Ibid. (citations omitted).

It has been noted that individuals suffering from schizophrenia account for between 5 and 10 per cent of homicides.[114] However, because of the relative rarity of homicide in the community the risk of such individuals committing an act of homicide is between 1 and 4 in 10,000.[115] The significance of these figures becomes apparent when it is noted that the homicide rate in most Western nations is between 1 and 4 in 100,000.[116] In effect, this signifies that there is a tenfold increase in the level of risk of an act of homicide occurring by individuals suffering from schizophrenia than by any other group. In particular, amongst those suffering from such a mental disorder, a failure to maintain a treatment regime, substance abuse, active symptoms and a failure to comply with medical directives, may result in an increase of violent behaviour.[117]

Disposition: societal protection

A concern with societal protection is also apparent in the disposition of a person found not guilty on the ground of insanity. Where an accused successfully pleads insanity, this is held, procedurally, to constitute an acquittal. However, the accused will not generally be allowed to go free as is the norm with acquittals. Under the 'governor's pleasure' system the detention of an accused who successfully pleads insanity is usually for an indefinite period, at the governor's pleasure.[118] In most instances this has resulted in an accused being confined in prison until a decision is made regarding his or her disposition.[119] The result of this procedure is that subsequent to the acquittal of an accused the court is relieved of any further jurisdiction. In such a case the accused is in the hands of the Executive, which from then on has the pivotal decision-making role. This is intended to ensure that public safety is the primary consideration when decisions about discharge are made.[120] The indefinite nature of the period of detention consequent upon a finding

114 P.E. Mullen and J. Ogloff, 'Assessing and Managing the Risks of Violence Towards Others' in *New Oxford Textbook of Psychiatry*, ed. M. Gelder et al. (2nd edn, Oxford, 2009) 1991, 1995, citing P.E. Mullen, 'Schizophrenia and Violence: From Correlations to Preventative Strategies' (2006) 12 *Advances in Psychiatric Treatment* 239.

115 Ibid.

116 Mullen (n. 111) 297.

117 P.E. Mullen, 'A Reassessment of the Link Between Mental Disorder and Violent Behaviour, and its Implications for Clinical Practices' (1997) 31 *Australian and New Zealand Journal of Psychiatry* 3.

118 *Trial of Lunatics Act 1883* (UK) 46 & 47 Vict, c 38.

119 A. Frieberg, 'The Disposition of Mentally Disordered Offenders in Australia: "Out of Mind, Out of Sight" Revisited' (1994) 1 *Psychiatry, Psychology and Law* 97.

120 Bronitt and McSherry, *Principles of Criminal Law* (n. 19) 253; cp. C.R. Williams, 'Psychopathy, Mental Illness and Preventive Detention: Issues Arising from the *David* Case' (1990) 16 *Monash University Law Review* 161, justifying detention on the basis of treatment.

of mental impairment has tended in the past to result in unwillingness on the part of accused to raise the defence of mental impairment.[121]

Given the manifest injustice of indefinite detention in cases of mental impairment amenable to treatment, certain jurisdictions have legislatively introduced a range of dispositional options.[122] For example, in both New South Wales and Tasmania, courts may order that an accused be detained in a hospital setting as part of a therapeutic regime.[123] In Victoria, the statutory formulation of the mental-impairment defence was implemented alongside the introduction of a range of dispositional options and brought about the abolition of the governor's pleasure system of indefinite detention.[124]

While the earlier practice under the governor's pleasure system was to vest the decision-making role in the Executive, the current Victorian legislation, which I will use as an example of modern trends relating to disposition, now reveals that all decisions concerning the duration of an accused's detention are solely matters for the court. The principle which the court must apply in deciding the disposition of an accused person under the Act is 'that restrictions on a person's freedom and personal autonomy should be kept to the minimum consistent with the safety of the community'.[125] In deciding the disposition of an accused matters which a court will take into account will include not only the safety of members of the public,[126] but also the question of 'whether there are adequate resources available for the treatment and support of the person in the community [in addition

121 R. Murugason and L. McNamara, *Outline of Criminal Law* (Sydney, 1997) 21, citing *Sullivan* [1983] 2 All ER 673; cp. *R v Falconer* (1990) 171 CLR 30, 63 per Deane, Dawson JJ, noting that it is more often in the prosecution's interest, rather than the accused's, to raise the issue of mental impairment.

122 *Mental Health (Criminal Procedure) Act 1990* (NSW) s 39; *Criminal Code* (NT) s 431; *Criminal Law Consolidation Act 1935* (SA) s 269O; *Crimes (Mental Impairment and Unfitness to be Tried) Act 1997* (Vic) s 23; *Criminal Law (Mentally Impaired Accused) Act 1996* (WA) s 22; cp. Qld and Tas, where indefinite detention is still applicable (*Criminal Code* (Qld) s 647, which however provides for a diversionary scheme, pursuant to the *Mental Health Act 2000* (Qld) ss 58, 288, to the Mental Health Court; *Criminal Justice (Mental Impairment) Act 1999* (Tas) s 21).

123 *Mental Health Act 1990* (NSW) s 101(1)(b), read with *Mental Health (Criminal Procedure) Act 1990*, s 39, allowing for court directed 'hospital orders'; *Criminal Code* (Tas) s 382.

124 Recommendations of the Community Development Committee of the Parliament of Victoria, *Inquiry into Persons Detained at the Governor's Pleasure*, Report No 57 (Melbourne, 1994) formed the basis of the Victorian *Crimes (Mental Impairment and Unfitness to be Tried) Act 1997* (Vic); see J. Lightfoot, 'Striking the Balance: The Abolition of the Victorian Governor's Pleasure System' (1998) 5 *Psychiatry, Psychology and Law* 265.

125 *Crimes (Mental Impairment and Unfitness to be Tried) Act 1997* (Vic) s 39.

126 *Crimes (Mental Impairment and Unfitness to be Tried) Act 1997* (Vic) ss 32(2), 40 (1)(c)(d).

to] any other matters the court thinks relevant'.[127] Where an accused is found 'not guilty because of mental impairment' (the special verdict), the accused must be either released unconditionally or held subject to supervision orders.[128] The use of supervision orders is designed to facilitate a structured, court-supervised process leading ultimately to the release of an accused.[129] A court may impose one of two types of supervision orders, either a custodial supervision order or a non-custodial supervision order.[130] Where a custodial supervision order is imposed the accused must be either remanded in 'an appropriate place', that is, a mental health service, or committed to 'custody in a prison'.[131] The court must not make a supervision order committing a person to 'an appropriate place' unless it has requested and received a 'certificate of available services' from the Secretary to the Department of Human Services.[132] A certificate of available services must 'state whether or not there are facilities or services available for the custody, care or treatment of the person.[133] A court must not make an order committing a person to custody in prison 'unless it is satisfied that there is no practicable alternative in the circumstances'.[134] Where a non-custodial supervision order is made the court may release the accused on 'conditions decided by the court and specified in the order'.[135] While all such orders are deemed to be indefinite,[136] as a safeguard a nominal term is also set. Such a nominal term is determined according to the maximum term of imprisonment applicable for the offence committed.[137] Where a person is still subject to a supervision order at the expiration of the nominal term, the court must conduct a 'major review' into the person's case.[138] As part of such a review the court can only vary a custodial supervision order down to a non-custodial supervision order, it cannot revoke it completely.[139] Application for a variation of a custodial supervision order to a non-custodial supervision order will only be considered where the person applying has completed at least

127 *Crimes (Mental Impairment and Unfitness to be Tried) Act 1997* (Vic) s 40(e).

128 *Crimes (Mental Impairment and Unfitness to be Tried) Act 1997* (Vic) ss 20, 23.

129 Fairall and Yeo, *Criminal Defences in Australia* (n. 19) 278; cp., for a similar system, *Criminal Code Amendment (Mental Impairment and Unfitness to be Tried) Act 2002* (NT).

130 *Crimes (Mental Impairment and Unfitness to be Tried) Act 1997* (Vic) s 26(2).

131 *Crimes (Mental Impairment and Unfitness to be Tried) Act 1997* (Vic) s 26(2)(a).

132 *Crimes (Mental Impairment and Unfitness to be Tried) Act 1997* (Vic) s 26(3), read with s 47.

133 *Crimes (Mental Impairment and Unfitness to be Tried) Act 1997* (Vic) s 47(2).

134 *Crimes (Mental Impairment and Unfitness to be Tried) Act 1997* (Vic) s 26(4).

135 *Crimes (Mental Impairment and Unfitness to be Tried) Act 1997* (Vic) s 26(2)(b).

136 *Crimes (Mental Impairment and Unfitness to be Tried) Act 1997* (Vic) s 27(1).

137 *Crimes (Mental Impairment and Unfitness to be Tried) Act 1997* (Vic) s 28; in the instance of murder the nominal term is 25 years.

138 *Crimes (Mental Impairment and Unfitness to be Tried) Act 1997* (Vic) s 35.

139 *Crimes (Mental Impairment and Unfitness to be Tried) Act 1997* (Vic) s 32 (by implication).

12 months 'extended leave' granted by the court.[140] Where a person is subject to a non-custodial supervision order he or she may apply to the court for a variation or revocation of the order.[141]

Because of the link between certain mental illnesses and violence, as currently understood, the following dispositional options present themselves. Where, on the one hand, the malfunctioning of the mind of an accused is caused by an external factor, that is transient and not likely to recur, he or she is entitled to an unconditional acquittal. Where, on the other hand, an accused experiences a malfunction caused by an internal factor whether he or she is to be held criminally liable or provided with the special verdict will be determined according to whether the malfunction was due to his or her fault. Where such malfunction is due to his or her fault or nature, he or she will be criminally liable and subject to punishment. Where however, the malfunction is caused by an internal factor not due to his or her fault or nature, the special verdict will apply and result in him or her being subject to a treatment regime. The above dispositional options reflect the community interest concerns informing the disease of the mind enquiry.

Arranged schematically the above analysis reveals the following dispositional options:

Table 3.2 Disease of the mind and disposition

Source of malfunction	**Potential verdict**	**Potential disposition**
Internal (not attributable to fault or nature of accused)	'Not guilty because of mental impairment'[a]	Treatment
Internal (attributable to fault or nature of accused)	Guilty	Punishment
External	Not guilty[b]	Acquittal

Notes:

[a] *Crimes (Mental Impairment and Unfitness to be Tried) Act 1997* (Vic) s 20(2).

[b] Where the malfunction results in the accused's conduct being involuntary.

However, it should not be thought that the law in paying regard to societal protection fails to concern itself with the issue of individual justice. The following section will address this issue. The first part of the section will comment on the significance of the distinction drawn above between the 'responsibility' and 'community interest' aspects of the disease of the mind enquiry. Succinctly stated, it will be argued that while these two aspects add complexity to the disease of the mind enquiry, they do not result in a state of irreconcilable tension.

---

140 *Crimes (Mental Impairment and Unfitness to be Tried) Act 1997* (Vic) ss 32(3), read with s 57.

141 *Crimes (Mental Impairment and Unfitness to be Tried) Act 1997* (Vic) s 31.

The extent to which social-defence considerations have an impact upon the disease of the mind enquiry will only be of tangential interest to the disposition of a mentally impaired acquittee. Nevertheless, concerns with societal protection will be relevant to the issue of disposition. The second part of the section will apply the distinction between an accused's responsibility and concerns with societal protection to highlight the way in which community interest concerns inform the disposition stage of the defence of insanity.

Societal protection and individual justice

Negotiating disease of the mind

I mentioned above that for certain contemporary theorists, the law consists of a number of contradictions which are kept from view by means of a sleight of hand. One such contradiction arises when it is sought to view the criminal law as a means of protecting individual rights and as a system of social control.[142] In the context of the insanity defence, this contradiction is most apparent in the way in which the law handles the issue of individual justice in order to secure social defence. According to these theorists the deterrent aspect of the law is addressed only to those rational autonomous individuals who may be deterred through the threat of punishment.[143] Those found incapable of either reasoning and choosing between right and wrong or controlling their conduct cannot be deterred by the threat of punishment and so should not be subject to criminal sanctions. However, rather than being released outright the criminal law continues to detain such individuals on the basis of community protection. That is, even though such individuals are found non-responsible, they are nevertheless considered to be fit subjects of our responsibility practices. Yet, such an approach results in policy issues being used in order to decide questions of responsibility and is thereby said to confuse two issues: the utilitarian issue of what to do with an acquittee who may be dangerous in the future and the moral question of the conditions for ascription of criminal responsibility.[144] Moreover, the conflation of issues of responsibility and questions of disposition results in the subsuming of individual justice under broader social defence considerations.[145]

In contrast to the approach adopted by theorists such as Lacey and Norrie, this chapter argues that the law genuinely reconciles claims arising from communal,

142 See Norrie, 'Simulacra of Morality?' (n. 4).

143 Norrie, *Crime, Reason and History* (n. 5) 178.

144 I.G. Campbell, *Mental Disorder and Criminal Law in Australia and New Zealand* (Sydney, 1988) 129; see G. Zdenkowske, 'Community Protection through Imprisonment without Conviction: Pragmatism versus Justice' (1997) 3 *Australian Journal of Human Rights* 8.

145 Norrie, *Crime, Reason and History* (n. 5) 178.

moral and professional imperatives in the context of the disease of the mind enquiry. While there is complexity in the law as a result of the various demands arising from these imperatives, any resulting tension arising from such demands and complexity may be resolved. The way in which the law manages to resolve the tension arising between notions of individual justice and societal protection will involve distinguishing between the purposes served by the responsibility and community interest aspects of the disease of the mind enquiry respectively.

The responsibility aspect of the enquiry reflects the moral concern that an individual who lacks the capacity for responsible conduct should not be punished. Where an individual lacks the ability or capacity to know the nature and quality or wrongness of his or her act or to control such an act, then he or she cannot be held morally responsible. Further, as such an individual cannot know or understand what he or she is doing or control his or her actions, a basic assumption of criminal law that individuals exercise rational choice is not established. As a result, those individuals who are found to be mentally impaired are exempted from criminal liability. The community-interest aspect of the enquiry reflects the societal concern that members of the community should be safeguarded from those individuals who may re-offend because of their mental illness. As seen above, the community-interest aspect of the disease of the mind enquiry is revealed through the use made of an objective standard and of the notion of recurrence in judicially formulated tests aimed at determining whether an accused is suffering from a disease of the mind.

The approach argued for in this chapter recognizes that the demands arising from the moral and communal imperatives associated with the insanity defence relate to different aspects of the disease of the mind enquiry. The fact that the judgment of responsibility and community interest aspects of the disease of the mind enquiry address different issues accounts for the relative complexity in determining the correct characterization of an individual's state of disease, disorder or mental disturbance. However, while the judgment of responsibility and community-interest aspect of the enquiry provide complexity this does not necessarily mean that they are therefore contradictory. In particular, the judgment of responsibility will turn on the question of an individual's responsibility while the community-interest aspect of the enquiry will be concerned with the conceptually distinct question of societal protection. Where an individual's state of disease, disorder or disturbance results in the requisite incapacities he or she is held, pursuant to the judgment of responsibility, to be non-responsible. To this extent the issue of individual justice is addressed. However, in addition to establishing the non-responsibility of an accused the disease of the mind enquiry addresses the question of community interest. The community-interest aspect of the disease of the mind enquiry is concerned with securing community protection in the light of the potential recurrence of an individual's mental illness and associated violence. Consequently, and in keeping with the law's concern in securing community protection, a finding of non-responsibility due to a disease of the mind will result only in a qualified acquittal. The next section will show how the non-responsibility of an accused and societal protection concerns are both accommodated in the disposition stage of the defence.

Special verdict

As with the disease of the mind enquiry, the law distinguishes between an accused's non-responsibility and the community-interest considerations at the time of his or her disposition. The way in which the law distinguishes between the responsibility and the community-interest aspects at the disposition stage is brought out most clearly by considering the special-verdict model of disposition adopted by the Victorian legislation.[146]

Two models have been distinguished in respect of the verdict following a finding of insanity or, non-responsibility: the 'special-verdict' model, and the 'mental-incompetence' model.[147] The special-verdict model indicates that, while the accused is not criminally culpable, he or she is nevertheless deemed to require oversight on the basis of community protection. To this extent the special-verdict model is best viewed as a system of preventive detention.[148] For example, the Victorian *Crimes (Mental Impairment and Unfitness to be Tried) Act 1997* states the significance of a finding of mental impairment as follows: 'If the defence of mental impairment is established, the person must be found not guilty because of mental impairment'.[149] As a result, in the context of indictable offences a Victorian court may order the immediate detention of an accused 'found not guilty because of mental impairment'.[150]

In contrast, the mental-incompetence model is not underpinned by an assumption that those accused who satisfy the insanity defence require detention. The question posed by this model is whether the accused was 'mentally incompetent to commit the offence'. For example, in South Australia a person is mentally incompetent to commit an offence, if at the time of the offence he or she is suffering from a mental impairment resulting in the relevant incapacities.[151] The mental-incompetence model allows for a range of dispositional options on the basis of court-supervised

---

146 *Crimes (Mental Impairment and Unfitness to be Tried) Act 1997* (Vic) s 20(2).

147 W. Brookbanks, 'Insanity' in *Psychiatry and Law*, ed. Brookbanks and Simpson (n. 111) 123, 148.

148 Bronitt and McSherry, *Principles of Criminal Law* (n. 19) 253; see *Veen v R (No 2)* (1988) 164 CLR 465, 472; *R v Carr* [1996] 1 VR 585; *McGarry v R* (2001) 207 CLR 121.

149 *Crimes (Mental Impairment and Unfitness to be Tried) Act 1997* (Vic) s 20(2).

150 Most courts of summary jurisdiction do not have power to order detention. Where an accused is found insane the charge is dismissed and the accused given an unconditional discharge (*Lynch v Hennicke* (1985) Tas R (NC 5) 175; *Medlin v Samuels* [1971] SASR 223). Contrast NSW, where on a finding of insanity a magistrate may dismiss the charge or discharge the accused unconditionally or conditionally (*Mental Health (Criminal Procedure) Act 1990* (NSW) s 32(1)).

151 *Criminal Law Consolidation Act 1935* (SA) 'S 269C-Mental Competence'.

assessments of risk.[152] Moreover, the provision of such a range of dispositional options by the legislature, while not conclusive proof, is evidence of the fact that community-interest considerations are only one factor that a court will consider in determining whether a particular mental condition should be characterized as a disease of the mind.

In its discussion of defences to homicide, the VLRC remarked on the proposed introduction of a new plea of 'guilty but mentally impaired'.[153] The commission considered the introduction of the new plea of guilty but mentally impaired specifically in the context of cases dealt with 'by consent'. The 'by consent' process already occurs in the majority of homicide cases involving mentally impaired accused and signifies that both the prosecution and the defence agree that the accused should be provided with the special verdict of not guilty because of mental impairment.[154] The purpose of the proposed new plea would be to bypass the need for a trial, by consent or otherwise, and allow the accused to proceed to the disposition stage.

However, in its final report the commission expressed the view that to change the current finding of not guilty because of mental impairment[155] to a plea of guilty but mentally impaired would be 'inappropriate'. According to the commission, 'it was wrong to label someone who was mentally impaired as "guilty". Someone affected by a mental impairment ought not to be found criminally responsible.'[156] The clear implication of the commission's finding is that while the issue of an accused's responsibility will be relevant to the nature of the verdict it remains a distinct question to that of his or her disposition. The disposition of a mentally impaired individual is determined according to concerns with community protection.

While based on the special-verdict model, the Victorian legislation shares with the mental-incompetence model the provision of a range of dispositional options. Again, the introduction of dispositional options by the Victorian legislation suggests that the issue of societal protection is only one of several factors a court will consider in deciding what to do with an accused acquitted on the basis of mental impairment. An accused who has been found not guilty due to mental impairment and who does not represent a danger to members of the public may be unconditionally released. Even a person who has been given a custodial supervision order may have, subject to certain conditions being satisfied, his or her custodial supervision order varied to a non-custodial one. Ultimately, a person may apply

152 *Criminal Law Consolidation Act 1935* (SA) 'Division 4: Disposition of Persons Detained to be Liable to Supervision under this Part: ss 269O–269VA'.

153 Victorian Law Reform Commission, *Defences to Homicide: Final Report* (n. 73) 5.72.

154 Ibid. 5.69.

155 *Crimes (Mental Impairment and Unfitness to be Tried) Act 1997* (Vic) s 20(2).

156 Victorian Law Reform Commission, *Defences to Homicide: Final Report* (n. 73) 5.73.

for the revocation of the non-custodial order. By providing a range of dispositional options the structured, court-supervised process found in the Victorian legislation reduces the inherent risk of indefinite detention faced by accused putting evidence of mental impairment before the courts.

However, notwithstanding the liberal disposition regime of the Victorian legislation, several commentators have remarked on an implicit conservatism in court and review-body decisions to release mentally impaired acquittees.[157] For example, it has been noted that where an accused has committed homicide 'there are no cases of [non-custodial] orders being made in any case of mental impairment which have arisen since the introduction of the legislation'.[158] As a result a mentally impaired acquittee who has committed homicide will not be released immediately but will be detained on the basis of community protection. That is, in the context of the Victorian Act the perceived likelihood of a recurrence of violent behaviour by mentally impaired acquittees will preclude their release on non-custodial orders.[159]

Conclusion

I have argued above that the disease of the mind enquiry involves three aspects: a judgment of responsibility, clinical evidence and community interest. The judgment of responsibility articulates the moral intuition that it is wrong to punish an individual whose mental condition precludes him or her from choosing to engage in criminally proscribed conduct or for failing to exercise his or her ability to control such conduct. The clinical expertise of psychiatrists permits expert evidence to be used in diagnosing an individual's mental condition, treatability and, if an accused is detained after the special verdict, evaluating the likelihood of any future acts of violence by such an individual. The community-interest aspect of the disease of the mind enquiry centres on the protection of members of society from the possible recurrence of violence posed by mentally impaired acquittees. In the light of the differing issues and demands raised by each of these three factors the disease of the mind enquiry gives rise to various tensions. I have chosen to focus on the tension arising in respect of the judgment of responsibility's concern with individual justice and the community-interest aspect's concern with societal protection.

---

157 See B. McSherry, 'Criminal Detention of those with Mental Impairment' (1999) 6 *Journal of Law and Medicine* 216; I. Freckelton, 'Decision-Making about Involuntary Psychiatric Treatment' (1998) 5 *Psychiatry, Psychology and Law* 249; Fairall and Yeo, *Criminal Defences in Australia* (n. 19) 278; Victorian Law Reform Commission, *Defences to Homicide: Options Paper* (n. 19) 5.34.

158 Victorian Law Reform Commission, *Defences to Homicide: Options Paper* (n. 19) 5.34 n 752.

159 Ibid. 5.34.

I have argued that the law manages to reconcile this tension by acknowledging that the question of an accused's responsibility is a distinct question to that of societal protection. While the judgment of responsibility will address the question of an individual's responsibility, the community-interest aspect of the enquiry will be concerned with the issue of societal protection. While both are parts of the disease of the mind enquiry they remain conceptually distinct: while an accused's non-responsibility reflects the judgment of responsibility aspect of the enquiry, societal protection reflects the community-interest aspect of the enquiry.

I have also argued that the disposition of a mentally impaired acquittee is a distinct issue from that of the disease of the mind enquiry. Nevertheless, the law maintains the distinction between an accused's responsibility and community-interest concerns at the disposition stage of the defence also. The way in which the distinction between individual responsibility and societal protection operates at the disposition stage of the defence was analysed in the final section through an examination of the special-verdict model as applied in the Victorian Act.

The next chapter will apply the above insights to an analysis of the problems posed by states of drug-induced psychosis.

Chapter 4
Drug-Use and the Defence of Insanity

Introduction

The question of whether someone who has suffered from drug-induced psychosis can use the defence of insanity is a pressing legal question which has arisen in several recent criminal trials in Victoria.[1] This chapter will critically examine several approaches which have been adopted in answer to this question before proposing a principled approach by way of conclusion.

The previous chapter highlighted three factors which it was suggested the criminal law endeavours to balance in determining which conditions will satisfy the legal expression 'disease of the mind'. One of these is what was referred to as a judgment of responsibility. The judgment of responsibility allows us to determine the question of an agent's moral and legal responsibility. The judgment of responsibility precludes punishing an accused individual whose mental condition renders him or her incapable of either knowingly choosing between right and wrong or controlling his or her conduct. The judgment of responsibility will be reflected in the scope of criminal-law defences dealing with individuals accused of engaging in criminal conduct. For example, the boundaries of the defence of insanity will seek to determine, according to principles of criminal responsibility, when an individual's mental state will result in him or her being held non-responsible and as a result not liable to criminal sanctions. The present chapter will apply the judgment of responsibility to instances of drug-induced psychosis in order to clarify the proper scope of the defence of insanity. This will involve determining when the voluntary use of a drug leading to a state of psychosis will satisfy the judgment of responsibility factor informing the disease of the mind enquiry.

This chapter will analyse the various issues which arise as a result of attempts to raise a defence of non-responsibility for criminal conduct performed subsequent to voluntary drug use resulting in psychosis. As will be discussed in more detail in Chapter 5, the scope of the defence of insanity may be altered in one of two ways: either by restricting or expanding those states of mental malfunction which will be recognized as diseases of the mind or by restricting or expanding those conditions considered sufficiently incapacitating for the purposes of the defence. Instances of psychosis due to drug use involve the paradigmatic instance of

---

1 *R v Sebalj* [2003] VSC 181(Unreported, SC Vic, Smith J, 5 June 2003); *R v Sebalj* [2004] VSC 212 (Unreported, SC Vic, Williams J, 11 June 2004); *R v Sebalj* [2006] VSCA 106; *R v Barrett* [2005] VSC 176; *R v Martin* [2005] VSC 497.

cognitive incapacity, namely a psychotic state, and for this reason do not present any particular definitional issues in regards to the defect of reason aspect of the defence as traditionally understood.[2] Consequently, the present discussion will focus on whether states of psychosis arising from drug use should be recognized as instances of disease of the mind.

The present chapter draws on material previously presented in two articles on drug use and the defence of insanity either authored or co-authored by myself.[3] The first, co-authored with Carroll, McSherry and Wood, acknowledged that there were a wide range of approaches to the issue of drug use and the defence of insanity in various legal jurisdictions. However, it was recognized as a structural point that three broad approaches to the problem were discernible: liberal, conservative and intermediate. This paper analysed legal, expert witness and policy perspectives relating to the three approaches developed by the three co-authors and myself, which will be discussed below. The paper was exploratory in scope and endeavoured to provide 'an overview of possible approaches that the law may take [so as] at the very least move the debate forwards'.[4] The single authored paper, while acknowledging the broad concerns of the group paper, aimed to 'explore some of the underlying conceptual issues faced by legal theorists in responding to the voluntary consumption of psychoactive drugs'.[5] This paper used the three broad approaches adopted in the group paper re-naming them 'causal irrelevance', 'settled insanity' and 'meta-responsibility', in keeping with each approach's defining characteristic.

The present chapter adopts the structure of three broad approaches used in the two papers in order to develop the current substantive argument. However, the substantive argument of this chapter differs from that of the preceding papers in reflecting the central concerns of this book. Both of the earlier papers highlighted the various difficulties faced by all three approaches without endorsing one in particular. As a result, and in contrast to the earlier papers, this chapter will endeavour to present a principled response to the question of when drug-induced psychosis should be characterized as a disease of the mind. Moreover, by analysing the above approaches to the issue of an accused's responsibility for states of drug-induced psychosis, it will be possible to develop the account of those factors informing the disease of the mind enquiry outlined in Chapter 3 above.

---

2 *R v Sebalj* [2006] VSCA 106 para 19 per Maxwell P, citing Mental Health Review Board Hearing No 230190: X01:300512 (Appeal of Gary Ian Patrick Webb), *Decisions of the Mental Health Review Board Victoria* (1987–91) vol. 1, 177–8.

3 A. Carroll et al., 'Drug-Associated Psychoses and Criminal Responsibility' (2008) 26 *Behavioural Sciences and the Law* 633; S. Yannoulidis, 'Drug Use and the Defence of Mental Impairment: Some Conceptual and Explanatory Issues' (2006) 18 *Bond Law Review* 165.

4 Carroll et al., 'Drug-Associated Psychoses and Criminal Responsibility' (n. 3) 634.

5 Yannoulidis, 'Drug Use and the Defence of Mental Impairment' (n. 3) 166.

I begin with an outline of the nature of the problem presented by instances of psychosis arising from drug use and the approach to be adopted in this chapter.

Drug-induced psychosis

The voluntary consumption of psychoactive drugs may result in what has been termed a drug-induced psychosis.[6] The term 'drug-induced psychosis' will be used to describe a state of psychosis arising from the ingestion of psychoactive substances which is due to either the intoxicating effects of the substance, or the short-term symptoms associated with the use of such a substance subsequent to its physiological excretion or due to the chronic use of such a substance operating independently of either of the above.

In considering the issue of drug-induced psychosis a distinction may be drawn between two distinct types of question, one clinical, the other normative. In order to adequately frame the enquiry, I will begin by outlining the distinction between these two questions in respect of the use of drugs leading to psychosis. The first question asks whether the state of psychosis is due to the immediate effects of a drug or exists independently of the effects of the consumption of a drug. The first question arises as a result of the fact that states of psychosis arising from drug use have been classified according to whether they have been caused by one of two distinct types of reaction: an acute-onset psychotic state that resolves within a relatively short time-frame when an individual stops using the drug and a chronic psychotic state occurring with a history of prolonged usage.[7] That is, a psychotic state may be due to the immediate intoxicating effects of a drug following its consumption or the relatively short-term symptoms associated with the use of a drug subsequent to its physiological excretion. Alternatively, a psychotic state may arise due to the chronic use of drugs and operate independently of either the intoxicating effects of a drug or the short-term symptoms associated with the use of a drug subsequent to its physiological excretion. Such a question is clearly a matter for expert evidence.

The second question asks whether the defence of insanity should be available to an accused who has voluntarily consumed drugs which have produced either an acute or chronic psychotic state. This latter question raises normative issues falling outside the exclusive purview of contemporary clinical research. In particular, the normative issues raised by this latter question concern the proper scope of the defence of insanity. This chapter is concerned with this second question which it will seek to answer by an analysis of the various problems posed by states of drug-induced psychoses. Three approaches in respect of establishing an accused's

6 R. Scott and W. Kingswell, 'Amphetamines, Psychosis and the Insanity Defence: Disturbing Trends in Queensland' (2003) 23 *Queensland Lawyer* 151.

7 Ibid. 4.

responsibility for a state of drug-induced psychoses are discernible: Causal Irrelevance, Settled Insanity and Meta-Responsibility.

Causal Irrelevance

The first approach to the issue of when to characterize a drug-induced psychosis as a disease of the mind which I will consider was that proposed by the VLRC during its examination of homicide offences committed by people with mentally impaired functioning.[8] Succinctly stated, the commission adopted the view that the causal antecedents of an accused's behaviour should be irrelevant to the question of his or her responsibility. According to the commission, in keeping with the defence's true purpose, if there is a cognitive failure on the part of an accused during the commission of the offence non-responsibility should follow as a matter of principle. That is, the VLRC claims that the source of a state of mental malfunction should make no difference to the non-responsibility of an accused. Where an accused experiences the relevant incapacities due to a state of mental malfunction, this will be sufficient to render him or her non-responsible. According to the VLRC the question of an accused's non-responsibility will be determined by his or her incapacity not the cause of such incapacity. The relevant time-frame on this view is that concurrent with when the offending conduct is performed.

Settled Insanity

A second alternative approach to the issue of when to characterize a drug-induced psychosis as a disease of the mind is referred to as settled insanity. Settled insanity holds an accused non-responsible where a state of mental malfunction is diagnosable independently of drug use.[9] Those theorists who argue for recognition of this approach hold that evidence of a state of settled insanity may be ascertained through evidence of a fixed, stable state of mental malfunctioning independent of an accused's drug use. That is, the test of settled insanity is predicated on a finding of a state of mental malfunction both before and after the offending conduct has been performed. Such a state is indicative of the existence of a mental malfunction independent of the effects of an intoxicant operating at the time of the offence.

Meta-Responsibility

A third approach holds an accused responsible where he or she has, through his or her culpable behaviour, created the conditions of his or her own defence.

---

8 Victorian Law Reform Commission, *Defences to Homicide: Final Report*, Report No 94 (Melbourne, 2004), 'Chapter 5: People with Mentally Impaired Functioning who Kill'.

9 J. Reid Meloy, 'Voluntary Intoxication and the Insanity Defence' (1992) 20 *The Journal of Psychiatry and Law* 439.

Such an approach has been put forward by Edward Mitchell in the course of his discussion of the notion of meta-responsibility.[10] Focusing on prior conduct, Mitchell argues that an accused is responsible where he or she has engaged in prior culpable behaviour that in turn creates the conditions of the defence relied upon. The relevant time-frame according to this view is that which occurs before the offending conduct is performed. Mitchell's views will be examined below. In contrast to the VLRC view, meta-responsibility holds that the causal antecedents of an accused's behaviour will be determinative of his or her responsibility. Where an accused's prior culpable behaviour causes a state of mental malfunction which results in the relevant incapacities, then he or she should not be accorded a defence of insanity.

The proposed argument

In the concluding remarks to this chapter it will be argued that any attempt to clarify the proper scope of the insanity defence in the context of drug-induced psychoses must take into account the various factors informing the disease of the mind enquiry. Consequently, the approach endorsed by this chapter will use the insights of the previous chapter in respect of the factors which inform the disease of the mind enquiry.

It will be argued that of the three approaches above that which is most in accord with the insights of Chapter 3 is the approach referred to as meta-responsibility. However, it will also be shown that the doctrine of meta-responsibility is in need of further elaboration. In particular, the formulation of meta-responsibility put forward by Mitchell will be shown to fail to take into account the conditions under which responsibility is ascribed, diminished or lost. Hence, while advocating Mitchell's general approach the final substantive section of this chapter will seek to extend the doctrine of meta-responsibility to account for these conditions.

The opening sections of the chapter will begin with an analysis of the three different approaches which have been adopted in respect of assigning criminal responsibility in cases of drug-induced psychosis. The latter sections of the chapter will analyse the nature of an individual's responsibility for a state of drug-induced psychosis and finish by arguing for a preferred approach. However, before proceeding to detail the relative strengths and weaknesses of the three broad approaches above the next section will provide an overview of the current approach adopted by courts to the question of states of mental malfunction arising in the context of illicit drug use.

10 E. Mitchell, 'Meta-Responsibility and Mental Disorder: Causing the Conditions of One's Own Insanity Plea' (1999) 10 *Journal of Forensic Psychiatry* 597; E. Mitchell, *Self-Made Madness: Re-Thinking Illness and Criminal Responsibility* (Aldershot, 2004); E. Mitchell, 'Culpability for Inducing Mental States: The Insanity Defence of Dr Jekyll' (2004) 32 *The Journal of the American Academy of Psychiatry and the Law* 63.

Intoxication and insanity

The consumption of intoxicants resulting in a temporary mental malfunction will not give rise to the defence of insanity as such a state of mental malfunction will not be recognized as a 'disease of the mind'.[11] The leading case is *R v Sebalj*.[12] In *Sebalj*'s case the accused was found guilty of the murder of his girlfriend while in a state of paranoid psychosis resulting from his attempt to withdraw from the use of drugs. The accused was a user of various addictive drugs, such as amphetamines and cannabis, for several years prior to the killing of his girlfriend. During an attempt to extricate himself from his addiction to drugs the accused developed aural and visual hallucinations associated with psychosis. After he was referred to a hospital by police officers, his psychotic state was diagnosed. After treating the accused with medication to alleviate both his anxiety and psychosis, hospital staff released him in the care of his girlfriend. Arrangements were made by hospital staff for a nurse from the crisis assessment team to meet the accused later that evening. Upon arriving that evening the nurse was unable to gain access despite making repeated telephone calls to the accused. The accused finally emerged from the bungalow which he shared with the deceased with blood spattered on his clothes. It was held on the facts that he had stabbed his girlfriend in the belief that she was allowing someone who had come to kill him to enter.

At his trial there was 'uncertainty as to how that element should be approached in the trial because of uncertainty as to the scope of the statutory defence of "mental impairment"'.[13] After determining Parliament's intent in passing the Act, Justice Smith noted that, 'the term "a mental impairment" should not be construed as changing the common law but construed as referring to the concept of "a disease of the mind" used in the common law defence of insanity'.[14] As a result the court held that a state of drug-induced psychosis will not give rise to the defence of insanity. In the instant case the court held that as the psychosis was brought about by means of an external agent voluntarily consumed the accused was not entitled to raise the defence. In particular, as the accused's psychosis had arisen due to drug use, it did not fit the definition of mental impairment which, following the common law, required the illness to be a disease of the mind.[15] Consequently, in the absence of the defence of mental impairment the accused was sentenced to 15 years imprisonment for murder.[16]

Given that the use of such an intoxicant in such cases is voluntary and advertent, courts in those situations have been reluctant to find the relevant defendants

---

11 P.A. Fairall and S. Yeo, *Criminal Defences in Australia* (4th edn. Chatswood, NSW, 2005) 238.

12 [2003] VSC 181.

13 Ibid. para 3.

14 Ibid. para 14.

15 Ibid.

16 *R v Sebalj* [2004] VSC 212 (11 June 2004) per Williams J.

non-responsible. By refusing to recognize a state of non-responsibility for such culpable behaviour courts are paying heed to what I have referred to in Chapter 3 as the responsibility aspect of the disease of the mind enquiry. In particular courts are reluctant to recognize a state of non-responsibility arising due to the fault or nature of a defendant. This was recognized by Sholl J, who noted that, while there may be cases which are problematic, 'states of drunkenness of itself, anger or other transient passions, excitability arising from temperament' have never been regarded as arising from a disease of the mind.[17]

The following sections will analyse three approaches to the question of whether the voluntary consumption of an illicit intoxicant leading to a psychotic state should be allowed to give rise to the defence of insanity.

Causal irrelevance

This section will consider the VLRC's approach to this question. The first part will outline the VLRC's position while the second will note several objections which have been raised to this view.

VLRC and disease of the mind

In the context of clarifying the current scope of mental impairment, the VLRC turned its attention to the definition of the term 'disease of the mind'.[18] The VLRC expressed the view that the interpretation of statutory formulations as merely legislative re-statements of the common law result in formulations that are too narrow.[19] In particular, the VLRC objected to the interpretation by the Supreme Court of Victoria in two recent cases of the expression 'mental impairment' as found in the Victorian Act.[20] In both *R v R*[21] and *R v Sebalj*,[22] the Supreme Court interpreted the statutory expression 'mental impairment' as 'merely a legislative restatement of the common law'.[23] The commission argued that adopting a common-law definition of mental impairment would not provide a sufficient

---

17 *R v Meddings* [1966] VR 306, citing *Porter* (1933) 55 CLR 182 per Dixon CJ.

18 Victorian Law Reform Commission, *Defences to Homicide: Final Report* (n. 8) 5.34.

19 Ibid. 5.35.

20 *Crimes (Mental Impairment and Unfitness to be Tried) Act 1997* (Vic) s 20; while not defined, 'mental impairment' is the terminology employed in the Victorian statute replacing the common-law defence of insanity.

21 *R v R* [2003] VSC 187 (Unreported, SC Vic, Teague J, 5 March 2003).

22 *R v Sebalj* [2003] VSC 181 (Unreported, SC Vic, Smith J, 5 June 2003).

23 Victorian Law Reform Commission, *Defences to Homicide: Final Report* (n. 8) 5.34.

level of flexibility in the application of the defence.[24] By way of example, the commission cited the case of *R v Sebalj*.[25]

The VLRC argued that as a result of the narrowness with which the statutory defence of mental impairment had been defined, the accused had been deprived of the defence. The VLRC held that the cause of an accused's incapacity was irrelevant to the question of whether a defence should be available to him or her. As a result of the lack of flexibility of the defence, the accused had been denied a defence to which he was entitled. The VLRC noted that the punishment of an individual who lacks the requisite capacities for responsible conduct is an injustice.[26]

The VLRC expressed the view that fear that a broad interpretation of the legal expression 'disease of the mind' or its statutory equivalent 'mental impairment' would open the 'floodgates' to undeserving accused was unfounded.[27] According to the VLRC, the reason why a 'floodgates' argument is unfounded is because it is the nature of the requisite incapacities which must result from a mental disorder characterized as a disease of the mind which keep the defence within 'strict limits'.[28] Consequently, it would require an accused to be more than 'adversely impaired to a material degree by alcohol or drugs' in order to satisfy the defence.[29] In keeping with the rules' formulation, that which would be required is a lack of capacity to understand the nature and quality of the act or that it was wrong.

The VLRC held that the causal antecedents of an accused's behaviour are irrelevant to the issue of his or her responsibility. According to the VLRC, where there is a cognitive failure which arises from a disease of the mind which satisfies the elements of the defence then the accused should be entitled to the defence. In order to ensure that there was a sufficient degree of flexibility in the application of the defence the VLRC suggested that the definition of mental impairment should be broader then the common law definition of disease of the mind.

As a result, the VLRC called for statutory intervention to alter the current narrow interpretation and to this end proposed that the following new definition of the expression 'mental impairment' be inserted into the Victorian Act:[30]

> 7. Definition of 'mental impairment' inserted
> In section 3(1) of the *Crimes (Mental Impairment and Unfitness to be Tried) Act 1997* insert the following definition –
> '"mental impairment" includes, but is not limited to, a disease of the mind'.

---

24 Ibid. 5.35.

25 [2003] VSC 181.

26 Victorian Law Reform Commission, *Defences to Homicide: Final Report* (n. 8) 5.42.

27 Ibid. 5.39.

28 Ibid.

29 Ibid.

30 Ibid. 'Recommendation 38' 217.

By broadening the scope of the defence so as 'to include, but not be limited to, a disease of the mind', the VLRC believed that the defence would thereby be available to deserving accused. The next section will critically examine the arguments put forward by the VLRC in support of such statutory intervention.

VLRC: indeterminate and over-inclusive

Notwithstanding the call for statutory amendment by the VLRC, the commission did acknowledge that there are two objections to allowing a person whose psychosis is induced by alcohol or drugs voluntarily consumed to rely on the defence of mental impairment.[31] First, given that the effects of an intoxicant may only be temporary with no lasting mental malfunction, it would be inappropriate to characterize such effects as a disease of the mind for the purposes of the defence. Second, there is a moral objection to allowing a person to benefit from conditions which he or she has been responsible for bringing about. The VLRC's response to each of these objections will be considered in turn.

In response to the first objection the commission argued that at common law the duration of a mental disorder will not be determinative of whether or not it is to be characterized as a disease of the mind.[32] The commission was correct to take this view. There is no requirement that a state of mental malfunction be permanent in order for the defence of insanity to be established. The defence is available in instances where the state of mental malfunction is permanent as well as in instances where it is only temporary.[33] Subject to what will be said below, all that is required in order for the defence of insanity to be established is that the state of mental malfunction characterized as a disease of the mind caused the relevant incapacities, as defined, at the time of the offence.[34] The fact that the mental malfunction was temporary will not preclude such a state from being characterized as a disease of the mind.

Of more interest is the related fact noted by the commission that in *Sebalj's* case the accused's drug-induced psychosis 'subsequently developed into a schizophrenic illness requiring ongoing treatment'.[35] The implication of this view, while not explicitly stated by the VLRC, is that the accused had a predisposition or vulnerability to psychosis which was triggered by drug-use and resulted in a fully fledged schizophrenic illness. Indeed, expert evidence was tendered in *Sebalj's* case indicating that it would have been the view of many psychiatrists that the accused

31 Ibid. 5.37.

32 Ibid. 5.38, citing *R v Porter* [1933] 55 CLR 182.

33 *R v Kemp* [1957] 1 QB 399, 407 per Devlin J.

34 *R v Sullivan* [1983] 2 All ER 673, 677 per Lord Diplock.

35 Victorian Law Reform Commission, *Defences to Homicide: Final Report* (n. 8) 5.38.

suffered from schizophrenia even before the drug-induced psychotic episode.[36] However, the commission failed to note that there are problems associated with determining whether a predisposition, or vulnerability, to drug-induced psychosis is indicative of the existence of an underlying pathological infirmity of mind.[37] The nature of these problems will be considered during the course of the analysis of the doctrine of settled insanity below.

In particular, the analysis will consider the problems associated with determining whether a predisposition to drug-induced psychosis is indicative of the existence of an underlying mental disorder. Succinctly stated, it will be argued there that there is no necessary causal relationship between an accused's predisposition to psychosis, a state of psychosis following the voluntary use of an intoxicant and the existence of an underlying mental disorder. Consequently, there is no means of determining whether a drug-induced state of psychosis is sufficient to establish an underlying pathological infirmity of mind and so give rise to the defence. Moreover, it will also be argued that an accused's lack of control over his or her predisposition to psychosis is not necessarily exculpatory.

The second objection which the commission noted in allowing drug-induced psychosis to be recognized as a disease of the mind was the 'moral argument that a person ought not to be able to raise the mental impairment defence if they were responsible for causing their condition'.[38] The commission recognized that this was an issue which rendered drug-related states of mental impairment problematic. As the commission put it, there is a great deal of difficulty in restricting the notion of responsibility in cases of voluntary drug taking.[39] For example, in the instant case, the accused himself was directly responsible for the psychosis as he had originally chosen to engage in the use of drugs. Paradoxically, it was his endeavour to cure himself of his addiction and the method of immediate withdrawal he had chosen in order to achieve this which had ultimately brought on the psychotic episode leading to the death of his girlfriend. Nevertheless, the commission stated that it did not think this should be a 'consideration in applying the defence of mental impairment'.[40] The commission argued that where the requisite incapacity is established an accused's drug-induced state of mental impairment should be sufficient to ground the defence of mental impairment.[41]

In particular, the commission was of the view that the court's ruling on mental impairment in the case of *Sebalj* failed to acknowledge the defence's 'underlying

---

36 Ibid. citing *R v Sebalj* [2004] VSC 212 (Unreported, SC Vic, Williams J, 11 June 2004) para 24.

37 *R v Radford* (1985) 42 SASR 266, 274 per King CJ.

38 Victorian Law Reform Commission, *Defences to Homicide: Final Report* (n. 8) 5.37.

39 Ibid. 5.43.

40 Ibid. 5.40.

41 Ibid. 5.42.

conceptual purpose'.[42] As expressed by the commission: 'the purpose of the defence is to ensure that people are excused from criminal responsibility when their cognitive functions are so affected that they are unable to understand what they are doing or that it is wrong'.[43] Such a purpose, according to the commission, would preclude taking into account the causal antecedent of the state of impairment. The commission held that what is determinative for the operation of the defence is the cognitive deficiency that gives rise to the requisite incapacities, not how such incapacities came about.[44] For now, I would argue that adopting the VLRC approach would result in a state of over-inclusiveness which would provide a defence to undeserving accused. By focusing exclusively on the mind of the accused at the time of the offence, without paying due regard to the precise cause of the drug-induced psychosis, all accused who experienced a psychotic response to the voluntary use of drugs would receive the benefit of the defence.

The second objection concerned the moral intuition that it would be unjust to allow a person to benefit from conditions which he or she has been responsible for bringing about. The question of an accused's responsibility for an act performed while incapacitated where he or she has brought about such incapacity through a voluntary act will be discussed below. It will be argued that not only does the VLRC view expressed above run counter to the current legal position, it is also mistaken. Succinctly stated, the reason why the VLRC is mistaken is that it fails to take into account an individual's 'meta-responsibility' for bringing about a state of non-responsibility.

This section has considered the VLRC's response to the two objections noted above in allowing a person whose psychosis is induced by voluntarily consumed drugs to rely on the defence of mental impairment. As will be seen both of these objections have given rise to two different approaches to the question of whether drug-induced psychosis should be allowed to ground the defence of insanity. Hence, the following two sections will analyse the VLRC's response by considering these two differing approaches.

Settled insanity

The first part of this section will begin with an account of the doctrine of 'settled insanity' as it is has been developed in certain American cases. The second part will consider refinements to the doctrine as proposed in the work of J. Reid Meloy. The third and final part of this section will then critically examine Meloy's suggestions in order to determine the utility of the doctrine of settled insanity as an approach in respect of the issues raised by instances of drug-induced psychosis.

42 Ibid. 5.44.

43 Ibid.

44 Ibid.

Settled insanity

In certain instances courts have held that the chronic use of an intoxicant that produces a state of psychosis operative both before and after the state of intoxication may be characterized as a state of settled insanity, rather than a case of intoxication.[45] In such cases the chronic use of substances results in a long-lasting or permanent organic brain condition rather than a state of intoxication resulting from the ingestion of a drug or alcohol. It is the long-lasting or permanent nature of the mental condition as distinct from the effects of the intoxicant which determines its characterization as a state of insanity rather than intoxication. For example, in *State v Hartfield*,[46] it was held that an accused could plead insanity where his voluntary intoxication by either alcohol or drugs had resulted in a permanent state of mental malfunction which precluded him from knowing right from wrong. Settled insanity is predicated on the idea that certain chronic users of intoxicants experience during the commission of the offence a state of drug-induced psychosis, which is independent of the effects of an intoxicant.[47] Consequently, the settled-insanity approach focuses on the mental state of the accused both before and after the criminal conduct.

The principal concern with the use of the doctrine of settled insanity concerns the difficulty in distinguishing the point at which a state of mental malfunction arising from the voluntary use of an intoxicant may be said to be symptomatic of an underlying pathological infirmity of mind. For the purposes of settled insanity, instances of drug-induced psychoses that are used to ground a defence of insanity require there to be both temporal proximity between the intoxicant and the psychotic symptoms, as well as satisfying the requirement that the state of psychosis exists independently of the consumption of the intoxicant. As a result there are two aspects to the issue of drug-induced psychosis which the doctrine of settled insanity must answer, one temporal, the other causal. First, what must be the temporal relationship between the use of an intoxicant and any subsequent psychotic symptoms in order for a state of settled insanity to be established? Moreover, if a 'prolonged or permanent persistence of substance-related symptoms' is a necessary requirement of a state of settled insanity how is this to be reconciled with the fact that states of temporary insanity excuse?[48] Second, how are the effects of the intoxicant to be distinguished from the effects of mental disorder? That is, how is a state of intoxication arising through the ingestion of a drug to be distinguished from an underlying pathological infirmity of mind due to chronic drug use?

In respect of the first question a temporal dimension has been viewed by certain commentators as determinative of whether a condition will be characterized

45 *State v Harden* (1971) 260 Kan. 365.

46 *State v Hartfield* (1990) 300 SC 469.

47 *People v Free* (1983) 447 NB 2d 218.

48 *R v Kemp* [1957] 1 QB 399, 407 per Devlin J.

as one of settled insanity. For example, according to the American Psychiatric Association's *Diagnostic and Statistical Manual of Disorders*:

> If the symptoms precede the onset of substance use or persist during extended periods of abstinence from the substance, it is likely that the symptoms are not substance induced. As a rule of thumb, symptoms that persist for more than 4 weeks after the cessation of acute Intoxication or Withdrawal [*sic.*] should be considered to be manifestations of an independent non-substance-induced mental disorder or of a Substance-Induced Persisting Disorder.[49]

The essential feature of a 'Substance-Induced Persisting Disorder' is 'prolonged or permanent persistence of substance-related symptoms that continue long after the usual course of Intoxication or Withdrawal has ended'.[50] Consequently, according to the DSM-IV-TR, in establishing whether an individual's psychotic symptoms are the direct physiological effect of substance use or characteristic of a state of settled insanity, the temporal relationship between substance use and a state of psychosis may be determinative.[51]

Similarly, Russ Scott and William Kingswell have argued that even if it is accepted that an external factor may cause acute psychosis, this alone will not be sufficient to satisfy the disease of the mind enquiry.[52] According to the authors, and in keeping with what was said by King CJ in *R v Radford*,[53] what is required for a finding of a disease of the mind is something more than 'a temporary disorder or disturbance of an otherwise healthy mind caused by external factors'.[54] As a result Scott and Kingswell contend that drug-induced psychosis should only be characterized as a disease of the mind when the symptoms of psychosis have persisted for longer than 28 days and in the absence of positive urine drug testing.[55]

However, some courts have held that, where psychosis is caused by an intoxicant, the precise time during which the symptoms associated with the psychosis are present will not be determinative of whether such a condition is to be characterized as a disease of the mind. For example, in *People v Kelly*,[56] the defendant's use of drugs during a two-month period resulted in a state of psychosis operative both before and after the murder of her mother. In that instance, the Californian

---

49 American Psychiatric Association, *Diagnostic and Statistical Manual of Mental Disorders* (4th edn, text revision, Washington, DC, 2000) 210 (DSM-IV-TR).

50 Ibid. 201.

51 Ibid.

52 Scott and Kingswell, 'Amphetamines, Psychosis and the Insanity Defence' (n. 6) 157.

53 (1985) 42 SASR 226.

54 Ibid. 274, applied *R v Falconer* (1990) 171 CLR 30, 49 per Mason CJ, Brennan and McHugh JJ.

55 Scott and Kingswell, 'Amphetamines, Psychosis and the Insanity Defence' (n. 6) 175.

56 (1973) 10 Cal. 3d 565.

Supreme Court reversed the trial court ruling requiring that the defendant's state of psychosis be both 'settled' and 'permanent' before it was recognized as giving rise to the defence of insanity. The Supreme Court held that in order for the defence of insanity to be raised all that was required was that the state of psychosis was 'settled' even if not permanent. The court defined a 'settled' state of mental disorder as one arising where 'the mental disorder remains even after the effects of the drug have worn off [regardless of] whether the period of insanity lasted several months or merely a period of hours'.[57] Consequently, where psychotic symptoms arising from voluntary drug use extend beyond the state of intoxication itself, such a state of psychosis may be sufficient to give rise to the defence of insanity regardless as to whether such symptoms are permanent or not.[58] For example, in *People v Skinner*,[59] the Supreme Court of California considered the case of a defendant who claimed that, as a result of a state of intoxication, he had experienced a state of psychosis which caused him to lack the capacity for criminal responsibility. Expert evidence was tendered by the defendant indicating that such a psychotic response could last for up to eight days after cessation of use. In delivering its judgment the court affirmed that a temporary state of psychosis brought about by intoxicants was not a settled state of insanity as would be expected from chronic use. The court held that: 'It appears logical that settled must mean fixed and stable for a reasonable duration'.[60] With respect to the causal issue, the central concern in such cases is how to clinically distinguish a state of intoxication arising through the ingestion of a drug from a long-standing or permanent brain condition arising from drug use? What is needed is a clear indication of when an accused's state of mental malfunction exists independently of the effects of the ingested intoxicant. The court attempted to answer this question in *Skinner* by holding that the state of psychosis must 'not [be] solely dependent on the recent injection or ingestion and duration of the effects of the drug'.[61] However, while requiring that the mental state not be solely dependent on the effects of the intoxicant consumed the court failed in *Skinner* to provide means by which to ascertain whether this was indeed the case in any given instance.[62]

The court proceeded to outline the criteria considered relevant to a state of settled insanity which would give rise to an insanity defence:

1. The condition must be fixed and stable;
2. The condition must last for a reasonable period of time;

---

57 Ibid. 577; cp. *Porecca v State* (1981) 43 A 2d 1294.

58 *People v Wagoner* (1979) 89 Cal. App. 3d 605, *People v Schneider* (1979) 95 Cal. App. 3d 671.

59 *People v Skinner* (1986) 185 Cal. App. 3d 1050.

60 Ibid. 1063.

61 Ibid.

62 Meloy, 'Voluntary Intoxication and the Insanity Defence' (n. 9) 449, citing *People v Skinner* (1986) 185 Cal. App. 3d 1050, 1063.

3. The condition must not be solely dependent on the ingestion and duration of the drug;
4. The condition must meet the legal definition of insanity.[63]

The discussion of the above criteria has been taken up in the work of Meloy.[64]

Meloy on settled insanity

For Meloy '"settled insanity" becomes the legal point at which voluntary behaviour creates a state of mind that negates culpability for criminal behaviour'.[65] However, according to Meloy, both temporal and causal problems remain with the formulation in *Skinner*. In relation to the temporal issue Meloy notes that the court in *Skinner*, in seeking to address the ambiguity inherent in the term 'settled', employed two terms, 'fixed' and 'stable'. However, all three terms, 'settled', 'fixed' and 'stable' were synonyms for 'unchanging' and were for that reason 'semantically ambiguous and clinically meaningless'.[66] In providing such alternatives, the court had merely substituted semantically equivalent words and had failed to create a new distinction aiding clarification.[67] According to Meloy, what was needed was a clear indication of the requisite 'period of time' before which an accused's condition would be characterized as 'settled'. While the Supreme Court in *Kelly* had removed the requirement that the state of psychosis be permanent in order for it to be characterized as a state of settled insanity, it had failed to make explicit the requisite temporal dimension.

In respect of the causal issue Meloy acknowledges that distinguishing the intoxicating effects of an ingested drug from a state of mental malfunction existing independently of the effects of an intoxicant 'is a clinically very difficult question to answer'.[68] In particular, Meloy notes that 'there is no clinical interview technique, psychological test, or central nervous system measure (CAT scan, PET scan, MRI, EEG, etc.) that can retrospectively sort out the various factors that cause a mental state and weigh their contribution, whether drug related or not, to a criminal act.'[69] A consequence of this uncertainty is that 'the question would fall, as is often the case when the law reaches and psychiatry attempts to grasp, to the speculation of retained experts'.[70] In order to remedy the court's shortcomings in

63 *People v Skinner* (1986) 185 Cal. App. 3d 1050, 1063.

64 Meloy, 'Voluntary Intoxication and the Insanity Defence' (n. 9).

65 Ibid. 439.

66 Ibid. 449, citing *People v Skinner* (1986) 185 Cal. App. 3d 1050, 1063.

67 Ibid.

68 Ibid.; see J.M. Fabian, 'Metamphetamine Motivated Murder: Forensic Psychological/Psychiatric and Legal Applications in Criminal Contexts' (2007) 35 *Journal of Psychiatry and Law* 443, 449.

69 Meloy, 'Voluntary Intoxication and the Insanity Defence' (n. 9).

70 Ibid.

Skinner in respect of both of these issues Meloy proposes 'that courts turn to the scientific literature for direction [in order] to formulate a judicial principle that can be applied to the facts in any one particular case'.[71] So as to formulate such a general principle Meloy uses by way of example the case of individuals who chronically use psycho-stimulants such as amphetamines and cocaine. Motivating Meloy's choice of example is the fact that the use of such drugs will give rise to delusions, the most paradigmatic symptom of psychosis the archetypal instance of mental illness.[72]

Meloy begins by citing five studies that support the view that 'subjects who become paranoid while using psycho-stimulants are predisposed to the development of such psychosis in the absence of pharmacological stress'.[73] One study cited found that drug users who developed psychosis had pre-morbid histories and symptoms comparable to those of schizophrenic patients, while a comparison group of drug users who did not develop such symptoms used drugs without psycho-mimetic properties.[74] Another study indicated that acutely psychotic subjects who had used hallucinogens within three years of admission were more sensitive to psychosis if they had a family history of mental illness.[75] A further study found that a diagnosis of paranoid schizophrenia was more likely to occur amongst those patients with schizophrenia who abused cocaine than amongst those patients with schizophrenia who did not.[76] Other researchers again hypothesized that sub-clinical psychotic symptoms may influence an individual's choice of drugs and be present prior to drug use.[77] The final body of research cited by Meloy involved a sample group of 20 cocaine-addicted men. Of this group, those who developed paranoia were found to have 'significantly correlated elevations on two measures of psychosis proneness'.[78] According to Meloy the significance of such studies is that they 'support a relationship between

---

71 Ibid. 450.

72 Ibid.; see *Sebalj* [2006] VSCA 106 para 19 per Maxwell P.

73 Meloy, 'Voluntary Intoxication and the Insanity Defence' (n. 9) 450.

74 Ibid., citing M. Tsuang, J. Simpson and Z. Kronfol, 'Subtypes of Drug Use with Psychosis: Demographic Characteristics, Clinical Features, and Family History' (1982) 39 *Archives of General Psychiatry* 141.

75 Meloy, 'Voluntary Intoxication and the Insanity Defence' (n. 9) 450, citing M.B. Bowers and M.E. Swigar, 'Vulnerability to Psychosis Associated with Hallucinogen Use' (1983) 9 *Psychiatry Research* 91.

76 Meloy, 'Voluntary Intoxication and the Insanity Defence' (n. 9) 450, citing K. Brady et al., 'Cocaine Abuse among Schizophrenic Patients' (1990) 147 *American Journal of Psychiatry* 1164.

77 Meloy, 'Voluntary Intoxication and the Insanity Defence' (n. 9) 451, citing A.T. McLellan, G.E. Woody and C.P. O'Brien, 'Development of Psychiatric Illness in Drug Abusers' (1979) 301 *New England Journal of Medicine* 1310.

78 Meloy, 'Voluntary Intoxication and the Insanity Defence' (n. 9) 451, citing S. Satel and W. Edell, 'Cocaine-Induced Paranoia and Psychosis Proneness' (1991) 148 *American Journal of Psychiatry* 1708.

measurable psychosis proneness and subsequent psychotic symptoms following the use of psycho-stimulants'.[79] Consistent with the scientific literature Meloy suggests that the following judicial principle should be formulated and applied to individual cases: 'the concept of "settled insanity" should be limited to cases in which a predisposition to psychosis can be substantially demonstrated'.[80] The principle argues for the presence of a 'predisposition' or vulnerability to psychosis as a necessary condition of settled insanity. Meloy acknowledges that while the retrospective nature of the evidence required to prove such a predisposition will be difficult to acquire, such a difficulty need not be insurmountable.[81] In particular, an accused's vulnerability could be established by means of an examination of his or her individual and familial psychiatric history prior to the consumption of drugs, along with any available psychological test results.[82] Following the judicial principle a failure to provide evidence indicative of a predisposition to psychosis would preclude the accused from raising a defence of settled insanity in the context of voluntary intoxication.

According to Meloy, several advantages would follow from the adoption of a judicial principle which focuses on an accused's vulnerability prior to his or her state of intoxication.[83] First, such an approach would eliminate any definitional problems associated with the term 'settled'. In particular, on the approach advocated there would be no need to resort to equally ambiguous synonyms such as 'fixed' and 'stable' to define what is meant by 'settled'. Second, such an approach would avoid any arbitrariness associated with determining the period of time an accused's state of psychosis must be operative in order for it to be characterized as a reasonable period of time. On Meloy's account a diagnosable psychotic disorder at the time of the offence will be sufficient where such a disorder is found to be indicative of an individual's predisposition to psychosis. Third, a focus on an accused's measurable psychosis proneness will ensure that any external factors other than his or her consumption of an intoxicant will be highlighted. By ensuring that the concept of settled insanity is limited to cases in which an internal predisposition to psychosis is demonstrated, any external factor contributing to an accused's mental state beyond the consumption and effect of a drug will be more readily recognized.[84] In this way the causal issue raised by states of settled insanity will be answered given that the proposed principle provides a means by which to distinguish the effects of intoxication from mental states not solely dependent on the ingestion and duration of a drug.

On Meloy's view, where there is no recognized predisposition to psychosis, an accused's mental malfunction subsequent to drug use will be viewed as the

79 Meloy, 'Voluntary Intoxication and the Insanity Defence' (n. 9) 451.

80 Ibid.

81 Ibid.

82 Ibid.

83 Ibid.

84 Ibid.

direct result of the effects of the ingestion and duration of the intoxicant. In such an instance the voluntary consumption of the intoxicant without more will be viewed as determinative of his or her culpability. That is, the absence of a clinical history of psychiatric or psychological data evincing a predisposition to psychosis will indicate that an accused is not eligible for an insanity defence in a case of drug-induced psychosis. Without such evidence the fact that an individual has a diagnosable psychotic disorder at the time of the crime will not be sufficient to raise the defence.[85] The reason for this is that on Meloy's account the condition under which such an individual commits the offence will be one which is solely dependent on the ingestion and duration of the drug. According to Meloy however, where there is a predisposition to psychosis things are different. In particular, an accused's condition in such a case will not be viewed merely as the direct result of the effects of voluntary drug usage. Given that the accused has a predisposition to psychosis, his or her state of psychosis is not solely dependent on voluntary drug use.

Meloy believes that a further benefit of his account of settled insanity is that it readily answers the moral objection to providing the defence to an accused who is responsible for causing the very conditions of the defence. According to Meloy, where an accused's vulnerability or predisposition to psychosis is established, a defence of settled insanity should be available in the context of voluntary intoxication. According to Meloy a benefit of such an approach is that it 'attenuates the volitional problem of "settled insanity" [by recognizing] that an accused's biological proneness to psychosis is beyond his [or her] volitional control and therefore becomes the most salient factor in his [or her] exculpation'.[86] That is, for Meloy, a further advantage in adopting the concept of settled insanity is that it would most readily address the issue of prior culpability in the context of drug-induced psychosis. For Meloy the exculpatory force of the defence is to be found in the fact that the existence of a vulnerability or predisposition to psychosis renders his or her 'proneness to psychosis beyond his [or her] volitional control'[87] while in a psychotic state.

The exculpatory force of the defence is to be found in the fact that settled insanity explicitly acknowledges that 'his biological proneness to psychosis is beyond his volitional control and therefore becomes the most salient factor in his exculpation'.[88] Given that an accused's proneness to psychosis is beyond his or her control, he or she should therefore not be held responsible for any offences performed as a result of such psychosis.

The next section will consider the merits of Meloy's view that a predisposition to psychosis must be shown in order to ground a defence of mental impairment

85 Ibid.
86 Ibid.
87 Ibid.
88 Ibid. 452.

in the case of drug-induced psychosis following voluntary intoxication and the concomitant benefits which he believes follow from this.

Limits to settled insanity

The use by Meloy of an accused's predisposition to psychosis in establishing a state of settled insanity is based on the belief that where a predisposition is established, any resulting state of psychosis from intoxication may be attributed to an underlying cause. In such a case the intoxication may be said to have triggered or acted on an already existent 'underlying pathology of the mind'. For this reason, and in keeping with common law, an accused in such a situation would be entitled to the defence.[89] However, as Meloy concedes, notwithstanding the research cited, there may not be a sufficient scientific basis to support a relationship between measurable psychosis proneness and subsequent psychotic symptoms as a result of drug use.[90] Consequently, it will be difficult to establish a necessary causal relationship between a predisposition to psychosis and a psychotic response following the voluntary use of an intoxicant. A psychotic response may result from an accused's predisposition to psychosis following drug use. Equally however, a psychotic response may result from an accused's use of an intoxicant without any necessary causal contribution from his or her predisposition to psychosis. In fact, it has been remarked that the high rate of co-morbidity between psychopathological states and substance abuse reflect common contributing factors and brain substrates.[91] At the very least, in cases of co-morbidity the task of differentiating between psychosis emanating from an underlying condition and a psychotic response without any contribution from an accused's predisposition to psychosis following drug use will be problematic. As has been noted in the context of methamphetamine use:

> In jurisdictions that recognise substance induced states relevant to insanity, diagnostic considerations would include comorbid diagnoses in addition to methamphetamine abuse and dependence, [however] differentiating psychotic features emanating from the psychotic disorder versus the methamphetamine induced psychosis may be difficult for the forensic clinician to assess.[92]

Consequently, there will be difficulty in ascertaining with the requisite degree of certainty whether it is in fact an underlying pathology of the mind that has been triggered or whether it is the effects of the intoxicant which is operative

89 *Re: Bromage* (1990) 48 A Crim R 79; *R v Meddings* [1966] VR 306 (SC, Vic).

90 Meloy, 'Voluntary Intoxication and the Insanity Defence' (n. 9) 452.

91 N.D. Volkow, 'Drug Abuse and Mental Illness: Progress in Understanding Co-Morbidity' (2001) 158 *American Journal of Psychiatry* 1181.

92 Fabian, 'Metamphetamine Motivated Murder' (n. 68) 449; Cp *R v Sebalj* [2006] VSCA 106, para 13 per Vincent JA, para 18 per Maxwell P.

independent of an underlying pathology of the mind. This puts pressure on Meloy's claim that there is a causal relationship between a predisposition to psychosis and a psychotic response following the voluntary use of an intoxicant. At the very least it highlights the impracticality of being able to 'substantially demonstrate' a causal relationship between a predisposition to psychosis and a state of settled insanity.

Equally, Meloy argues that as an accused's proneness to psychosis is beyond his or her control he or she should therefore not be held responsible for any offences performed as a result of such psychosis. The fact that an accused has no volitional control of his or her biological proneness to psychosis will not necessarily be exculpatory. In order for a lack of volitional control over such biological proneness to provide a defence to an accused it must be shown that there is a causal connection between an individual's biological proneness to psychosis and a psychotic response following the voluntary use of an intoxicant which has resulted in criminal conduct. However, as just noted, a psychotic state following drug use may be caused by an accused's predisposition to psychosis or be caused by the use of the intoxicant without any input from his or her predisposition to psychosis. Consequently, as a causal link between biological proneness, intoxication and psychosis has not been established it cannot be said that an accused's lack of volitional control of his or her biological proneness constitutes 'the most salient factor in his [or her] exculpation'.

Further, as Meloy notes, equally problematic is the nature of the evidence relied upon to determine an individual's psychosis proneness. In particular, given that such evidence is reliant on the 'more overt measures of individual or familial mental disorder before drug use there [is] a substantial risk of false negatives'.[93] That is, as a result of a 'lack of measurement sensitivity', individuals who are in fact psychosis prone may, due to a lack of relevant information, be found not to be psychosis prone. Moreover, Meloy concedes that the evaluation of the risk of false negatives arising is currently beyond the reach of extant research.[94]

However, the issue of an accused's volitional control of his or her conduct is one which remains central to the issue of an accused's responsibility. For example, the issue of an accused's volitional control was remarked on in the context of the Colorado Supreme Court case of *Bieber v People*.[95] In *Bieber*,[96] the accused argued that he had experienced an amphetamine induced delusional disorder at the time of the offence which caused temporary insanity. The Colorado Supreme Court held that as the accused had 'actively and voluntarily contracted' his mental disturbance his actions could not be excused.[97] The court held that an individual who voluntarily ingests substances is aware of the potential consequences of his or her behaviour and is morally culpable for both consuming the substance and

93 Meloy, 'Voluntary Intoxication and the Insanity Defence' (n. 9) 452.
94 Ibid.
95 *Bieber v People* (1993) 856 P (2d) 811.
96 Ibid. 818.
97 Ibid.

the final result of such consumption. What the ruling in *Bieber* indicates is that an individual may be held responsible where he or she exercises control in bringing about a condition in which he or she is rendered incapable of knowing the nature and quality or wrongness of his or her action. An accused will exercise control where he or she acts voluntarily in consuming an intoxicant while being aware of the potential consequences of such consumption.

On what basis would the absence of an accused's volitional control of his or her biological proneness to psychosis exculpate? First, it would need to be established that it was in fact the accused's predisposition to psychosis which brought about the psychotic response. Second, it would need to be established that the accused was not aware of the potential consequence of bringing about the death of another. While the accused performs a voluntary act in consuming the substance it remains an open question whether he or she foresees that by so doing he or she will bring about as a result of a state of psychosis, for example, the death of another person.

The various necessary conditions which need to be satisfied in order for an accused to be held responsible for the effects of a state of drug-induced psychosis will be discussed further in the final substantive section of this chapter.

The above analysis has revealed three things. First, that an individual who consciously acts while knowing the consequences of his or her actions may be held responsible for bringing about a condition in which he or she is rendered incapable of knowing the nature and quality or wrongness of his or her act. Second, that there is no necessary causal relationship between an accused's predisposition to psychosis and his or her psychotic response following the voluntary use of an intoxicant. Third, and consequently, an accused's lack of volitional control over his or her biological proneness to psychosis is not necessarily exculpatory. What would be required to exculpate an accused for a state of drug-induced psychosis on the basis of his or her proneness would be a causal connection between the state of psychosis and the proneness and foresight by the accused as to the potential consequences of his or her behaviour.

In addition to the question of whether a predisposition to psychosis is symptomatic of an underlying infirmity of mind for the purpose of the defence of insanity, the VLRC acknowledged in its *Defences to Homicide Report* the moral objection to allowing an accused who has voluntarily consumed drugs to raise the defence. The next section will consider in greater detail an accused's responsibility for an act performed while incapacitated where he or she has brought about such a state of incapacity.

Meta-responsibility

Edward Mitchell has sought to outline an argument for denying the defence of insanity to those accused who have brought about a state of non-responsibility.[98]

98 Mitchell, 'Meta-Responsibility and Mental Disorder' (n. 10).

Mitchell argues that where an accused has culpably created the conditions of his or her own defence he or she should be liable on the basis of his or her 'prior fault' and for this reason should not be allowed to raise a defence of non-responsibility. According to Mitchell such an accused should be held responsible for his or her state of non-responsibility. This section will consider the merit of Mitchell's view.

Mitchell on meta-responsibility

Mitchell begins his discussion of an accused's responsibility for bringing about his or her state of non-responsibility with a remark by Fitzjames Stephen who in the context of formulating an irresistible-impulse test of insanity wrote:

> If it is not, it ought to be the Law of England that no act is a crime if the person who does it is at the time … prevented either by defective mental power or by any disease affecting his mind from controlling his own conduct, *unless the absence of the power of control has been produced by his own default.*[99]

Mitchell refers to this notion of an individual's responsibility for bringing about a state of non-responsibility as meta-responsibility. Meta-responsibility seeks to capture the intuition that 'a defendant's criminal responsibility may to a certain extent be under autonomous control'.[100] Such control will manifest itself in the context of an accused's autonomy, advertence and autogeny of mental disorder. That is, according to Mitchell, an individual's capacity to self-regulate, be aware of and bring about a mental disorder will be sufficient to constitute the control required for meta-responsibility.

According to Mitchell any difficulty which the idea of prior fault in mental disorder might invoke is due to the belief that 'mental disorder is something that "happens to us", rather than something we "do"'.[101] For Mitchell such a view of the aetiology of mental disorder has its origins in the medical model of mental disorder which is said to remove culpability from the patient and focuses on empirically verifiable psychopathological conditions and pharmacological treatment regimes.[102] However, as Mitchell notes, the assumption that madness is in no way blameworthy is erroneous as 'disorders such as drug-induced psychosis throw immediate suspicion on the validity of such an argument that the mentally disordered are in no way culpable for their unfortunate situation and concomitant criminal responsibility'.[103] Varieties of meta-responsibility include 'consensual'

---

99 Mitchell, 'Culpability for Inducing Mental States' (n. 10) 66, citing J. Fitzjames Stephen, *A History of the Criminal Law of England* (1883) (emphasis added).

100 Mitchell 'Meta-Responsibility and Mental Disorder' (n. 10) 598.

101 Ibid. 602, citing T.S. Szasz, *Law, Liberty and Psychiatry* (New York, 1963).

102 Mitchell 'Meta-Responsibility and Mental Disorder' (n. 10) 602.

103 Ibid. 603.

meta-responsibility and 'purposive' meta-responsibility.[104] 'Consensual' meta-responsibility corresponds to such 'traditional problems of clinical management' as medication non-compliance, substance abuse, ignoring medical advice and the like.[105] 'Purposive' meta-responsibility involves an individual's 'acquiescence in mental disorder' and incorporates the anti-psychiatric notion that mental disorder is the manifestation of wilful behaviour on the part of an accused in an attempt to determine his or her personal situation.[106] For the purposes of this chapter I will only be concerned with Mitchell's account of 'consensual' meta-responsibility and so will not comment on 'purposive' meta-responsibility.

According to Mitchell, in cases of consensual meta-responsibility an individual does not have as his or her intention the creation or exacerbation of mental disorder. Rather, through the pursuit of sensual appetites an individual is said to consent to the creation or exacerbation of mental disorder as a side effect. However, 'consent' is not to be understood in this context as implying that the side effect has been consciously chosen or that it has even entered consciousness.[107] That is, an individual's advertence is not directed towards the mental disorder itself but rather to the pursuit of some other purpose. In such cases an individual's meta-responsibility will apply in respect of those of his or her actions which arise before the offending conduct and are accompanied by a state of negligence or recklessness.[108] Mitchell uses the example of an individual who wishes to satisfy his or her hunger by cooking a meal.[109] A side effect of satisfying his or her hunger is the generation of dirty dishes. While such an individual does not intend to generate the dirty dishes, he or she consents to doing so rather than give up his or her purpose or the means chosen. In the above example, the dirty dishes are not the mental disorder itself but the concomitant criminal responsibility associated with the offending conduct.[110]

Instances of consensual meta-responsibility may arise in the context of severe disorders and medication non-compliance. For example, cases of severe disorder may result in a lack of insight on the part of the patient. Such a lack of insight may lead to a belief that the individual does not need any medication. In turn, such a belief may result in the individual refusing to take his or her medication, which would then further exacerbate the disorder. Where a mental disorder results in a lack of insight or medication non-compliance, Mitchell refers to this as

104 Ibid.

105 Ibid.

106 Ibid., citing R.D. Laing, *The Self and Others* (Harmondsworth, 1969); T.S. Szasz, *Insanity: The Idea and its Consequences* (New York, 1997).

107 Mitchell 'Meta-Responsibility and Mental Disorder' (n. 10) 603, citing M.D. Slodow, 'Criminal Responsibility and the Noncompliant Psychiatric Offender: Risking Madness' (1989) 40 *Case Western Reserve Law Review*, Comment, 271.

108 Mitchell 'Meta-Responsibility and Mental Disorder' (n. 10) 611.

109 Ibid. 604.

110 Ibid.

'disorder-mediated meta-responsibility'.[111] Disorder-mediated meta-responsibility will reflect the degree of an individual's 'autonomous control' and so give rise to varying degrees of responsibility.

After outlining the theoretical basis of meta-responsibility Mitchell turns his attention to one suggested means by which to better understand the operation of the concept of meta-responsibility in a court-room setting.

Understanding meta-responsibility

Mitchell focuses his attention on the approach to meta-responsibility which has been suggested by the American criminal-law scholar Paul Robinson.[112] Robinson defends a view which he refers to as the doctrine of 'creating the conditions of one's own defence'.[113] For Robinson, the question is whether an accused who has committed an offence while in a state of non-responsibility should be held responsible for bringing about the conditions of his or her own defence? Robinson proposes a general principle to govern all such cases. On Robinsons' analysis, while an accused may, strictly speaking, be held non-responsible for the offence, he or she will nevertheless be liable for the earlier conduct which culpably caused the conditions of the defence. The doctrine takes as the most critical factor an accused's culpability at the time he or she causes the conditions of his or her defence rather than at the time of the offence.[114] As Robinson states:

> Where the actor is not only culpable as to causing the defence conditions, but also has a culpable state of mind *as to causing himself to engage in the conduct constituting the offence*, the state should punish him for causing the ultimate justified or excused conduct. Under this analysis, one need simply consider whether, at the time that the actor engages in his initial conduct in causing the defence conditions he has a culpable state of mind as to causing the conduct constituting the offence.[115]

Robinson's 'causing the conditions of one's own defence' doctrine is ultimately reliant on the view that where an accused causes the conditions of his or her own defence and attendant upon the creation of these conditions he or she has the required fault element of the offence, he or she will be guilty of the completed offence. Such an account is analogous to the doctrine of 'innocent agency' whereby the excused accused is the 'innocent agent' who is caused to engage in

111 Ibid. 605.

112 Ibid. 614.

113 P.H. Robinson, 'Causing the Conditions of One's Own Defence' (1985) 71 *Virginia Law Review* 1.

114 Ibid. 27.

115 Ibid. (emphasis in original).

criminal conduct by the accused's prior, culpable actions.[116] On such an analysis an accused will be liable for the ultimate offence given that he or she has acted to bring about the offending conduct with the requisite culpable state of mind with respect to such conduct.

For example, a hypothetical case cited by Robinson involves an accused who knows of his propensity to violent behaviour when intoxicated. Upon forming the decision to kill his wife such an accused may drink excessively, knowing that by so doing he will become violent and kill her. It may in fact be the case that, as a result of his state of intoxication at the time of the killing, he will be found to lack the requisite mental element of the offence. In such a case on Robinson's analysis, notwithstanding that he lacks the requisite fault element for the offence, he will be liable for the death of his wife given that he has culpably caused the conditions of his own defence.

However, as Robinson notes his account is not limited to those instances where the accused intends the commission of the offence:

> This analysis properly accounts for different degrees of culpability as to the ultimate criminal conduct. If at the time of causing the conditions of the excuse the actor is reckless as to ultimately causing a death, he may properly be held liable for reckless homicide. If the actor should know, but does not, that a notoriously insane hypnotist may give him a hypnotic suggestion to kill, the actor is negligent as to the death when he undergoes hypnosis and kills pursuant to such a suggestion.[117]

Nevertheless, according to Mitchell one problem with Robinson's doctrine of holding a defendant responsible for the earlier conduct which culpably caused the conditions of his or her defence is its failure to give 'definition to "earlier" – just how far should we look back in history to find prior fault on the actor's part?'[118] That is, according to Mitchell, what Robinson's account of creating the conditions of one's defence fails to provide is a relevant time-limit on the search for an event's cause. Mitchell recognizes that a solution will need to be provided to the question of how broadly to frame the time period during which one may look back in order to determine a defendant's responsibility. Ultimately, Mitchell acknowledges 'that some practical limit will have to be set (on a case-by-case basis) necessarily delimited by an evidentiary test of relevance'.[119]

In order to allow his conception of meta-responsibility to be used in a court room Mitchell formalizes his account into what he refers to as a 'double product test'.[120] Mitchell phrases his test as follows:

116 Ibid. 54.
117 Ibid. 55.
118 Ibid.
119 Mitchell, 'Culpability for Inducing Mental States' (n. 10) 66.
120 Mitchell, 'Meta-Responsibility and Mental Disorder' (n. 10) 616.

> 1. Everyone is presumed sane and to possess a sufficient degree of reason to be responsible for their crimes until the contrary is proven.
>
> 2. To establish a defence on the ground of insanity, it must be clearly proved that, at the time of committing the act, the party accused was laboring under such a defect of reason, from disease of the mind, as (a) not to know the nature and quality of the act he was doing; or (b) if he did know it, that he did not know what he was doing was wrong.
>
> 3. If the defect of reason or disease of the mind has been substantially self-induced then a defence of insanity shall be denied to the accused.[121]

Hence, according to both Mitchell and Robinson, in order to determine an accused's meta-responsibility his or her state of mind should be considered at the time at which he or she creates the conditions of his or her own defence. Where an accused's offending conduct is the product of a state of non-responsibility and such a state of non-responsibility is the product of an act of the accused ('substantially self-induced') the defence of insanity will not be available in respect of the offending conduct.

Drug-induced psychosis and responsibility

The defence of insanity is not merely an attempt to ascertain whether an accused is suffering from a mental illness but rather involves a question of responsibility.

There is an intuitive attractiveness to the notion of meta-responsibility as a means of delimiting an accused's responsibility for a state of drug-induced psychosis. One reason for this is that responsibility is historical, that is, the reasons why an individual will be held non-responsible will be in part determined by how his or her state of non-responsibility came about. It is an historical, rather than a 'time-slice' view of events, that is determinative of criminal responsibility.[122] The causal connection between such a series of events will be delimited, as Mitchell notes, by an evidentiary test of relevance between the accused's earlier conduct and the proscribed outcome.[123] Where an accused has voluntarily consumed an intoxicant, the causal connection between his or her act of consumption and any resulting consequence remains extant. In the event that such an accused's cognitive capacities have been impaired such a result remains the result of a voluntary act of the accused.

---

121 Ibid. 616–17.

122 See J.M. Fischer and M. Ravizza, *Freedom and Responsibility* (Cambridge, 1998), for a detailed account of 'historical' views of responsibility.

123 Ibid. 16.

Another reason why meta-responsibility has an intuitive appeal is that the notion of prior fault underpinning an accused's meta-responsibility captures that aspect of the disease of the mind enquiry referred to in Chapter 3 as the judgment of responsibility. The judgment of responsibility holds that it would be wrong to punish an individual who is incapable of either knowing and choosing between right and wrong or controlling his or her action. However, as argued in Chapter 3, the responsibility factor of the disease of the mind enquiry also distinguishes between a responsible accused and a non-responsible accused on the basis of whether the state of mental malfunction which precludes him or her from knowing right from wrong or choosing right from wrong is due to his or her fault or nature. Where an accused's state of mental malfunction results in the relevant incapacities as a result of his or her fault or nature, then such a state will not be characterized as a disease of the mind. Consequently, an accused will be guilty for behaviour which occurs in a state of mental malfunction where such behaviour is brought about by his or her fault. Where however, the state of mental malfunction resulting in the requisite incapacities does not result from his or her fault or nature, then such a state should be characterized as a disease of the mind. Given that he or she is incapable of either acting rationally or controlling his or her behaviour the judgment of responsibility precludes punishing him or her. In such circumstances an accused should be provided with the special verdict.

However, a question which has yet to be answered is: what is the nature of the requisite fault which an accused must engage in before he or she will be denied the defence? In particular, what aspect of his or her conduct must the fault relate to?

This section will seek to utilise the approaches adopted by Robinson and Mitchell to meta-responsibility discussed above in order to determine both the nature of the fault required and to which aspect of the accused's conduct such fault must relate to before he or she may be held responsible. By proceeding in this way it is hoped that a principled approach to the question of drug-induced psychosis may be developed. The first part of this section will briefly outline the views expressed by Robinson and Mitchell in respect of that aspect of an accused's conduct to which his or her fault must relate. This will be followed by an analysis of two recent cases indicating what at common law has been considered sufficient to ground liability for states of drug-induced psychosis. The following section will then apply the above analysis to an instance of conduct performed in a state of drug-induced psychosis. It is hoped that by so doing it will be possible to determine what elements will need to be satisfied in order to raise a defence for criminal conduct engaged in during an episode of drug-induced psychosis. The final part of this section will apply the results of this analysis to the case of *R v Sebalj*.

Culpably creating one's own defence

Both Robinson and Mitchell approach the issue of an accused's responsibility for a state of drug-induced psychosis from the perspective of his or her prior fault.

However, as will be seen, each of these authors regards the fault of the accused as relating to a different aspect of his or her conduct.

As noted above, in the course of developing a general principle of prior fault Robinson formulates his doctrine of 'creating the conditions of one's defence'. On Robinson's account, an accused will be liable for conduct which culpably creates the conditions of his or her defence rather than for the offence itself. An accused's culpability in creating the conditions of his or her defence will be grounded in his or her having the requisite fault element of the completed offence at the time of the conduct. That is, liability will be imposed on the basis of the actor's earlier conduct in culpably causing the conditions of his or her own defence. Hence, while he or she may be held non-responsible for the offending conduct itself, he or she will be held criminally liable for bringing about such conduct with the requisite fault element.

Consequently, on Robinson's account, in order to determine whether an accused has a defence to an offence committed in a state of non-responsibility brought about through his or her prior conduct the question to be asked is:

> (1) Did the accused intend to bring about a state of non-responsibility intending thereby to commit, or reckless or negligent as to whether he or she would commit, an offence?

That is, for Robinson an accused will not have a defence where he or she intends to create the conditions of his or her defence knowing or foreseeing that he or she would commit, or ought to have foreseen that he or she would commit, the consequent offence.

It will be noted that on Robinson's account an accused will not be punished where he or she has not foreseen or been negligent as to the consequences of his or her action. That is, a lack of recklessness or a lack of advertence on the part of an accused in respect of the consequences of his or her action will be sufficient to raise a defence. However, it will be required that the accused did intend to bring about a state of non-responsibiliity. It will not be sufficient on Robinson's account that he or she was merely reckless or negligent in respect of bringing about such a state.

In order to capture both advertent and inadvertent conduct on the part of an accused in respect of the creation of the conditions of his or her defence, Mitchell's formulation does not require an accused to intend to bring about a state of non-responsibility. Meta-responsibility will be established even where an accused's non-responsibility arises from his or her state of negligence or recklessness.

That is, for Mitchell meta-responsibility will apply to those actions occurring before the offending conduct even where such actions are accompanied by negligence or recklessness. It will be sufficient for an accused to be held responsible on this account for conduct which occurs in a state of non-responsibility if he or she intends the act which brings about a state of non-responsibility while reckless or negligent as to creating the state of non-responsibility. Hence, for Mitchell, the question to be asked in order to determine whether an accused has a defence to a charge of criminal conduct arising during a state of non-responsibility brought about through his or her prior fault is:

> (2) Did the accused intend the act which brought about the state of non-responsibility while reckless or negligent as to whether such a state of non-responsibility would ensue?

Meta-responsibility will be established even where an accused does not have as his or her *intention* the creation of a state of non-responsibility.

Unlike Robinson who requires that an accused must be shown to have intended to bring about the state of non-responsibility, Mitchell's account does not require intention on the part of an accused for bringing about his or her condition of non-responsibility. For Mitchell it will be sufficient if the accused intended to perform the act which brings about his or her state of non-responsibility subject to him or her having foreseen, or ought to have foreseen, that by so doing such a state would ensue. In this way Mitchell's account, unlike Robinson's, captures both an accused's advertent and inadvertent conduct in respect of his or her state of non-responsibility. A result of such a formulation is that an accused will be denied the defence of non-responsibility for criminal conduct occurring while in a state of drug-induced psychosis where he or she foresees, or ought to have foreseen, that such a state of non-responsibility may result from voluntary drug use.

In addition to the views of Robinson and Mitchell the common law has also sought to qualify the requisite fault element required for prior fault before an accused will be found liable for the consequences of his or her earlier conduct.

Common-law cases

Several common-law cases have dealt with the issue of an accused's state of non-responsibility arising from voluntary drug use. For example in *R v Barrett*,[124] the defendant was found guilty of the murder of his long-time girlfriend resulting from a series of attacks over the course of several days. Evidence at the trial included the testimony of a forensic psychiatrist who noted that the defendant suffered from morbid jealousy, which had increased with amphetamine use. This same psychiatrist noted that while the defendant 'had reached the point of having insight into this relationship [between the jealousy and drug use, he] had not been willing or able to take the next step of doing something about it, most significantly by eliminating amphetamine use'.[125] Psychiatric evidence was tendered by the defence that the defendant suffered from a 'genuine psychiatric condition' namely 'a psychotic disorder secondary to poly-substance dependence'.[126] Defence

---

124 [2005] VSC 176; the facts of the case are taken from the sentencing hearing in the Supreme Court.

125 Ibid. para 3.

126 Ibid. para 12.

counsel further 'submitted that both the psychotic disorder and morbid jealousy [of the defendant] were features of, and a consequence of, [his] drug use'.[127] Such drug use, according to defence counsel, resulted in a 'mental illness' which was a 'genuine condition whether "self-induced or otherwise"'.[128] While acknowledging that 'drug use was not an excuse', defence counsel submitted that 'a long standing drug addiction had produced a condition of psychosis'.[129] While the disorder was described as a 'serious psychiatric illness', the defence of insanity was not raised, the defence proceeding on the basis of reckless murder.

In his analysis of the evidence, Whelan J began by noting that the mere fact of a diagnosis of drug-induced psychosis does not of itself entail an absence or reduction of a defendant's moral culpability.[130] In fact, according to Whelan J, mental illness may be an aggravating factor rendering an offender a 'greater danger to the community'.[131] Whelan J drew the following conclusions:

> 3. Your mental disorder is substantially self-induced.
>
> 4. You had been aware of the relationship between your mental disorder, your drug use and your violence for some time prior to this offence.[132]

His Honour held that the longstanding character of the defendant's psychosis was an important factor to be taken into account in moderating the aims of general deterrence. However, general deterrence was not eliminated 'given the self-induced character of your psychiatric condition and your insight into your condition'.[133]

In *R v Barrett*, notwithstanding the accused's state of drug-induced psychosis, he was held responsible for the commission of the offence, as the condition had been brought about by the defendant himself in a voluntary fashion. Further, while the defendant was fully aware of the relationship between his mental disorder, jealousy (and concomitant violence) and drug use, he had not been willing to control this by eliminating his drug use.

Another case where previous drug use led to a case of drug-induced psychosis is *R v Martin*.[134] In *Martin*, the defendant drove a truck on the wrong side of the road for over 50 km before colliding with an on-coming vehicle and killing the driver on impact.[135] At the time of these events the defendant was found to be floridly psychotic due to the ingestion of illegal drugs immediately before the

---

127 Ibid.
128 Ibid.
129 Ibid.
130 Ibid. para 24, citing *R v Maccia* [2005] VSCA 20, para 28–32 per Winneke P.
131 [2005] VSC 176, para 24.
132 Ibid. para 29.
133 Ibid. para 30.
134 *R v Martin* [2005] VSC 497.
135 The facts of the case are taken from the sentencing hearing in the Supreme Court.

events. At his trial for the murder of the other driver, the jury failed to find the defendant guilty of murder, returning a verdict of manslaughter. Evidence was tendered by the defendant relating to a history of experiencing serious psychotic symptoms associated with visual and auditory hallucinations and delusional beliefs. The defendant's history revealed difficulties with both substance abuse and mental health. During a period of approximately eight years, between 1995 and 2003, the defendant was admitted to a public psychiatric unit over 15 times. Such admissions were characterized by psychotic symptoms such as auditory hallucinations and persecutory delusions subsequent to illicit drug use. At the time of these admissions the defendant's psychosis was diagnosed as drug induced and thought to co-exist with an anti-social personality disorder.[136] Drugs used during this period included both cannabis and amphetamines.

A report tendered during the trial by a senior consultant psychiatrist indicated that the defendant had been told on numerous occasions that his 'continued use of illicit substances was initiating and perpetuating episodes of mental illness. The seriousness of his behaviour was explained to [the defendant], yet he displayed a reckless regard for the repeated unambiguous medical advice made to him.'[137] The court accepted the opinion of both the senior consultant and other psychiatrists that the cause of the psychotic episode during the period of the offences was the consumption of drugs.[138]

It was suggested by defence counsel that the fact that the defendant was psychotic at the time of the offence lowered his moral culpability.[139] Bongiorno J rejected this submission and held that mitigation of punishment because of serious psychiatric illness at the time of an offence will depend upon such a condition being 'beyond the control' of the person being sentenced.[140] His Honour gave the following reasons for refusing to lower the defendant's moral culpability on the basis of his drug-induced psychosis: 'In the circumstances of this case, the fact that you voluntarily took illegal drugs such that they caused you to become dangerously psychotic in circumstances where you knew or ought to have known that that was a likely result is an aggravating factor'.[141]

His Honour held that while the defendant was psychotic at the time of the offence, such a state was brought about by the voluntary ingestion of illegal drugs.[142] Further, based upon earlier medical advice, the defendant knew, or ought to have known, that his behaviour in taking the drugs would result in a risk of his becoming psychotic and consequently placing both himself and others in danger. Not only was the risk of such danger predictable, it was in fact predicted by the

136 *R v Martin* [2005] VSC 497, para 17.
137 Ibid. para 21.
138 Ibid. para 22.
139 Ibid.
140 Ibid.
141 Ibid.
142 Ibid.

senior consultant several years prior to the time of the offence. It was as a direct result of the defendant's refusal to acknowledge such warning, and his decision to persist in drug taking, that the current offence had been committed. Consequently, the defendant could not rely upon the effect of his drug-taking, his psychosis, as a ground for mitigation.

As in *Barrett*,[143] the court in *Martin*[144] highlighted the fact that drug-induced psychosis will not reduce an accused's culpability where it is the result of a defendant's voluntary ingestion of an intoxicant which he or she knows will result in a risk of psychosis. However, in addition to *Barrett*'s subjective knowledge requirement, *Martin* indicates that it will be sufficient for an accused to be held liable if he or she ought to have known that his or her drug use will result in a risk of psychosis. As Bongiorno J's reasoning in *Martin* reveals, it will be sufficient for a defendant to be held responsible for the killing of an individual if 'the defendant knew, or ought to have known, that his [or her] behaviour in taking the drugs would result in a risk of his [or her] becoming psychotic and consequently placing both himself and others in danger'.[145] In both of the cases analysed, the defendant showed a disregard of the obvious connection between their substance abuse and psychiatric condition by refusing to control their use of drugs.[146]

Consequently, on the basis of the above cases the question to be asked in order to determine whether an accused has a defence to a charge of criminal conduct arising during a state of non-responsibility brought about through his or her prior fault is:

> (3) Did the accused intend or foresee, or ought the accused to have foreseen, that by performing the act he or she might enter a state of non-responsibility and commit an offence?

Defences to drug-induced psychosis

On the basis of the analysis of the work of Robinson and Mitchell, on the one hand, and common-law cases, on the other, various options present themselves in respect of what an accused must show in order to establish a defence for conduct arising from a state of drug-induced psychosis. This part will consider the merits of each in turn.

On Robinson's account a defence will arise where it is shown that the accused did not

143 [2005] VSC 176.
144 [2005] VSC 497.
145 Ibid. para 23.
146 *Barrett* [2005] VSC 176, para 29; *Martin* [2005] VSC 497, para 23.

(1) Intend to bring about a state of drug-induced psychosis by his or her voluntary drug use knowing or foreseeing that he would commit, or ought to have foreseen that he would commit, an offence during such a state of psychosis.

According to Mitchell, several problems are apparent with Robinson's account. First, if Robinson's doctrine is to be used as a general principle, it will need to hold responsible those individuals who have engaged in inadvertent conduct; that is, conduct the consequences of which they may not have foreseen.[147] However, this may involve punishing blameless conduct of which the defendant may not have foreseen the consequences.[148] In order to avoid such a result, Robinson's doctrine must be restricted to the case where an accused has culpably caused the conditions of his or her defence by intending the consequences of his or her actions.

However, if Robinson's account is to be restricted to such instances rather than providing a general principle it will be restricted to those defendants displaying 'Dutch Courage' or who are 'Grand Schemers'.

The 'Dutch Courage' defendant is the type of individual described in Robinson's example above. For example, he or she may become intoxicated in order to summon the courage required to commit the offence in question.[149] The 'Grand Schemer' refers to a defendant who places him or herself in a position in order to create the conditions of his or her own defence. For example, a defendant may intentionally provoke his or her victim in order to ensure a retaliatory response from the victim, whom he or she then kills. Having originally brought about the victim's response the defendant then seeks an excuse such as self-defence or provocation.[150] Unless we are prepared not to hold a defendant liable for bringing about the conditions of his or her own defence recklessly or negligently, Robinson's suggested formulation of 'creating the condition of one's defence' will be overly narrow as a general doctrine.

In contrast to Robinson's proposal, for Mitchell a defendant will have a defence where it is shown that the accused did not

(2) Intend to voluntarily consume drugs which brought about a state of drug-induced psychosis knowing or foreseeing that he or she would bring about a state of psychosis, or ought to have foreseen that he or she would bring about such a state.

It will be sufficient on this account to hold an accused responsible for conduct which occurs in a state of psychosis if he or she has voluntarily consumed drugs which bring about a state of psychosis provided that he or she is reckless or negligent in

---

147 Mitchell 'Meta-Responsibility and Mental Disorder' (n. 10) 615; see *R v O'Connor* (1980) 146 CLR 64.

148 Ibid.

149 Ibid.; see *A-G (Northern Ireland) v Gallagher* [1963] AC 349.

150 Ibid.; see *R v Voukelatos* [1990] VR 1, 19; *Allwood* (1975) 18 A Crim R 120, 132–3 per Crockett J.

respect of bringing about such psychosis. However, as Nigel Walker has remarked, such an approach to 'prior fault' 'raises genuine issues for retributively minded moralists'.[151]

As Walker expresses the concern:

> It is one thing to hold a person punishably culpable for an accomplished act, or even an attempt. It is quite another thing to hold him punishably culpable for doing something which merely risked an unintended and far from certain result. Even if his act or behaviour made the result more probable than it would have been, what was the real increase in probability, and could he possibly have estimated it?[152]

In particular, to hold an individual criminally liable and subject to criminal sanctions for an outcome to which he or she has not adverted and which a reasonable person may not have adverted to merely on the basis of a causal link between his or her conscious act and a resulting outcome may be problematic.

Succinctly stated, the problem arises from the fact that 'the transfer of a pre-existing intention and/or recklessness from one time to another is one thing; the deeming of that transfer is another'.[153] At common law it is not correct to say that there may be an automatic transfer of deemed fault to a proscribed result from previous behaviour.[154]

However, it may be argued that given that the effects of drug taking are so widely known an accused that places him or her self in such a situation has in fact satisfied the subjective fault requirement of advertence in respect of the criminal conduct. Yet, as Mathew Goode has remarked, such a claim of common knowledge grounding advertence in reality amounts to '*constructive* or *deemed* fault or culpability. The accused *must be taken to know* that a high degree of intoxication may lead to some kind of violence'[155]

The common law view endeavours to meet the above criticism by holding that a defendant will have a defence to an offence committed as a result of voluntary drug use which has resulted in a state of drug-induced psychosis where it is shown that the accused did not

> (3) Intend or foresee or could not have foreseen that by taking drugs he or she might enter a psychotic state *and* commit the offence.

---

151 N. Walker, 'Book Review: Mitchell, EW (2003) *Self-Made Madness: Rethinking Illness and Criminal Responsibility*' (2005)16 *Journal of Forensic Psychiatry and Psychology* 612.

152 Ibid. 614.

153 M. Goode, 'On Subjectivity and Objectivity in Denial of Criminal Responsibility: Reflections on Reading *Radford*' (1987) 11 *Criminal Law Journal* 131,147.

154 *R v O'Connor* (1980) 146 CLR 64, 80 per Barwick J.

155 Goode 'On Subjectivity and Objectivity' (n.153) 14 emphasis in original.

Where the prosecution establishes that the accused has performed the act voluntarily and knew, or ought to have known, that by so doing he or she risked becoming psychotic and committing an offence an accused's moral culpability will be established. Subject to the elements of the offence being satisfied he or she will be subject to criminal sanctions.

The attractiveness of the common law position is in part due to the fact that it does not allow a defendant to raise a defence merely on the basis that he or she has not subjectively adverted to the consequences of his or her voluntary drug taking. Equally, however, the common law position also acknowledges that, it will not be sufficient to deem fault from the accused's prior conduct to a proscribed result on the basis of a 'double product' test. It would be morally impermissible to hold the defendant liable for those consequences unless the accused intended, foresaw or was negligent in respect of those consequences.

R v Sebalj*: responsibility for drug-induced psychosis*

As noted above, the VLRC has argued in its *Defences to Homicide: Final Report*[156] that the case of *R v Sebalj*[157] shows that the interpretation of the expression 'mental impairment' in the Victorian Act[158] as merely a re-statement of the common law is unnecessarily restrictive. Turning to the facts of *Sebalj*, the defendant was held responsible for the death of his girlfriend which he caused while in a state of psychosis. The cause of the psychosis was only indirectly related to his previous drug use, as it arose as a result of his endeavours to wean himself from the influence of drugs.

The VLRC noted that, as a result of the narrowness with which the statutory defence of mental impairment was defined, the defendant was deprived of a defence to which he was entitled. According to the VLRC the purpose of the defence is to ensure that those individuals whose cognitive functions are so affected that they do not know what they are doing or that it is wrong should be excused.[159] Hence, the punishment of an individual who lacks the requisite capacities for responsible conduct is an injustice.[160] The VLRC argued that the cause of an accused's behaviour is irrelevant to the question of his or her non-responsibility. What is determinative of criminal responsibility is the cognitive deficiency which results in the relevant incapacities not how such cognitive deficiency came about.[161]

---

156 Victorian Law Reform Commission, *Defences to Homicide: Final Report* (n. 8) 5.35.

157 [2003] VSC 181 (Unreported, SC Vic, Smith J, 5 June 2003).

158 *Crimes (Mental Impairment and Unfitness to be Tried) Act 1997* (Vic) s 20.

159 Victorian Law Reform Commission, *Defences to Homicide: Final Report* (n. 8) 5.44.

160 Ibid. 5.42.

161 Ibid.

Such an argument by the VLRC stands in contrast to the view put forward in Chapter 3 in respect of the judgment of responsibility factor informing the disease of the mind enquiry. The judgment of responsibility holds that an accused whose mental condition precludes him or her from knowingly choosing between right and wrong or from controlling his or her conduct is not a fit subject of our responsibility practices. That is, unlike most criminal-law defences which excuse, the boundaries of the defence of insanity determine when an individual will be exempted from criminal responsibility.[162] However, where such a mental condition has been brought about through the fault or nature of the accused, the judgment of responsibility indicates that the accused will not be accorded the defence.

In the case of *Sebalj*,[163] the accused voluntarily consumed illegal drugs at an earlier point in time whose effect was causally relevant at the time at which he killed his girlfriend. However, it remains an open question whether his state of psychosis had been brought about through his fault so as to preclude the condition of his mental state at the time of the killing from being characterized as a disease of the mind. As formulated above, the question to be asked in determining whether *Sebalj* has a defence is:

> did he intend or foresee, or ought he to have foreseen, that as a result of voluntary drug-taking he might enter a psychotic state and commit the offence?

On the facts of the case there is a degree of uncertainty as to what precisely would need to be established in order to show that *Sebalj* was at fault. Would it be sufficient to show that he foresaw, or was negligent, that his withdrawal from drugs would lead to a state of psychosis and the death of his girlfriend? Or, would it need to be established that he foresaw, or was negligent, that at some point in time after commencing drug use he would decide to withdraw and that as a result of his withdrawal he would become psychotic and kill his girlfriend?

The judgment of responsibility will hold an accused responsible for those states he or she brings about in a conscious and voluntary fashion, even if as a result of such a state he or she is rendered incapacitated. The judgment of responsibility is in no way compromised by holding an individual criminally responsible for offences committed by him or her while in a state of non-responsibility brought about by him or her while rational and autonomous. This will also apply whether or not the accused is in a state of drug-induced psychosis as a result of his or her rational and autonomous conduct. However, in a case such as *Sebalj*, our moral intuitions flounder as the accused may be considered to be less blameworthy for his state of psychosis, given that it occurred in the context of drug withdrawal.

162 The distinction between excuses and exemptions in the context of the criminal law will be discussed in more detail in Chapter 6 in the context of the partial defence of impaired consciousness.

163 [2003] VSC 181 (Unreported, SC Vic, Smith J, 5 June 2003).

However, the problems associated with a case such as *Sebalj* do not undermine the utility of the approach which this chapter has argued for. The force of this approach is readily recognizable in its application to cases such as *Barrett*[164] and *Martin*.[165]

Moreover, as the VLRC acknowledged, part of the reason for the definitional narrowness evinced by courts is a desire to ensure that the defence remains circumscribed in its scope. The nature of the public policy considerations that are operative in this context were remarked upon by Smith J in *Sebalj*:[166]

> Unless some limits are imposed on the term 'a mental impairment', the statutory defence and the statutory regime would apply wherever the mind of a person charged with an offence had been adversely impaired to a material degree by alcohol or drugs. This would be a dramatic and extremely wide-ranging change to the law and vast numbers of the accused people could seek to rely on and be made subject to the statutory regime.[167]

However, as noted above, the VLRC argued that such a floodgates argument was unfounded.[168] The VLRC argued that it was the elements of the defence, the lack of knowledge as to the nature, quality and wrongness of an act, rather than the meaning of 'mental impairment', which determine the boundaries of the defence.[169] As such, it would be unlikely that individuals who are only 'adversely impaired to a material degree by alcohol or drugs' would be able to use the defence.[170]

The VLRC are correct to suggest that the defence may be restricted by means of those elements of the defence of insanity which are considered sufficiently incapacitating. Equally, the results of an accused's mental impairment will need to be sufficiently incapacitating before the defence will be allowed to be raised. However, as noted in the introduction to this chapter, instances of psychosis due to drug use do not present definitional issues in respect of this aspect of the defence. In the context of the present discussion, that which is of concern is determining when an accused may raise a defence of non-responsibility for his or her criminal conduct subsequent to voluntary drug use which has resulted in psychosis. This is a preliminary question to that of whether the resulting incapacity from voluntary drug use will be deemed sufficient to ground a defence. The issue which voluntary drug use resulting in a state of psychosis raises is whether such a state of psychosis should be recognized as a disease of the mind.

---

164 [2005] VSC 176.

165 [2005] VSC 497.

166 [2003] VSC181 (Unreported, SC Vic, Smith J, 5 June 2003).

167 Ibid. para 10.

168 Victorian Law Reform Commission, *Defences to Homicide: Final Report* (n. 8) 5.39.

169 Ibid. 5.18, 5.39.

170 Ibid. 5.39.

Chapter 3 has argued that whether psychosis arising from drug use will be characterized as a disease of the mind will, according to the judgment of responsibility, be determined according to whether it is due to the fault of the accused. Where such states of psychosis are due to the fault of the accused then the defence should not be available. However, where such states arise through no fault of the accused then such a state will not be recognized as a disease of the mind. This chapter has formulated a question which may be asked in order to determine whether an individual who has brought about a state of drug-induced psychosis through the voluntary use of drugs, has in fact the requisite fault: did the accused intend or foresee, or could have foreseen that he or she would enter a psychotic state and commit the offence? The purpose of the question is to clarify the proper scope of the defence of insanity in such cases. Such a question will ensure that the fact that an accused has experienced a state of cognitive incapacity will not be sufficient for him or her to seek to avoid criminal punishment.

Conclusion

I began my analysis by distinguishing between two types of question. The first is a question to be answered on the basis of clinical evidence: whether a diagnosable mental disorder exists independently of the consumption of drugs. The fact that an accused suffers from cognitive incapacity is not, in and of itself, conclusive. What needs to be established is a causal nexus between such cognitive incapacity and an underlying disease of the mind. The second question is whether an individual who has voluntarily consumed drugs that have led to a state of impaired reasoning powers should be viewed as suffering from a disease of the mind. These are difficult questions, not only because they raise complex, indeterminate clinical issues, but because by their nature they bring into sharp relief the nature of our responsibility practices.

The VLRC approach outlined above focuses exclusively on an accused's state of mind at the time of the offence. The law clearly requires that an accused's mental disorder cause the wrong in question.[171] However, I have argued that the VLRC's call for a broadening of the definition of disease of the mind so as to include all states where an individual's drug use results in a state of incapacity is over-inclusive. The VLRC's approach would provide a defence to individual's whose rational and voluntary behaviour, according to the judgment of responsibility aspect of the disease of the mind enquiry, warrants punishment.

Meloy has endeavoured to delimit the enquiry by postulating a state of settled insanity as a precondition of an accused raising a defence of mental impairment. I have argued that an attempt to rely on current scientific research as a means of formulating judicial principles results in a failure to appreciate the true nature

171 *R v Kemp* [1957] QB 399, 407 per Devlin J.

of the defence. The defence of mental impairment is not an attempt to ascertain whether an accused is suffering from a mental illness.

Finally, Mitchell and Robinson approach the issue from the perspective of an accused's prior fault in becoming intoxicated. There is an intuitive attractiveness to the notion of prior fault as a means of delimiting an accused's responsibility for drug-induced psychosis. To this extent meta-responsibility will result in an accused who has consented to his or her incapacity being held responsible and criminally sanctioned.

I have argued that it is by using the judgment of responsibility aspect of the disease of the mind enquiry that a principled response may be provided to the question of drug-induced psychosis. Consequently, I have endeavoured to show that where an accused has brought about his or her, own incapacity in a rational and voluntary fashion, he or she should be held responsible. The correlation of rational and voluntary conduct to a particular category of liability is the purpose served by the judgment of responsibility. Such a purpose is served by holding an accused who has engaged in voluntary drug use resulting in a state of psychosis responsible where he or she has intended or foreseen, or ought to have foreseen, that such drug use may lead to psychosis and the commission of an offence.

This chapter has addressed the scope of the insanity defence by considering the disease of the mind element of the defence. The next chapter will continue this investigation in the context of the introduction of an independent volitional limb to the M'Naghten rules.

Chapter 5
Volitional Insanity: Involuntariness, Injustice and Cognitive Impairment

Introduction

In this chapter I will argue that an individual may suffer from a mental disorder which will allow him or her to know the nature, quality and wrongness of his or her act and yet nevertheless be precluded from acting voluntarily. I will argue that where an accused's lack of capacity to act voluntarily arises independently of a cognitive defect but is due to a mental disorder that is characterized as a disease of the mind, the defence of insanity should be available. That is, where an individual who suffers from a disease of the mind is rendered incapable of voluntary conduct, even where he or she knows the nature and wrongness of his or her act, the defence of insanity should be acknowledged at common law.

As will be set out below the extent to which involuntary conduct arising from mental disorder is recognized as a disease of the mind in order to ground the defence of insanity varies amongst Australian jurisdictions.[1] In particular, while most code jurisdictions have a separate volitional limb added to their insanity defence, the common law has not treated involuntary conduct arising from mental disorder as an independent limb of the insanity defence. Moreover, endeavours to broaden the defence at common law in order to allow volitional disorders to ground the defence have, with certain exceptions which are discussed below, not been successful.

The present discussion is motivated by the view that the refusal of the common law to recognize states of volitional impairment without any cognitive impairment as sufficient to ground a defence of non-responsibility may result in the punishment of morally innocent individuals. Individuals who lack the capacity for voluntary conduct due to mental disorder lack the capacity for

---

1 While various expressions are used throughout Australian jurisdictions, for ease of usage the expression 'defence of insanity' will be used to cover all instances: in the Commonwealth, ACT, Northern Territory and Victoria 'mental impairment' is the correct expression: *Criminal Code* (Cth) s 7.3(1); *Criminal Code* (ACT) s 28; *Criminal Code* (NT) s 43C; *Crimes (Mental Impairment and Unfitness to be Tried) Act 1997* (Vic) s 20; in New South Wales 'mental illness': *Mental Health (Criminal Procedure) Act 1990* (NSW) s 38; in Queensland, Western Australia and Tasmania 'insanity': *Criminal Code* (Qld) s 27; *Criminal Code* (WA) s 27; *Criminal Code* (Tas) s 16; in South Australia 'mental incompetence': *Criminal Law Consolidation Act 1935* (SA) s 269C, 269E.

responsible action and, by implication, cannot be deterred by the threat of punishment. Hence, in punishing such individuals the law, I would argue, is in fact punishing the morally innocent. Nevertheless, certain commentators have maintained that the common law's failure to recognize an independent volitional limb as sufficient to ground an insanity defence does not result in injustice as all instances of involuntary conduct arising from mental disorder involve some form of cognitive impairment.

In response to this claim I will highlight an instance of a psychiatrically recognized diagnostic category, pyromania, which is characterized by volitional impairment without any accompanying cognitive impairment which renders an individual suffering from such a state incapable of self-control. From this position I will maintain that if a conservative reading of the M'Naghten rules leads to the punishment of individuals who lack the capacity for self-control, it would be best to expand our understanding of the rules in order to provide such individuals with a defence of non-responsibility. The reasons why the law should acknowledge volitional disorders characterized by a 'lack of capacity for control' as sufficient to ground the defence will be analysed in this chapter in the context of the diagnostic category of pyromania. I will argue that an individual who suffers from pyromania may lack the capacity to control his or her conduct without necessarily suffering from any form of cognitive defect.

The chapter begins with an account of the requirement under both code jurisdictions and at common law that conduct be voluntary before criminal responsibility is established. This is followed by an overview of the way in which the common law has responded to instances of involuntary conduct arising from a disease of the mind. The following section will proceed to examine the operation of the volitional limb of the insanity defence in the code jurisdictions.

The final two parts will analyse the diagnostic category of pyromania as a particular example of an impulse-control disorder that gives rise to involuntary conduct on the part of the sufferer. The analysis will consider the degree to which this diagnostic category reveals a lack of cognitive capacity while satisfying the various aspects of the disease of the mind enquiry. The analysis concludes that the diagnostic category of pyromania satisfies the various aspects of the disease of the mind enquiry while indicating that an individual suffering from pyromania does not experience a lack of cognitive capacity. On this basis it is concluded that an individual suffering from the diagnostic category of pyromania should be allowed to raise a defence of volitional insanity at common law.

Insanity and involuntary conduct

The centrality of voluntariness to criminal liability is recognized in both common law and code jurisdictions as a matter of legal principle.[2] Doctrinally it is said that all criminal conduct requires proof of a physical element. The physical element of criminal conduct must be performed voluntarily. Conduct is only voluntary where it is the product of the will of the person performing the conduct.[3] For example, under the criminal codes of Queensland and Western Australia a person is not criminally responsible for 'an act or omission' occurring 'independently of the exercise of the person's "will"'.[4] Consequently, under the codes an accused is not responsible where his or her act occurs independently of his or her will.

The High Court in *R v Falconer*[5] has held that the requirement under the Western Australian Code that an accused's conduct be the result of the exercise of his or her will in order for him or her to be held criminally responsible is the same as the common-law requirement for conduct to be voluntary. As expressed by Mason CJ, Brennan and McHugh JJ:

> Mrs Falconer is criminally responsible for discharging the gun only if that act were 'willed', that is, if she discharged the gun 'of [her] own free will and by decision' (per Kitto J in *Vallance* at 64) or by 'the making of a choice to do' so (per Barwick CJ in *Timbu Kolian* at 53). The notion of 'will' imports a consciousness in the actor of the nature of the act and the choice to do an act of that nature.[6]

Where a person's conscious mind directs an act, he or she does the act by will or choice. In such a case a person makes a decision to engage in particular conduct.

Unwilled conduct may occur in several different ways. For example, the Commonwealth Criminal Code states that:

> (3) The following are examples of conduct that is not voluntary:
> 'a spasm, convulsion or other unwilled bodily movement;
> an act performed during sleep or unconsciousness;

---

2 *Criminal Code* (ACT) s 15; *Criminal Code* (NT) s 31; *Criminal Code* (Qld) s 23; *Criminal Code* (Tas) s 13(1); *Criminal Code* (WA) s 23; *Woolmington v DPP* [1935] AC 462; *Ryan v R* (1967) 121 CLR 205.

3 *Criminal Code* (Cth) s 4.2(2).

4 *Criminal Code* (Qld) s 23(1)(a); *Criminal Code* (WA) s 23. The operation of the voluntariness requirement in the other Australian jurisdictions will be discussed below.

5 (1990) 171 CLR 30.

6 Ibid. 39 per Mason CJ, Brennan and McHugh JJ.

> an act performed during impaired consciousness depriving the person of the will to act'[7]

Where an accused's mental disorder is characterized as a disease of the mind and results in involuntary conduct he or she is obligated to raise a plea of insanity rather than involuntariness.[8] In pleading the insanity defence an accused is debarred from an outright acquittal and is, subject to what is to be outlined below, a candidate for a qualified acquittal.

To the extent that a finding of insanity results in a qualified rather than outright acquittal the disposition of an accused whose act is involuntary due to a disease of the mind represents a departure from the above mentioned general principle of criminal liability. Such a departure from the general principle of voluntariness as a necessary element of criminal liability is necessitated by a policy concern with societal protection it being incumbent on the law to protect the community from 'dangerous' people.[9] As noted in Chapter 2, the dispositional aspect of the disease of the mind enquiry seeks to ensure social-defence considerations receive appropriate attention whenever there is a finding of insanity. Consequently, individuals suffering from a disease of the mind are considered to be appropriate targets of therapeutic intervention rather than punishment. In this way both the individual's and society's interests are served: the former by being provided with appropriate treatment the latter by ensuring that such an individual is, where needed, kept in a secure facility.

However, having raised the issue of insanity, it is incumbent on the accused to satisfy the requirements of the defence on the balance of probabilities.[10] In particular, the accused must show that the nature of the mental malfunctioning arising from the state of mental impairment (disease of the mind) is one that is, depending on the jurisdiction, recognized by the M'Naghten rules[11] or a statutory formulation of the insanity defence.[12]

Under the current law where an accused seeks to raise a defence of non-responsibility on the basis of involuntariness resulting from mental disorder there are two matters that warrant notice: the first concerns the displacement of principle by policy; the second, the requirement on the part of the accused to satisfy the elements of the defence as stipulated in the relevant jurisdiction. This results in the counter-intuitive position that not only is a volitional disorder precluded from giving

---

7 *Criminal Code* (Cth) s 4.2 'Voluntariness'.

8 *Criminal Code* (Qld) s 23(1)(a) read with s 27; *Criminal Code* (WA) s 23A read with s 27; *Criminal Code* (Cth) s 7.3(6); *Bratty v A-G (Northern Ireland)* [1963] AC 386; *Hawkins* (1994) 179 CLR 500.

9 *R v Stone* (1999) 134 CCC (3d) 353, 440–441.

10 Though note s 21 (3) *Crimes (Mental Impairment and Unfitness to be Tried) Act 1997* (Vic), party raising defence bears onus of rebutting presumption of sanity.

11 *R v M'Naghten* (1843) 10 Cl and Fin 200; 8 ER 718.

12 *Criminal Code* (Qld) s 27; *Criminal Code* (WA) s 27; *Criminal Code* (Cth) s 7.3.

rise to an outright acquittal, but also in order for an accused to obtain a qualified acquittal, he or she must ensure that the nature of the resulting malfunction arising from his or her mental disorder is one which is recognized as an incapacitating condition by the defence of insanity in the relevant jurisdiction. This may prove problematic where an accused's mental disorder results in involuntary conduct and the relevant jurisdiction defines the requisite incapacitating conditions of the defence of insanity restrictively so as not to include states of involuntariness. Involuntary conduct arising from mental disorder is not a recognized limb of the defence of insanity at common law. However, the common law has endeavoured to take into account an accused's incapacity to control his or her conduct in establishing the defence of insanity. This will be considered further in the following section. In contrast to the common law, code-jurisdiction formulations provide an explicit volitional limb in respect of an accused's incapacity to control his or her actions. This will be considered further in the section after.

Common-law approaches

Common-law courts have adopted two means by which to refuse to recognize involuntary conduct arising from mental disorder as sufficient to ground the defence of insanity. First, and most conspicuously, courts have refused to acknowledge a claim of involuntary conduct arising from a mental condition characterized as a disease of the mind as a sufficiently incapacitating condition for the purpose of establishing the defence of insanity. At common law, it is only where volitional disorders leading to involuntary conduct reveal an absence of the requisite kinds of knowledge that such disorders will support an accused's claim. A second approach adopted by courts at common law by which to restrict the scope of the insanity defence is to refuse to characterize mental disorder giving rise to involuntary conduct as a disease of the mind.

Notwithstanding the above, courts have endeavoured to ensure a more liberal interpretation of the defence for the benefit of defendants experiencing involuntary conduct arising from mental disorder. In particular, courts will characterize an accused's involuntary conduct arising from mental disorder as evidence of a lack of the requisite kinds of knowledge required to ground a defence of insanity at common law. This is the approach adopted in most common-law cases.[13]

A more radical approach which has been adopted by courts on occasion is to reject the current scope of the insanity defence and hold that a volitional disorder should be recognized as an independent limb of the insanity defence sufficiently

---

13 *Sodeman v R* (1936) 55 CLR 192, 214–15; *Brown v A-G (SA)* [1959] ALR 808 (HCA).

incapacitating for the purposes of the defence. Such an expansionary approach has been applied in some common-law cases.[14]

Volitional disorder: evidence of defect of reason

At common law, involuntary conduct arising from a mental disorder may only be used as evidence of insanity, it will not establish the defence of insanity.[15] As Dixon J observed in *Sodeman v R*:

> If [the accused] is able to understand the nature of his [or her] act and to know that the act is wrong, an incapacity through disease of the mind to control his [or her] actions affords no excuse and leaves the prisoner criminally responsible.[16]

Similarly, Latham CJ stated that:

> The direction explains that uncontrollable impulse in itself is not a defence, but that uncontrollable impulse resulting from mental disease which brings about or is associated with an incapacity to know the nature and quality of an act or to know that it is wrong amounts to insanity which constitutes a defence. In my opinion this is an accurate state [*sic.*] of law. Such an impulse may be one manifestation of mental disease. It may have the effect of destroying or preventing knowledge of the nature and quality of the act done or knowledge that the act is wrong. In such a case, insanity is established, but by reason of the latter feature of the case and not by reason of uncontrollable impulse per se. This principle of law is frequently criticized, especially by medical and other scientific men, but a Court must administer the law as it finds it.[17]

Consequently, the fact that there is a volitional disorder characterized as a disease of the mind will not, at common law, give rise to an insanity defence unless such a disorder precludes the accused from knowing either the nature and quality or wrongness of his or her act. Where an accused establishes the requisite absence of knowledge he or she will receive a qualified acquittal. Where an accused fails to establish the requisite absence of knowledge the defence will not be available and he or she will be convicted.

However, while there is no recognized common-law defence of involuntary conduct arising from mental disorder, courts have been prepared to consider the evidentiary import of a range of mental disorders by recognizing that one type of

14 *HM Advocate v Kidd* (1960) JC 61, 70–1; *Doyle v Wicklow County Council* [1974] IR 55, 71, citing *People (A-G) v Hayes* (Unreported, CCC, 30 Nov. 1967).

15 *A-G (SA) v Brown* [1960] AC 432 (PC).

16 (1936) 55 CLR 192, 214.

17 Ibid. 203–4.

mental disorder may provide evidence of the existence of another.[18] For example, rather than being considered to be instances of mutually exclusive types of malfunctioning, evidence of involuntary conduct arising from mental disorder has been held to lend support in establishing a state of cognitive impairment and thereby satisfy the requirements of the M'Naghten rules. This section will consider two High Court cases in which the court has viewed an accused's involuntary conduct arising from a mental disorder as evidence of a state of cognitive impairment which will satisfy the defence of insanity.

In *Sodeman*, Dixon J noted that:

> It is important to bear steadily in mind that if through disorder of the faculties a prisoner is incapable of controlling his relevant acts, this may afford the strongest reason for supposing that he is incapable of forming a judgment that they are wrong, and in some cases even of understanding their nature.[19]

Sodeman makes it clear that involuntary conduct arising from a mental disorder may provide evidence as to both an accused's incapacity to know the nature of his or her act, as well as his or her incapacity to know that an act is wrong.

The evidentiary approach adopted in *Sodeman* has found subsequent support in the High Court case of *Brown v A-G (SA)* where it was stated that: 'Uncontrollable impulse ... may afford strong ground for the inference that a prisoner was labouring under such a defect of reason from disease of the mind as not to know that he [or she] was doing what was wrong'.[20] However, the claim that various types of mental disorder may be symptomatic of one another falls short of establishing that involuntary conduct arising from mental disorder, independent of the operation of a cognitive defect, will provide exculpation. That is, the approach adopted in both *Sodeman* and *Brown* remains hostage to the psychiatric facts being a certain way. In particular, on the *Sodeman/Brown* approach, a defence will be available to an accused only where the accused's disease of the mind gives rise to involuntary conduct and such involuntary conduct is accompanied by a lack of knowledge as to the nature or wrongness of his or her act.

However, notwithstanding the use to which the evidentiary approach has been put, the M'Naghten rules have been criticized by various courts as failing to provide a sufficiently comprehensive test of insanity.[21] Yet, any detailed discussion of the type of mental malfunction that may satisfy the M'Naghten rules should

---

18 P.A. Fairall and S. Yeo, *Criminal Defences in Australia* (4th edn, Chatswood, NSW, 2005) 261.

19 *Sodeman* (1936) 55 CLR 192, 214–15.

20 [1959] ALR 808 (HCA).

21 *Oxford* (1840) 173 ER 941; *H.M. Advocate v Kidd* (1960) JC 61, 70–1; *Doyle v Wicklow County Council* [1974] IR 55, 71, citing *People (A-G) v Hayes* (Unreported, CCC, 30 Nov. 1967).

be cognizant of a comprehensive range of mental disorders.[22] On its face there is no reason to believe that, as per *Sodeman* and *Brown*, the only varieties of mental malfunction which may be experienced by an accused are those where an accused's involuntary conduct is accompanied by a lack of knowledge. For example, a psychiatric condition may be envisaged wherein the accused knows that his or her act is wrong, yet he or she is not able to act voluntarily. In fact, psychiatric diagnostic manuals have tentatively recognized such states with discrete diagnostic categories. In such instances an accused's involuntary conduct may be viewed as occurring independently of his or her lack of knowledge as to the nature or wrongness of his or her conduct. One such category, pyromania, will be discussed below. In the light of the clinical recognition of such a state, common-law courts have on occasion endeavoured to accommodate involuntary conduct arising from mental disorder by acknowledging a defence of insanity arising from a state of volitional disorder independent of the M'Naghten rules' knowledge requirement. Several such cases will be considered in the next section.

Case law: expansionary developments

Certain jurisdictions, such as Ireland and South Africa, which have adopted the M'Naghten rules have considered them to be non-exhaustive pronouncements of the law and have judicially recognized involuntary conduct arising from mental disorder as sufficient to ground the defence of insanity.[23]

An example of a case in a common-law jurisdiction which seeks to recognize involuntary conduct arising from mental disorder as an independent ground for the defence of insanity is to be found in the Supreme Court of Ireland case of *Doyle v Wicklow County Council*.[24] In *Doyle* a 17-year-old boy had deliberately burnt down an abattoir intending to destroy both the premises and contents. Medical evidence established that the accused was suffering from a mental disorder which prompted him to set fire to the premises as a means of protest against the slaughter of animals in the belief that he was justified in so doing, although he knew his act to be forbidden by society or contrary to law.[25]

The Supreme Court in *Doyle* recognized that a defendant may know that his or her act is wrong, yet nevertheless be held to satisfy the requirements of the defence on the basis of involuntary conduct arising from a disease of the mind.

---

22 K.W.M. Fulford, 'Value, Action, Mental Illness, and the Law' in *Action and Value in Criminal Law*, ed. S. Shute, J. Gardner and J. Horder (Oxford, 1993) 279, 281.

23 Ireland: *O'Brien* [1936] IR 263; *Boylan* [1937] IR 449; *Doyle v Wicklow County Council* [1974] IR 55; South Africa: *R v Hay* (1899) 16 SC 290; *S v Kavin* 1978 (2) SA 731 (W). Both these jurisdictions have now enacted statutory provisions on insanity: *Irish Criminal Law (Insanity) Act 2006* (No. 11 of 2006) s 5(1); South Africa: *Criminal Law Procedure Act 1977* (No. 51 of 1977) s 78(1).

24 [1974] IR 55.

25 *S v. Kavin* 1978 (2) SA 731 (W).

Griffin J, in delivering the judgment of the court, specifically noted that, on the facts, it was the 'capacity of a man on the basis of his knowledge to act or refrain from acting' that was in issue.[26] As put by Griffin J, the key issue in *Doyle* was whether mental disorder precludes a defendant's capacity 'to act or refrain from acting' notwithstanding his knowing what he is doing and that it is wrong.[27] That is, unlike the High Court of Australia in *Brown*, the Supreme Court of Ireland in *Doyle* did not view involuntary conduct arising from a mental disorder as merely symptomatic of an absence of knowledge according to the operation of the M'Naghten rules.

Griffin J applied the reasoning of Henchy J in *People (A-G) v Hayes*[28] and stated that

> The [M'Naghten] rules do not take into account the capacity of a man on the basis of his knowledge to act or refrain from acting, and I believe it to be correct psychiatric science to accept that certain serious mental diseases, such as paranoia and schizophrenia, in certain cases enable a man to understand the morality or immorality of his act or the legality or illegality of it, or the nature and quality of it, but nevertheless prevent him from exercising a free volition as to whether he should or should not do that act.[29]

Further, having understood the 'capacity of a man to act or refrain from acting' in terms of the 'exercise of free volition', Griffin J stated that:

> If it is open to the jury to say that this man understood the nature and quality of his act, and understood its wrongfulness, morally and legally, but that nevertheless he was debarred from refraining from [acting] because of a defect of reason, due to his mental illness, it seems to me that it would be unjust, in the circumstances of this case not to allow the jury to consider the case on these grounds.[30]

That is, an accused lacks 'free volition' where he or she is 'debarred from refraining' from acting in a particular fashion. Hence, an accused that cannot will not to do the act or cannot do otherwise is taken to lack free volition. The absence of a capacity to do otherwise will ground a defence of insanity where the reason for such absence is mental illness. Consequently, according to the judgment in *Doyle*, an accused may raise a defence of insanity, independent of a lack of knowledge as to the nature, quality or wrongness of his or her act, where he or she is 'debarred from refraining from [acting] because of a defect of reason, due to

26 Ibid. 70.

27 Ibid.

28 Unreported, CCC, 30 Nov. 1967.

29 [1974] IR 55, 71.

30 Ibid. applied *People (DPP) v O'Mahoney* [1985] IR 517 (Supreme Court).

his [or her] mental illness'.[31] However, the judgment in *Doyle* fails to reveal how mental illness resulting in a defect of reason may debar an accused from refraining from acting and yet nevertheless allow him or her to know both the nature and quality of his or her act and understand its wrongness. The court merely points to 'correct psychiatric' evidence that will establish such mental malfunctioning.

In this respect it is interesting to note that Griffith J, stated, in *obiter*, that:

> Having regard to the findings of the learned Circuit Court judge and the [psychiatric] evidence, it seems to me that the respondents have not made out a case that legal insanity absolved the youth, who set fire to the abattoir, from criminal responsibility.[32]

While the issue of whether insanity has been established is a question of fact for a jury to consider, Griffith J's remarks suggest that the facts did not reveal incapacity on the part of the accused to refrain from acting. In particular, the ability to make a choice for a reason and act on such a choice for that reason presupposes the ability to exercise control.[33] Consequently, the accused's reason or motivation in burning down the abattoir as a means of protesting against the slaughter of the animals and his acting for that reason, would seem incongruent with the hypothesis that he was unable to exercise free volition.

It may be noted that to the extent to which the judgment in *Doyle* is reliant on psychiatric evidence it remains hostage to empirical evidence to the same degree as does the High Court approach in *Sodeman* and *Brown*. As noted above, the High Court cases of *Sodeman*[34] and *A-G (SA) v Brown*[35] make it clear that at common law, involuntary conduct arising from mental disorder may be used as evidence in establishing an accused's incapacity to know the nature and wrongness of his or her act. The High Court ruling in these latter cases is of interest only on the assumption that volition and cognition track one another. That is, these judgments indicate that volitional defects are symptomatic of cognitive defects. Conversely, a case such as *Doyle*[36] endeavours to expand the common-law defence by recognizing a state of mental disorder characterized by involuntary conduct independent of a lack of knowledge of the nature, quality or wrongness on the part of the accused. That is, the *Doyle* approach is of interest to the extent to which an accused may experience involuntary conduct arising from mental disorder without

---

31 [1974] IR 55, 71.

32 Ibid.

33 See *R v Falconer* (1990) 171 CLR 30, 40 per Mason CJ, Brennan and McHugh JJ, 'because we assume that a person who is apparently conscious has the capacity to control his [or her] actions, we draw an inference that the act is done by choice'.

34 *Sodeman v R* (1936) 55 CLR 192, 214–15 per Dixon J.

35 [1960] AC 432 on appeal to PC.

36 *Doyle v Wicklow County Council* [1974] IR 55.

any cognitive impairment. Hence, the Irish Supreme Court approach in *Doyle* is of interest only on the assumption that cognition may be separated from volition.

On both the *Sodeman/Brown* and *Doyle* approaches, the court is reliant on the psychiatric evidence being of a certain kind. However, legal rules governing the operation of the defence should not assume that mental disorders are discrete or finite. This is particularly so where the evidence in respect of the veracity of such a mental disorder remains ambiguous.

Nevertheless, there is an important asymmetry between the *Sodeman/Brown* and *Doyle* approaches. If in fact the common-law approach adopted by cases such as *Sodeman* and *Brown* is incorrect, and there are instances where an individual may suffer from a mental disorder characterized by involuntary conduct without any cognitive impairment, refusing to extend the defence to such an individual may result in injustice. It is only by extending the defence to states of involuntariness arising from mental disorder independent of a knowledge requirement that these individuals will be provided with a defence. Under the *Doyle* approach however, no harm will result if it is shown that there is no extant or verifiable mental disorder whose diagnostic criteria involve involuntary conduct without any cognitive defect on the part of an individual. No harm will result by introducing such an independent volitional limb as the introduction of such a limb will merely prove to be redundant in the absence of the requisite mental disorder. In such a case it is arguable that the common law should play it safe by recognizing an independent volitional limb giving rise to the defence of insanity alongside the M'Naghten rules rather than rely on the non-occurrence of a mental disorder characterized by volitional impairment.

However, by adopting the safe-guard suggested above we are confronted by an important trade-off. The trade-off stems from the fact there is no objectively verifiable means of distinguishing an impulse which was not resisted from an impulse which was irresistible: distinguishing those accused who 'could not' from those who 'would not'.[37] Consequently, by introducing an independent volitional limb we safeguard against the risk of punishing individuals who lack the capacity for voluntary conduct, yet, at the same time, a significant epistemic problem is raised regarding distinguishing those individuals who lack the capacity from those who choose not to exercise it. I will return to this issue when I come to consider various objections to the introduction of an independent volitional limb below.

The next section will outline the approach taken by the code jurisdictions in respect of involuntary conduct arising from mental disorder.

---

37 S. Bronitt and B. McSherry, *Principles of Criminal Law* (3rd edn, Pymont, NSW, 2010) 250.

Code-jurisdiction approach

The first part of this section will outline the various formulations of an independent volitional limb to the defence of insanity adopted by the code jurisdictions in Australia. This will be followed by a comment on various interpretations that have been suggested in respect of these volitional limb formulations. The final part of this section will consider the practical effect of the code formulations and provide a response to several objections that have been raised in respect of the provision of an independent volitional limb.

Code-jurisdiction formulations

An instance of a code jurisdiction adopting an independent volitional limb is to be found in the Tasmanian Criminal Code.[38] Section 16(1)(b) of the Tasmanian Code stipulates that the defence of insanity may be raised by an individual where 'the act or omission was done or made under an impulse which he or she was in substance deprived of any power to resist'. The Northern Territory Criminal Code[39] allows the defence to be raised by an accused that is 'not able to control his or her actions'.[40] Similarly, the Australian Capital Territory (ACT) has included an independent volitional limb to its criminal code.[41] The ACT Code stipulates that an accused may raise a defence of mental impairment where he or she 'could not control [his or her] conduct'.[42] In respect of the Queensland and Western Australian jurisdictions the M'Naghten rules were codified in section 27 of the Queensland and Western Australian Criminal Codes (Griffith Codes).[43] However, in contrast to the M'Naghten rules Griffith Code formulations of the insanity defence have recognized incapacity to control conduct as a separate basis for the insanity defence. An instance of a Griffith Code formulation adopting an independent volitional limb is to be found in section 27 of the Queensland Criminal Code:

> (1) A person is not criminally responsible for an act or omission if at the time of doing the act or making the omission the person is in such state of mental disease or mental infirmity as to deprive the person of capacity to understand what the person is doing, or of capacity to control the person's actions, or of capacity to know that the person ought not to do the act or make the omission.[44]

---

38 *Criminal Code* (Tas).

39 *Criminal Code* (NT).

40 Ibid. s 43(1)(c).

41 *Criminal Code* (ACT).

42 Ibid. s 28(1)(c).

43 *Criminal Code* (Qld); *Criminal Code* (WA).

44 *Criminal Code* (Qld); s 27(2) and the second paragraph of s 27 under the WA Code deal with partial delusions and for the purposes of this discussion will not be discussed. However, I note at this point that this aspect of the defence has in practice been rendered

Code jurisdictions, in keeping with the case at common law, hold that where an accused's involuntariness is caused by a disease of the mind only the defence of non-responsibility is open.[45] Consequently, in such an instance an accused cannot maintain that he or she is entitled to an acquittal on the basis of involuntariness.[46]

The Commonwealth Criminal Code defence of mental impairment is analogous to the Griffith Code formulations above:

> 7.3 Mental Impairment
>
> (1) A person is not criminally responsible for an offence if, at the time of carrying out the conduct constituting the offence, the person was suffering from mental impairment that had the effect that:
>
> (a) the person did not know the nature and quality of the conduct; or
>
> (b) the person did not know that the conduct was wrong …; or
>
> (c) the person was unable to control the conduct.[47]

The Commonwealth Code preserves the Griffith Code position in respect of the degree of impairment an accused must suffer in relation to his or her capacity to control before the defence is raised. Under both the Griffith and Commonwealth Codes an accused must be '*deprived* of the capacity', that is, be 'unable to', control his or her conduct in order for the defence to be established. By requiring a deprivation rather than an impairment of an accused's capacity, the Griffith and Commonwealth Codes further restrict the operation of this limb of the defence.[48] However, in keeping with both the common law and the Griffith Code under the Commonwealth Code, an accused choosing to raise evidence of mental impairment

---

largely superfluous, most cases being dealt with under s 27(1) of the Queensland code or the first paragraph of s 27 of the WA code: for a recent case noting the operation of this aspect of the defence, see *The State of Western Australia v Tarau* [2005] WASC 290, para 71–2 per Miller J.

45 *Criminal Code* (Cth) s 7.6, evidence of mental impairment may not be used to deny voluntariness.

46 *Falconer* (1990) 171 CLR 30, 47 per Mason CJ, Brennan and McHugh JJ; *Criminal Code* (Cth) s 7.6.

47 *Criminal Code* (Cth) s 7.3. The use of the expression 'mental impairment' by way of a heading to this section is to be understood as synonymous with 'insanity', while the use of the same expression in 7.3(1) ('suffering from mental impairment') is to be understood as synonymous with the common-law expression disease of the mind. For a like interpretation of the Victorian legislation employing identical terms, see *R v R* [2003] VSC 187 (5 June 2003) para 17–18 per Teague J.

48 See Fairall and Yeo, *Criminal Defences in Australia* (n. 18) 13.25, who argue that criticisms of current statutory formulations ('difficult conceptually to define and practically to apply') would be in part met by requiring a 'substantial' rather than total impairment of an accused's capacity to control his or her conduct.

in order to deny voluntariness must rely on the insanity defence.[49] Consequently, in such an instance an accused cannot maintain that he or she is entitled to an acquittal on the basis of involuntariness.[50]

In contrast to the common-law formulation of the insanity defence, code-jurisdiction formulations of the defence provide a more expansive definition of insanity. In particular, code formulations allow an accused to raise a defence of insanity by showing that he or she has been deprived of the capacity to control his or her conduct as a result of mental impairment.[51]

Interpreting lack of capacity to control

Despite some differences in terminology, all code jurisdictions recognize a lack of capacity to control conduct as an independent ground of establishing the insanity defence. The absence of capacity for self-control may be interpreted in one of two ways.[52] One interpretation views the absence of capacity for self-control as referring to those cases where the behaviour on the part of an accused is involuntary, that is, behaviour occurring independently of the exercise of the will.[53] This interpretation follows the High Court in *R v Falconer*,[54] where it was held that the requirement for voluntary conduct requires a person's conscious mind to have directed the act because the notion of voluntariness or will requires the act to be made by the accused '"of [his or her] own free will and by decision" (per Kitto J in *Vallance* at 64) or by "the making of a choice to do" so (per Barwick CJ in *Timbu Kolian* at 53). The notion of "will" imports a consciousness in the actor of the nature of the act and the choice to do an act of that nature.'[55] On such an interpretation of the code jurisdiction's limb the absence of a capacity to control is restricted to instances where an accused's incapacity for self-control is interpreted merely as involuntary conduct.[56] That is, conduct of which the accused was not conscious. Consequently, an interpretation of the capacity to control as conduct occurring independently of the will would restrict the operation of the code's second limb of the insanity defence to states of automatism. As expressed by Toohey J in *Falconer*:[57]

---

49 *Criminal Code* (Cth) s 7.3(6), evidence of mental impairment may not be used to deny voluntariness.

50 *Falconer* (1990) 171 CLR 30, 47 per Mason CJ, Brennan and McHugh JJ.

51 *Criminal Code* (Qld) s 27; *Criminal Code* (WA) s 27; *Criminal Code* (Cth) s 7.3.

52 The Tasmanian Code provision is in different terms referring to an accused who is 'deprived of any power to resist' an impulse to act or omit: *Criminal Code* (Tas) s 16(1)(b).

53 *R v Falconer* (1990) 171 CLR 30.

54 Ibid.

55 Ibid. 39 per Mason CJ, Brennan and McHugh JJ.

56 Ibid.

57 Ibid.

> Undoubtedly, automatism implies conduct which is involuntary. The use of descriptions such as 'automatism' should not obscure the fact that, in terms of the Code, where criminal responsibility is in issue, the question ultimately is whether the act or omission in respect of which an accused has been charged occurred independently of the exercise of his or her will. Automatism is merely a fact going to voluntariness: *Hall* (1988) 36 A Crim R 368 at 371.[58]

However, by defining the incapacity to control limb of the defence narrowly as conduct which is merely involuntary, the volitional limb adopted by code jurisdictions would be rendered redundant as acts which are performed in a state of unconsciousness are also those acts in respect of which the accused did not know their nature and quality.[59]

Another interpretation of an accused's capacity to control seeks to cover instances of 'irresistible impulse' arising from a state of mental impairment.[60] The notion of irresistible impulse was considered in *R v Moore*,[61] where it was held that:

> This section [*Criminal Code Act 1902* (WA) s 27] deals with the defence of insanity, and it shows in what cases persons who would otherwise be responsible for their acts are free from responsibility because they are insane. It treats as insane certain persons who under the old law would not have been treated as insane. It accepts the medical theory of uncontrollable impulse, and treats people who are insane to the extent that they have not the capacity to control their actions, whether from mental disease or natural mental infirmity, as being persons who are irresponsible.[62]

A similar approach was adopted in the Western Australian case of *Wray v R*,[63] where the court upheld an appeal against conviction on the basis of medical evidence that the accused was suffering from dementia praecox which deprived him of the capacity to control his actions.

Interpreting an incapacity to control conduct in terms of an irresistible impulse, rather than merely as an instance of involuntary conduct due to mental disease, would provide a defence to those individuals who are deprived of the capacity to resist engaging in proscribed conduct and yet who may still know the nature and

---

58 Ibid. 69–73.

59 T. Crofts and K. Burton, *The Criminal Codes: Commentary and Materials* (6th edn, Pyrmont, NSW, 2009) 10.390; E. Colvin and J. McKechnie, *Criminal Law in Queensland and Western Australia* (5th edn, Chatswood, NSW, 2008) 17.27.

60 *R v Moore* (1908) 10 WALR 64, 65–6; *Wray v R* (1930) 33 WALR 67, 68–9.

61 (1908) 10 WALR 64.

62 Ibid. 66 per McMillan J.

63 (1930) 33 WALR 67.

quality of their act. The introduction of a defence on the basis of an irresistible-impulse interpretation of capacity to control will be considered below.

Objections to a volitional limb

Bronitt and McSherry have noted that, even in those jurisdictions where an independent volitional limb is available, claims of irresistible impulse are rarely used.[64] The authors suggest that the rarity of the use of the volitional component in these jurisdictions is explainable given that an accused's lack of capacity to control must stem from a disease of the mind or a related concept. Yet, in those jurisdictions which do have an independent volitional limb, there is a reluctance to interpret a volitional disorder arising from, for example, an impulse-control disorder, as a disease of the mind for the purposes of the defence.

Moreover, as the authors remark, even where the issue has been raised, it has been relatively unsuccessful with only one reported case of an appeal against conviction succeeding.[65] Bronitt and McSherry hypothesize that such a relative lack of success may be attributable to the fact that the provision of an independent volitional limb 'might be perceived as an "easy out" for persons who are seeking an excuse for yielding to temptation'.[66]

The authors are correct in noting that not all states of mental disorder are necessarily acknowledged as diseases of the mind. However, this is due to the fact that the narrowness of psychiatric categorizations of mental disorder does not necessarily accord with the breadth of the expression disease of the mind and cognate terms as used at common law and in mental-health legislation.

Moreover, while determining the applicability of a diagnostic category to a condition suffered by a particular accused may accord with psychiatry's therapeutic rationale, this is not always congruent with the law's policy objectives. As a matter of policy, Ferguson points out, 'the public expectation that citizens must in general take personal responsibility for their conduct is an important value which is essential to the continued preservation of peace and order in our society'.[67] So, for example, where the capacity for control is set too low there is a risk that such public expectation will be destroyed, and a disproportionate number of individuals will not be held to the relevant standard. Hence the fact that an independent volitional limb is rarely used in those jurisdictions where it is extant may in fact be due to policy considerations. That is, the reluctance on the part of

64 Bronitt and McSherry, *Principles of Criminal Law* (n. 37) 249; see also R. Schopp, *The Psychology of Criminal Responsibility* (Cambridge, 1994) 201–3.

65 Bronitt and McSherry, *Principles of Criminal Law* (n. 37) 249, citing *Wray v R* (1930) 33 WALR 67.

66 Bronitt and McSherry, *Principles of Criminal Law* (n. 37) 249, quoting E.A. Tollefson and B. Starkman, *Mental Disorder in Criminal Proceedings* (Toronto, 1993) 41.

67 G. Ferguson, 'A Critique of Proposals to Reform the Insanity Defence' (1989) 14 *Queen's Law Journal* 135, 141.

judges to characterize a particular mental disorder as a disease of the mind may be attributable to extant policy considerations rather than a felt lack of need for the recognition of an independent volitional limb as such.

Further, it is sometimes argued that a reason why volitional disorders should not be allowed to ground the defence is because of the inherent difficulty of distinguishing an individual who chooses not to exercise his or her capacity to refrain from acting ('would not') from an individual who lacks the capacity to refrain from acting ('could not').[68] However, the difficulty of distinguishing an accused who has raised a bogus defence should not preclude the availability of an independent volitional limb to those who are deserving of the defence. Epistemic constraints, or what we may know of an accused's intention, or motivation, are a recurring problem in the criminal law.[69] Several commentators have remarked on similar concerns arising in other areas of criminal law with respect to questions of degree, such as determining the requisite loss of control required for the partial defence of provocation or in dealing with legal concepts such as 'knowledge' and 'negligence'.[70] The inherent difficulty of determining these issues in no way undermines the importance of such concepts to the criminal law. I will return to this issue in the context of pyromania below.

Moreover, an additional safeguard against bogus claims of involuntary conduct arising from mental disorder presents itself as a result of the degree of impairment required before a claim of involuntary conduct arising from the mental disorder will satisfy the defence. Given that the defence results in a finding of non-responsibility, it will be incumbent on the accused to satisfy the court to the requisite degree that his or her volitional impairment is sufficiently severe to warrant such a finding.[71] In this respect it is noteworthy that both the Griffith and Commonwealth Codes require that an accused be 'deprived' of the capacity to control his or her conduct.[72]

Another objection to the provision of an independent volitional limb is the claim that, as instances of volitional disorder amount to or involve a cognitive failure, the failure to provide an independent volitional limb will not necessarily deny an accused claiming incapacity to control his or her conduct a defence.[73] Bronitt and McSherry argue that, in keeping with modern psychological

68 A.S. Goldstein, *The Insanity Defence* (New Haven, 1967) 67–8, cited in Bronitt and McSherry, *Principles of Criminal Law* (n. 37) 250.

69 P. Cane, *Responsibility in Law and Morality* (Oxford, 2002) 44–9.

70 S. Yeo, 'The Insanity Defence in the Criminal Laws of the Commonwealth of Nations' [2008] *Singapore Journal of Legal Studies* 241, 254; Bronitt and B. McSherry, *Principles of Criminal Law* (n. 37) 250.

71 Ferguson 'A Critique of Proposals to Reform the Insanity Defence' (n. 67) 141.

72 *Criminal Code* (Qld) s 27; *Criminal Code* (WA) s 27; *Criminal Code* (Cth) s 7.3.

73 S. Morse, 'Diminished Capacity' in *Action and Value in Criminal Law*, ed. S. Shute, J. Gardner and J. Horder (Oxford, 1993), 265.

understanding, a person suffering from incapacity to control his or her conduct would not have his or her cognitive faculties unaffected.[74] On this account there can be no independent volitional disorder arising from a disease of the mind, as putative cases of exclusively volitional impairment will be found to involve cognitive failure. Loss of control tests wrongly

> assume that a person can know what he or she is doing is wrong, yet be unable to control his or her actions. In reality, such tests assume that cognition remains completely unaffected, and this contradicts not only the holistic standpoint of modern psychology but also the view that the ability to reason plays an essential part in controlling conduct.[75]

According to the above holistic model of mental functioning, a failure to provide an independent volitional limb will not result in injustice as an accused who claims incapacity to control his or her conduct will nevertheless still be able to raise a defence employing the current (cognitive) formulation of the M'Naghten rules.

However, there is no reason to doubt the existence of a serious mental disorder in certain cases precluding an individual from knowing the nature, quality and wrongness of his or her act while being prevented from exercising free volition in relation to such an act. While some mental disorders manifest a lack or impairment of cognitive capacity, this is not the case in all instances. I will argue in the next section that there are instances where a person suffering from some form of volitional disorder may have his or her capacity to conform to conduct severely restricted without any form of cognitive dysfunction. Consequently, there is no reason to doubt the existence of a serious mental disorder in certain cases precluding an individual from knowing the nature, quality and wrongness of his or her act while being prevented from exercising free volition in relation to such an act.

The next section will outline a category of psychiatric disorder characterized by volitional impairment without cognitive dysfunction, impulse-control disorder.

Impulse-control disorder: pyromania

This section will outline the characteristic features of the diagnostic category of impulse-control disorder. I will begin by remarking on the reasons why an individual who suffers from an impulse-control disorder should have the defence extended to him or her. This will be followed by an outline of the diagnostic features of one particular type of impulse-control disorder, pyromania, as they appear in two major classificatory manuals. However, before commencing with

---

74 See Bronitt and McSherry, *Principles of Criminal Law* (n. 37) 250 and citations.
75 Ibid.

the above analysis certain remarks will be made in respect of the use of diagnostic manuals in forensic settings.

Diagnostic manuals: clinical judgment in forensic settings

The central premise of this chapter is predicated on the conditional existence of a diagnostic category bearing the hallmarks of an irresistible impulse. In order to establish the recognition of such a diagnostic category, recourse will be had to two major diagnostic manuals. Consequently, the present chapter bears the onus of showing the relevance of diagnostic manuals in the context of courtroom settings. This section will seek to discharge this onus.

Michelle Pathé and Paul Mullen have warned of the dangers to which the use of diagnostic manuals in court-room settings may give rise.[76] In particular, the authors note two related problems stemming from the use of such manuals in criminal trials. One problem concerns the potential for a mechanical application of the diagnostic categories and criteria to be found in such manuals without clinical judgment. A second related problem concerns the possible misuse and misunderstanding of diagnostic categories and criteria when used in court-room settings. Each will be considered in turn.

Pathé and Mullen write that clinical training provides the expert witness with 'skills [which] extend beyond the mere recognition of mental state or behavioural aberrations which might fulfil the diagnostic criteria specified by one's preferred classificatory system'.[77] Such training 'equips the mental health professional to elicit, assimilate and articulate the experience of madness in a way that is understandable to the average person'.[78] This has led the compilers of the *Diagnostic and Statistical Manual of Mental Disorders*, to warn against the application of diagnostic categories, criteria and textual descriptions 'mechanically by untrained individuals'.[79] As the DSM-IV-TR notes, the specific diagnostic criteria are 'meant to serve as guidelines to be informed by clinical judgment and are not meant to be used in a cookbook fashion'. Attempting to use diagnostic manuals without the requisite specialized clinical training may give rise to a degree of 'uncritical diagnostic pigeon-holing'.[80]

Nevertheless, counterbalancing warnings against a too rigid application of diagnostic criteria is the DSM-IV-TR's recognition that these same criteria serve

76 M.T. Pathé and P.E. Mullen, 'The Dangerousness of the DSM-III-R' (1993) 1 *Journal of Law and Medicine* 47, 50.

77 Ibid.

78 Ibid.

79 American Psychiatric Association, *Diagnostic and Statistical Manual of Mental Disorders* (4th edn, text revision, Washington, DC, 2000) xxxii (DSM-IV-TR).

80 Ibid.

as a 'common language for communication'.[81] Similarly, Pathé and Mullen note that cross-clinician consistency in diagnoses has been improved by the extant diagnostic systems.[82] By their very nature diagnostic categories remain in a state of flux and remain open to review and modification as a result of new clinical insights and research. Nevertheless, and notwithstanding this relative state of flux, diagnostic manuals 'reflect a consensus about the classification and diagnosis of mental disorders' at the time of their publication.[83]

Moreover, there is no suggestion in case law that expert evidence will be constituted merely by classificatory diagnostic categories and corresponding criteria. Rather than relying solely on diagnostic manuals, other evidence, such as whether the accused had a motivation in committing the offence, will be considered in determining the ultimate issue. In fact,

> in assessing medical evidence a multitude of factors must be taken into account-including the standing of the expert, whether he expresses his opinion with conviction or with hedging, whether the opinion expressed in its nature seems reasonable or fanciful, whether it incorporates assumptions not founded upon the evidence given, and whether the evidence given, upon which the opinion is based, is to be believed.[84]

Consequently, fears that diagnostic manuals will be used in a mechanical fashion without clinical judgment may be overstated. The acceptance of expert evidence by triers of fact will require more than simply a recounting of diagnostic categories and criteria. The goal of explaining to a jury in a comprehensible fashion the 'experience of madness' will necessitate the expert witness to move beyond the limits of diagnosis alone.

According to Pathé and Mullen another problem in the use of diagnostic manuals such as the DSM-IV-TR or the ICD-10, is that neither manual provides satisfactory means by which to determine legal issues.[85] As the DSM-IV-TR notes, there are significant risks that diagnostic manuals may be misunderstood 'because of the imperfect fit between the questions of ultimate concern to the law and the information contained in a clinical diagnosis'.[86] In Chapter 3, I argued that the fact

81 Ibid. In this context note the use of both the DSM-IV-TR and World Health Organization, *The ICD-10 Classification of Mental and Behavioural Disorders: Clinical Descriptions and Diagnostic Guidelines* (Geneva, 1992) (ICD-10) by the same expert witness (Dr Schineanu) in two different cases involving an accused suffering from paranoid schizophrenia (*The State of Western Australia v Iley* [2006] WASC 107, para [46] (DSM-IV-TR); *The State of Western Australia v Wright* [2007] WASC 80, para [40] (ICD-10)).

82 Pathé and Mullen, 'The Dangerousness of the DSM-III-R' (n. 76) 50.

83 DSM-IV-TR (n. 79) xxxiii.

84 *Chester* (1982) A Crim R 296, 381 per Allan J approved *Hone v The State of Western Australia* [2007] WASCA 283, para 125 per Miller JA.

85 Pathé and Mullen, 'The Dangerousness of the DSM-III-R' (n. 76) 51.

86 DSM-IV-TR (n. 79) xxxiii.

that a state of mental malfunction is recognized as a diagnostic category is only one aspect of the disease of the mind enquiry. In order to establish a disease of the mind, in addition to expert evidence, both a judgment of responsibility will need to be considered as well as social defence concerns addressed. Consequently, a clinical diagnosis of a DSM-IV-TR mental disorder alone will not be sufficient to establish for legal purposes the existence of a disease of the mind.[87]

Moreover, whether the functional impairment experienced by an accused as a result of a disease of the mind will be viewed as exculpatory will be determined on the basis of an individual's capacity to meet a legal standard of non-responsibility. Such a determination cannot be made purely on the basis of a diagnostic category. Diagnostic categories encompass behaviours revealing a great deal of variation from a norm,[88] consequently, the fact that an accused's behaviour corresponds with a diagnostic category does not imply a particular level of impairment. In order to ascertain the level of impairment experienced by an accused, additional information will be required. Such information will establish the nature of the accused's functional impairment in addition to the way in which such impairment affects an accused's ability to exercise such a function.

There is clearly a difference between an expert opinion on how a particular mental disorder may affect an individual in the accused's position and an opinion as to whether or not the particular mental disorder did in fact affect the accused. While the former is a question for an expert witness the latter is a question of fact for a jury to be determined on the basis of expert evidence.[89] For example, in the context of the present chapter, 'even when diminished control over one's behaviour is a feature of the disorder, having the diagnosis in itself does not demonstrate that a particular individual is (or was) unable to control his or her behaviour at a particular time'.[90] Allowing an expert to decide whether an accused has performed the conduct voluntarily would amount to deferring the ultimate issue of his or her guilt or innocence to the expert rather than allowing the jury to decide the issue on the basis of the evidence.[91]

---

87 Ibid.; Pathé and Mullen, 'The Dangerousness of the DSM-III-R' (n. 76) 50.

88 This is the direct result of both the DSM-IV-TR and the ICD-10 adopting a 'categorical' model of classification. Such a classificatory system divides mental disorders into types based on criteria sets with defining features. However, no assumption is made by manuals using a 'categorical' model that all individuals described as having a particular disorder are alike. In fact, the DSM-IV-TR specifically emphasizes the heterogeneous nature of individuals sharing a diagnosis and 'emphasises the need to capture additional clinical information that goes beyond diagnosis' in order to capture the variety of clinical presentations (DSM-IV-TR (n. 79) xxxi, 'Limitations of the Categorical Approach').

89 Victorian Law Reform Commission, *Defences to Homicide: Options Paper* (Melbourne, 2003) 5.162.

90 Ibid.

91 *Haidley* [1984] VR 229, 235 per Young CJ. Though note that the ultimate issue rule has been abolished by s 80 of the Commonwealth *Evidence Act 1995*.

Such consistency has provided un-contradicted expert testimony with a degree of authority in the context of legal determinations. For example, there is ample case law indicating that where there is unchallenged medical evidence of facts which bring an accused person within the provisions of the insanity defence and there is no evidence to cast doubt on such medical evidence, a verdict which fails to give effect to those facts will not be supported by the evidence and will be set aside.[92] While juries are not bound to accept and act upon expert evidence, if there are no facts and no circumstances shown before them which throw doubt on the medical evidence the jury must accept such evidence.[93]

Equally however, where there are facts which would entitle a jury to either reject or differ from the opinion of the expert witness, a jury is not bound to accept the expert evidence. Justice Allan has pointed out:

> There is no rule of law that a verdict of guilty will be quashed as unsafe in any case in which the verdict is inconsistent with medical evidence called for the accused even where no medical evidence has been called for the Crown. Each case is unique. The totality of the evidence must be weighed: *Walton* (1978) AC 788.[94]

A consensus in respect of the classification and diagnosis of mental disorders provides legal determinations based on these disorders with a degree of reliability. The diagnostic manuals allow legal determinations to be made without 'recourse to un-grounded speculation about mental disorders and about the functioning of a particular individual'.[95] Additionally, diagnostic formulations have significant potential application to the dispositional phase of the criminal trial. Determinations at the dispositional phase will require clinical assessments on the basis of the diagnostic criteria in respect of whether the accused poses a further risk and whether he or she is treatable.[96]

Accordingly, despite the criticisms that have been made of the use of diagnostic manuals in the court room they serve the purpose of guiding deliberations. Therefore, the next section will now turn to the relevant diagnostic formulations in the DSM-IV-TR and the ICD-10 in order to explore the connection between certain impulse-control disorders and involuntariness.

---

92 *R v Matusevich* [1976] VR 470, 475 per Smithers J; *Taylor v R* (1978) 45 FLR 343; *R v Dick* [1966] Qd R 301; *Matheson v R* [1958] 1 WLR 474; *R v Michaux* [1984] 2 Qd R 159; *Hall* (1988) 36 A Crim R 368; *Hone v The State of Western Australia* [2007] WASCA 283.

93 *Bailey* (1977) 66 Cr App R 31 per Lord Parker CJ; *Chester* (1982) A Crim R 296, 380–1 per Allan J.

94 *Chester* (1982) A Crim R 296, 308 per Allan J.

95 Ibid.

96 L.L. Foust, 'The Legal Significance of Clinical Formulations of Fire-Setting Behaviour' (1979) 2 *International Journal of Law and Psychiatry* 371, 377.

Impulse-control disorders and involuntariness

One definition used to describe impulse-control disorders is 'harmful behaviours performed in response to *irresistible* impulses'.[97] The DSM-IV-TR however adopts a more cautious approach to the question of the characterization of such disorders. The essential feature of impulse-control disorders according to the DSM-IV-TR is

> the *failure to resist* an impulse, drive, or temptation to perform an act that is harmful to the person or to others. The person feels an increasing sense of tension or arousal before committing the act and then experiences pleasure, gratification, or relief at the time of committing the act. Following the act there may or may not be regret, self-reproach, or guilt.[98]

The DSM-IV-TR classifies impulse-control disorders residually as 'Impulse Control Disorders Not Elsewhere Classified'.[99] Such classification ensures that only 'disorders of impulse control that are not classified as part of the presentation of disorders in other sections of the manual' are noted.[100] The ICD-10 classifies impulse-control disorders under the rubric of 'Habit and Impulse Disorders'.[101] The ICD-10 also defines such disorders residually as those

> behavioural disorders that are not classifiable under other rubrics. They are characterized by repeated acts that have no clear rational motivation and that generally harm the patient's own interests and those of other people. The patient reports that the behaviour is associated with impulses to action that *cannot be controlled*.[102]

What is immediately apparent from the above three definitions of impulse-control disorders is the lack of a clear definition. While the first definition from the *New Oxford Textbook of Psychiatry* highlights the irresistible nature of these disorders, the DSM-IV-TR describes the essential feature of such disorders as involving a failure to resist. The ICD-10 defines impulse-control disorders as (self-reported) behaviour that cannot be controlled. Rather than 'providing a consensus in respect of the classification and diagnosis of mental disorders' as I have argued for above, the ambivalence expressed by these diagnostic and classificatory manuals in respect of the definitional features of impulse-control disorders provides reason

97 S. McElroy and P.E. Keck Jr, 'Habit and Impulse Control Disorders' in *New Oxford Textbook of Psychiatry*, ed. M.G. Gelder et al. (2nd edn, Oxford, 2009) 911, 911, emphasis added.

98 DSM-IV-TR (n. 79) 663.

99 Ibid. (emphasis added).

100 Ibid.

101 ICD-10 (n. 81) 211, 'F63 Habit and Impulse Disorders'.

102 Ibid. (emphasis added).

for concern.[103] Indeed, it has been remarked in respect of the varieties of impulse-control disorders that 'whatever, the clinical value of such classifications, none of these conditions has been established as a separate diagnostic entity'.[104] However, such concern may be overstated in the context of impulse-control disorders. Notwithstanding the variety of disorders recognized by the above diagnostic manuals as forming part of the classification of impulse-control disorders, current research indicates that such disorders share several common features. These features include 'in addition to irresistible impulses to perform harmful behaviours, features of trait impulsivity, trait compulsivity, and mood dysregulation, as well as obsessive compulsive mood, and addictive disorders'.[105] Moreover, McElroy and Keck conclude their analysis of impulse-control disorders by noting that:

> Growing research shows that the impulse control disorders are much more common than once thought to be. The consistency of the 'structure' of the irresistible impulse (a core disturbance of impulsivity and compulsivity) together with increasing research showing that it responds to certain treatments regardless of its 'content' (the specific impulse experienced), strongly suggest that it is an important psychopathological symptom, and that impulse control disorders are legitimate mental disorders that are in fact likely to be related despite their apparent differences.[106]

While there is ambivalence in respect of whether such conditions preclude an individual's capacity to control his or her conduct, this is not to deny the veracity of these conditions but merely to highlight the current state of uncertainty concerning their diagnostic criteria. For example, it has been remarked that in respect of the DSM-IV-TR criteria for pyromania 'the validity of this diagnostic criteria is unsubstantiated'.[107] However, the reason for this lack of substantiation is due to the fact that there are no 'systematic reports of a group of people with pyromania by [DSM-IV-TR and ICD-10] criteria sets'.[108] Nevertheless the clinical record indicates that

---

103 See *The State of Western Australia v Iley* [2006] WASC 107, para 58 per Johnson J, expressing concern as to the validity of psychiatric diagnosis where an accused seemingly has the capacity to deliberately mislead a qualified psychiatrist into believing that he was not experiencing symptoms though ultimately finding that it would be more difficult for such an accused 'to satisfy a psychiatrist that he was suffering from a symptomatic … illness when he was not'.

104 M. Gelder, P. Harrison and P. Cowen, *Shorter Oxford Textbook of Psychiatry* (5th edn, Oxford, 2006) 736.

105 McElroy and Keck Jr, 'Habit and Impulse Control Disorders' (n. 97) 911.

106 Ibid. 918.

107 DSM-IV-TR (n. 79) 671: Diagnostic criteria for impulse control disorder 312.33 'Pyromania', in *New Oxford Textbook of Psychiatry*, ed. M.G. Gelder et al. (n. 97) 744.

108 McElroy and Keck Jr, 'Habit and Impulse Control Disorders' (n. 97) 914.

> 'there are numerous case reports and case series of people with repetitive fire-setting behaviour who would probably meet these criteria for pyromania'.[109]

Consequently, any ambivalence in respect of the diagnostic criteria may be attributed to the current paucity of epidemiological studies, rather than contradictory understanding of the relevant criteria by various diagnostic and clinical manuals.

In the context of impulse-control disorders, it is apparent from the relevant psychiatric evidence that the criminal law is confronted by certain epistemic constraints. In particular, the criminal law attempts to distinguish between impulses which could be resisted but were not, from those which could not be resisted, that is, instances of impulsivity from compulsivity. I have suggested above that, as a matter of caution where psychiatric evidence is ambivalent in respect of the diagnostic criteria of a particular condition, it is incumbent on the criminal law to make provision for any resulting contingency on this basis. That is, until the precise nature of the diagnostic criteria of impulse-control disorders is established, the law should be prepared, as a matter of principle, to provide a defence. The provision of a defence for involuntary conduct arising from a state of mental disorder will act as a safeguard in the event that the diagnostic criteria of impulse-control disorders suggesting compulsion (irresistible impulse) are subsequently shown to be correct. However, even if the definitional criteria of impulse-control disorders are shown not to include instances of involuntary conduct but merely states of impulsivity on the part of individuals, the provision of the above defence will not be problematic. In such a case the existence of a law excusing involuntary conduct will merely prove to be redundant for individuals suffering from an impulse-control disorder given that such involuntariness is not a diagnostic feature of the condition.

Both the DSM-IV-TR and the ICD-10 include as instances of impulse-control disorders, intermittent explosive disorder, kleptomania (pathological stealing), pyromania (pathological fire-setting), pathological gambling, trichotillomania (pathological hair-pulling).[110] Further, both the DSM-IV-TR and the ICD-10 recognize a category of unspecified impulse disorders.[111] Of the extant types of impulse-control disorders recognized psychiatrically, the disorder of pyromania will be used by way of example in the ensuing discussion. A reason for preferring this variety of impulse-control disorder to another variety such as, for example, kleptomania, is that pyromania has far greater potential for large-scale harm to both person and property than most acts of stealing. As a result, there is a cogent reason why an individual who is charged with arson resulting in large-scale destruction or death would entertain raising the defence of insanity. Notwithstanding the prospect

---

109 Ibid.

110 DSM-IV-TR (n. 79) 663–77; ICD-10 (n. 81) 211–14.

111 DSM-IV-TR (n. 79) 677, 'Impulse Control Disorder Not Otherwise Specified'; ICD-10 (n. 81) 214, 'F 63.9: Habit and Impulse Disorder, Unspecified'.

of an indefinite or nominal term in a secure facility resulting from a successful insanity plea, such an individual may feel that this represents a more attractive alternative than the prospect of a proportional criminal sanction resulting from a finding of guilt. In contrast, an individual who is charged with an act of stealing will be unlikely to raise an insanity defence given that the consequences attendant upon a finding of insanity would, in most instances, prove to be more onerous than a proportionate criminal sanction following a finding of guilt.

Another reason for preferring pyromania as an example of an impulse-control disorder is the view that not all varieties of impulse-control disorders are suitable candidates for consideration as instances of volitional insanity. For example, while intermittent explosive disorder is a recognized category of impulse-control disorder, it paradigmatically involves a motivated response arising from a perceived threat to one partner's control of another. As I will argue in Chapter 6, where an individual makes a choice for a reason and decides to act on that reason, there is a rebuttable presumption that he or she has acted voluntarily. While such states may amount to instances of volitional impairment, they do not necessarily involve the complete loss of control demanded of cases of volitional insanity. Moreover, where an individual acts for a reason, such a reason is open to critical moral evaluation. Chapter 6 will provide examples which reveal that in keeping with certain excusatory defences in modern criminal law, an accused will be provided with a defence where the reasons for which he or she acts are found to be good reasons. The use of force in response to the threat of losing control of one's partner would not be considered to be a good reason.[112] Hence, for public-policy reasons the diagnostic category of intermittent explosive disorder should not be characterized as a disease of the mind. The recognition of intermittent explosive disorders as a disease of the mind grounding a defence of volitional insanity would challenge the public expectation that citizens must in general take personal responsibility for their conduct. The diagnostic category of pyromania does not raise the above issues and consequently will be used by way of example in the ensuing discussion.

Diagnostic category: pyromania

The offence of deliberate fire-setting, or the crime of arson, is a serious crime as it presents a threat to both property and life. The cost of arson in Australia has been calculated to be in the vicinity of $157m every year in direct property losses alone.[113] It has been noted in both England and Australia that there has

112 See B. McSherry, 'Men Behaving Badly: Current Issues in Provocation, Automatism, Mental Impairment and Criminal Responsibility' (2005) 12 *Psychiatry, Psychology and Law* 15.

113 R. Doley, 'Pyromania: Fact or Fiction?' (2003) 43 *The British Journal of Criminology* 781, citing Insurance Council of Australia, *Research into Insurance Fraud: Member Survey 1996/1997* (Sydney, 1998).

been an increase in the number of fires deliberately lit, with one arson fire being deliberately lit 'every hour of every day'.[114] A longitudinal study of convicted arsonists found that about 10 per cent of offenders were re-convicted for arson over the course of a 20-year follow-up period.[115]

One particular classification of arsonists distinguishes between three different groups:

> 1. Fire-setters who are free from psychiatric disorder and who start fires for financial or political reasons or for revenge: they are sometimes referred to as motivated arsonists.
>
> 2. So-called pathological fire-setters, who suffer from learning difficulties, mental illness, or alcoholism. This group accounts for about 10–15 per cent of arsons.
>
> 3. A third group who meet DSM-IV criteria for pyromania. These individuals obtain intense satisfaction and tension relief from fire-setting.[116]

It has been remarked by Doley that 'the main reason the pyromaniac differs from other arsonists is because they do not have a conscious motivation for their fire-setting, but are responding instead to what is described as an "irresistible impulse" to light fires'.[117] The diagnostic criteria for impulse-control disorder 312.33, pyromania, are as follows:

> A. Deliberate and purposeful fire setting on more than one occasion.
>
> B. Tension or affective arousal before the act.
>
> C. Fascination with, interest in, curiosity about, or attraction to fire and its situational contexts (e.g. paraphernalia, uses, consequences).

114 R. Doley, 'Pyromania: Fact or Fiction?' (n. 113) 781; H. Prins, 'Arson (Fire-Raising)' in *New Oxford Textbook of Psychiatry*, ed. M.G. Gelder et al. (2nd edn, Oxford, 2009) 1965, noting that 'the latest figures indicate a continuing worrying number of deliberate fires – some 91200 in 2004 … [while] figures from the Association of British Insurers (ABI) indicate "that the cost of commercial fire claims in 2005 was 791 million pounds" – a record'.

115 K. Soothill, E. Ackerley and B. Francis, 'The Criminal Careers of Arsonists' (2004) 44 *Medicine, Science and the Law* 27, cited in Prins, 'Arson (Fire-Raising)' (n. 114) 1968.

116 Gelder, Harrison and Cowen, *Shorter Oxford Textbook of Psychiatry* (n. 104) 744.

117 Doley, 'Pyromania: Fact or Fiction?' (n. 113) 800, citing A.O. Rider, 'The Firesetter: A Psychological Profile' (1980) 49 *FBI Law Enforcement Bulletin* 7.

> D. Pleasure, gratification, or relief when setting fires, or when witnessing or participating in their aftermath.
>
> E. The fire setting is not done for monetary gain, as an expression of socio-political ideology, to conceal criminal activity, to express anger or vengeance, to improve one's living circumstances, in response to a delusion or hallucination, or as a result of impaired judgment (e.g. Dementia, Mental Retardation, Substance Intoxication).
>
> F. The fire setting is not better accounted for by Conduct Disorder, a Manic Episode, or Antisocial Personality Disorder.[118]

Criterion A highlights the recurrent nature of the fire-setting in the context of pyromania in order to distinguish such fire-setting from other motivated acts of fire-setting. Criteria B, C and D distinguish the features of pyromania which account for its being characterized as an impulse-control disorder. Criteria E and F clarify the context in which pyromania may occur, so as to ensure that fire-setting that occurs in association with other mental disorders is excluded from the clinical definition of pyromania.

The ICD-10 defines pathological fire-setting as multiple acts of, or attempts at, setting fire to property or other objects, without apparent motive, in addition to a persistent preoccupation with subjects related to fire and burning.[119] The essential features of pyromania are:

> Repeated fire-setting without any obvious motive such as monetary gain, revenge, or political extremism;
> An intense interest in watching fires burn;
> Reported feelings of increasing tension before the act, and intense excitement immediately after it has been carried out.[120]

Epidemiological studies have revealed various rates of prevalence depending on the definition employed. In the largest study of pathological fire-setting conducted to date, 1,145 American case records of males 16 years of age and older were studied. The authors reported that 688 (60 per cent) could be classified as having broadly defined pyromania, but only 50 (4 per cent) as having the 'true' disorder.[121]

---

118 DSM-IV-TR (n. 79) 671. Pyromania appeared in the first edition of DSM (1952) as a supplementary term, disappearing completely in DSM-II (1968); reappearing under the category of 'Impulse Control Disorders Not Elsewhere Classified' in DSM-III (1980), DSM-III-R (1987), DSM-IV (1994) and in the current revision DSM-IV-TR (2000).

119 ICD-10 (n. 81) 212.

120 Ibid. 213.

121 McElroy and Keck Jr, 'Habit and Impulse Control Disorders' (n. 97) 914, citing N.D.C. Lewis and H. Yarnell, *Pathological Firesetting (Pyromania)*, Nervous and Mental

Of the 50 who 'approached true pyromania' they were able to give a 'classical description of the irresistible impulse' with subjects self-reporting that before they set fires there was 'mounting tension; restlessness; the urge for motion; conversion symptoms such as headaches, palpitations, ringing in the ears, and the gradual merging of their identity into a state of unreality'.[122] Studies suggest that pyromania is probably more common in males than females and usually begins in adolescence or early adulthood.[123] A review of the relevant literature reveals that the reported instance of pyromania is increasingly infrequent with the bulk of evidence supporting the view that there is a 'relatively rare incidence of the disorder'.[124] Nevertheless, all such evidence is subject to both definitional and methodological bias.[125] For example, as the definition of pyromania becomes increasingly focused, fewer arsonists will be characterized as pathological fire-setters. Further, if known arsonists form the sample group then, given that a large number of instances of arson remain unsolved, the sample group cannot be representative of the general population of arsonists most of who remain undetected.[126]

On the basis of clinical descriptions the course of pyromania may be either episodic or chronic.[127] To date there are no systematic treatment studies of pyromania.[128]

In the next section I will argue for the recognition of an independent volitional limb using by way of example the case of pyromania.

Pyromania and volitional insanity

As currently understood, at common law, even if an impulse-control disorder such as pyromania is recognized as a disease of the mind, the defence will fail unless the involuntary conduct arising from mental disorder is symptomatic of a cognitive

Disease Monograph 82 (New York: Coolidge Foundation, 1951).

122 McElroy and Keck Jr, 'Habit and Impulse Control Disorders' (n. 97) 914.

123 M. Leyoux, M. McLoughlin and J. Ades, 'Pyromania' in *Clinical Manual of Impulse Control Disorders*, ed. J. Hollander and D.J. Stein (Arlington, VA, 2006) 229, 231.

124 Doley, 'Pyromania: Fact or Fiction?' (n. 113) 801, 'Table 1: Reported Prevalence of Pyromania in the Psychiatric and Arson Literature' and references.

125 Ibid. 802–5; for an appraisal of methodological flaws afflicting earlier studies of pathological fire-setting thereby precluding sound epidemiologic conclusions, see J.L. Geller, J. Erlen and P. J. Pinkus, 'A Historical Appraisal of America's Experience with "Pyromania": A Diagnosis in Search of a Disorder' (1986) 9 *International Journal of Law and Psychiatry*, 201, 212.

126 Doley, 'Pyromania: Fact or Fiction?' (n. 113) 803–4, 'Figure 1: Number of Arson Offences Reported to Police Compared to Number of Arson Offences Cleared'.

127 Ibid.

128 S.L. McElroy and P.E. Keck Jr, 'Impulse Control Disorders' in *Gabbard's Treatments of Psychiatric Disorders*, ed. G.O. Gabbard (4th edn, Arlington, VA, 2007) 877, 880.

defect. In this section, I will argue that where such involuntary conduct arises independently of a cognitive defect from a mental disorder that is characterized as a disease of the mind the defence of insanity should be available. That is, where an individual who suffers from a disease of the mind is rendered incapable of voluntary conduct, even where he or she knows the nature and wrongness of his or her act, the defence of insanity should be acknowledged at common law. In particular, I will argue that an individual suffering from pyromania may know the nature, quality and wrongness of his or her act and yet nevertheless act involuntarily as a result of a mental disorder.

I will begin by positing that, if an individual suffers from pyromania, the best explanation for his or her repeated acts of fire-setting is that they are performed involuntarily. I will then argue that, even though such an individual's acts of fire-setting are performed involuntarily, he or she may know the nature, quality and wrongness of his or her act. I will end this section by noting the extent to which pyromania satisfies the relevant aspects of the disease of the mind enquiry as formulated in Chapter 3 above.

Involuntary conduct

While some writers have doubted the existence of individuals who satisfy the diagnostic category of pyromania,[129] others have more cautiously remarked that 'the validity of [the] diagnostic criteria is unsubstantiated'.[130] Such responses are in keeping with what was referred to above as the ambivalence expressed by diagnostic manuals in respect of the definitional features of impulse-control disorders in general. However, as indicated at that point, such ambivalence may be ascribed to a paucity of epidemiological studies rather than to contradictory understandings of the relevant criteria associated with the disorders. Nevertheless, the fact remains that there is a degree of uncertainty in respect of both the existence of individuals suffering from pyromania and, as a result, the validity of the criteria of this diagnostic category.

In the light of such controversy I will begin by distinguishing between two distinct claims: one empirical, the other theoretical. The empirical claim involves the assertion that there are individuals in the world who satisfy the diagnostic criteria of the diagnostic category of pyromania. In contrast, the theoretical claim proceeds on the conditional basis that 'if there are individuals in the world who satisfy the diagnostic criteria of pyromania then the view that they are acting involuntarily is the best explanation of their behavior'. In recognition of the uncertainty surrounding the existence of individuals who satisfy the diagnostic category, the argument presented below will proceed on a conditional basis. The

129 Geller, Erlen and Pinkus, 'A Historical Appraisal of America's Experience with "Pyromania"' (n. 125) 201 and references.

130 Gelder, Harrison and Cowen, *Shorter Oxford Textbook of Psychiatry* (n. 104) 744.

conditional basis of the claim is designed to allay concerns associated with the existence of individuals who both satisfy and validate the diagnostic criteria associated with pyromania. By proceeding on a conditional basis the argument recognizes and responds to the possible objection that there are no instances of fire-setting in the world which constitute pyromania. Moreover, the conditional argument also acknowledges that if there are instances of pyromania in the world, then the law should be able to provide for such a contingency and provide an accused suffering from such a condition with a defence where such a defence is warranted.

Consequently, by arguing on a conditional basis, I am not to be taken to be asserting that there are individuals in the world whose repeated acts of fire-setting satisfy the criteria associated with the diagnostic category of pyromania. There may in fact be no individuals in the world at large who do satisfy the necessary criteria for pyromania. However it is not a part of my argument that such individuals do in fact exist. Consequently, the mere assertion that there are no cases of fire-starting that involve individuals who suffer from pyromania in the real world is not a counter-argument to my view. Whether there are such individuals remains an empirical question to be answered by experts. What I am proposing is a best-explanation account of the behaviour of individuals who satisfy the diagnostic criteria of pyromania, if such individuals are found to exist in the world. As such my argument is to be taken as providing a theoretical point in respect of the behaviour of individual fire-setters given the possibility that such individuals exist and satisfy the diagnostic criteria of pyromania.

According to the diagnostic criteria associated with the diagnostic category of pyromania an individual who suffers from pyromania will engage in repeated acts of fire-setting characterized by 'deliberate and purposeful fire setting on more than one occasion'.[131] As noted earlier, this particular criterion highlights the recurrent nature of the fire-setting in the context of pyromania in order to distinguish such fire-setting from other acts of fire-setting. As expressed in the DSM-IV-TR a further diagnostic feature of pyromania is that 'the fire setting is not done for monetary gain, as an expression of socio-political ideology, to conceal criminal activity, to express anger or vengeance, to improve one's living circumstances'.[132] Similarly, the ICD-10 notes that an essential feature of pyromania is 'repeated fire-setting without any obvious motive such as monetary gain, revenge, or political extremism'.[133] It is, according to the diagnostic manuals, the absence of any obvious or characteristic motivation for personal or financial gain which further defines the repeated acts of fire-setting by an individual who suffers from the diagnostic category of pyromania. That is, one of the diagnostic features of pyromania is a lack of characteristic motivation on the part of an individual

---

131 DSM-IV-TR (n. 79) 671; ICD-10 (n. 81) 212, remarks on instances of 'repeated fire-setting' as a defining characteristic of pyromania.

132 DSM-IV-TR (n. 79) 671.

133 ICD-10 (n. 81) 212.

engaging in repeated acts of fire-setting. According to the diagnostic manuals, an individual who suffers from pyromania does not set fires for personal use or for monetary gain. Additionally, such an individual does not engage in repeated acts of fire-setting in order to express anger or for vengeance.

However, given the absence of an obvious motive such as that found in instances of personal or financial gain, it may be asked: why would an individual choose to engage in repeated acts of fire-setting unless he or she is motivated by a specific and characteristic reason for such behaviour? This chapter will argue that the best explanation of the diagnostic criterion of a lack of obvious or characteristic motivation for personal or financial gain for repeated acts of fire-setting committed by individuals who suffer from pyromania is that such acts are instances of involuntary conduct arising from a state of mental disorder. The above explanation is merely a hypothesis as to why an individual who satisfies the diagnostic criteria of pyromania might, in the absence of an obvious or characteristic motivation for personal or financial gain, engage in repeated acts of fire-setting. Consequently, the following conditional claim will be made:

> If there is an individual who satisfies the relevant criteria of the diagnostic category of pyromania, the best explanation for the lack of obvious or characteristic motivation for his or her repeated acts of fire-setting is that such acts are instances of involuntary conduct arising from a state of mental disorder.

What is not being asserted is the empirical claim that there are such individuals in the world. Succinctly stated the reason for making the conditional claim is that all the other obvious explanations, or motivations, in respect of an accused's repeated acts of fire-setting, are ruled out by the diagnostic criteria. If all the obvious motivations for such acts are ruled out, what else is left but involuntariness arising from a state of mental disorder?

One other matter that warrants discussion at this point is the evidentiary issue of whether an individual who is found to satisfy the diagnostic criteria is in fact acting involuntarily or merely choosing not to. It was noted above that an objection raised to the characterization of such volitional disorders as diseases of the mind in order to ground a defence of insanity is the difficulty of distinguishing an individual who chooses not to exercise his or her capacity to refrain from acting from an individual who lacks the capacity to refrain from acting. In respect of the conduct of an individual who suffers from pyromania, any evidentiary concerns in determining whether his or her conduct is in fact involuntary or whether he or she is merely refusing to act voluntarily may be overstated. In the case of pyromania, any difficulty in distinguishing between instances of irresistible impulse and instances where impulses were not resisted may be ameliorated by virtue of the diagnostic criteria associated with this particular category. For example, in the instance of an accused who claims to have started a fire as a result of pyromania, where such behaviour arises with a view to, for example, personal or monetary gain a necessary condition of the disorder is not met. In such an instance, it may be said that there is clear prima facie proof of criminality rather than behaviour symptomatic of pyromania. While not conclusive, the diagnostic criteria operate as a side-constraint in such instances by providing relatively stringent evidentiary hurdles which an accused must satisfy before being allowed to raise the defence. Consequently, any concerns as to whether the recognition of pyromania as a disease of the mind will result in the opening of the floodgates to unworthy claimants may be unfounded.

To reiterate, it has been noted that according to the relevant diagnostic manuals, a key diagnostic feature of pyromania is a lack of motivation for personal or financial gain for the repeated acts of fire-setting caused by an individual, if any, suffering from this condition. It has been claimed that the best explanation for such repeated acts of fire-setting which occur notwithstanding the absence of any obvious motivation is that these acts are involuntary acts due to a mental disorder. In support of this claim it has been argued that given the absence of a characteristic motivation for personal or financial gain no other obvious explanation presents itself in order to account for such repeated acts of fire-setting.

However, one possible objection presents itself in respect of the claim that the repeated acts of fire-setting associated with the diagnostic category occur in the absence of any obvious motive. It has been suggested that in an attempt to avoid the unpleasant aspects of dysphoria associated with rising tension, an individual suffering from pyromania may be motivated to succumb to an impulse to start a fire.[134] On this account it is said that where an individual experiences the effects of pyromania, he or she has a motive for his or her acts of repeated fire-setting.[135] The following response may be made in respect of this objection.

While the claim that an attempt to escape any unpleasantness associated with dysphoria may aim to provide an individual with a motivation for his or her repeated acts of fire-setting, such a claim fails to explain the onset of the state of dysphoria itself. The state of dysphoria experienced by an individual suffering from pyromania according to the diagnostic manuals is not chosen by such an individual. That is, the state of dysphoria arises independently of the exercise of an individual's will and is for this reason involuntary. Hence, the suggestion that the repeated acts of fire-setting are explicable in terms of an individual's avoidance of the unpleasant effects of a dysphoric state merely moves the issue of the voluntariness of such acts of fire-setting back one step: it does not show these acts of fire-setting themselves to be voluntary. If in fact the dysphoria is of such a degree of severity as to compel an individual to engage in repeated acts of fire-setting, he or she is again acting involuntarily. Moreover, as discussed in the context of drug-induced psychosis in Chapter 4, given that the acts of fire-setting do not arise through his or her fault, the state of dysphoria arising involuntarily, he or she cannot be held responsible for such acts. Alternatively, if in fact the degree of severity is not as great as to compel an individual to engage in repeated acts

134 Morse, 'Diminished Capacity' (n. 73) 256.

135 Ibid.

of fire-setting then this would suggest that the individual fire-setter has acted in a voluntary fashion in lighting the fires. On this alternative the objection is made out as there is motivation for the repeated acts of fire-setting which are undertaken voluntarily.

However, the above analysis highlights the empirical nature of the objection made by those who claim that it is an attempt to flee from a state of dsyphoria which motivates the pathological fire-setter's actions. In particular, the objection is seen to be reliant on the existence of a causal connection between an accused's experience of an involuntary state of dysphoria and his or her repeated acts of fire-setting. Hence, before the objection may be made, it would need to be established that the repeated acts of fire-setting by the individual are explicable by his or her attempt to escape from the unpleasant experience of this state of dysphoria. Where the effects of the dysphoria are so severe as to compel an individual to light a fire, the act of fire-setting itself remains involuntary. It is only where the effects of dysphoria fall short of compulsion and cause the individual fire-setter to act voluntarily that the objection is established. However, nothing has been shown to indicate that the repeated acts of fire-setting themselves are not involuntary and do not arise independently of an individual's experience of dysphoria.

Both the DSM-IV-TR and the ICD-10 readily acknowledge a state of dysphoria as a criterion of pyromania.[136] According to the DSM-IV-TR, an individual with this disorder will experience:

> B. Tension or affective arousal before the act.
>
> D. Pleasure, gratification, or relief when setting fires, or when witnessing or participating in their aftermath.[137]

The ICD-10 notes as part of the diagnostic guidelines for pyromania the following 'essential feature':

> (c) reported feelings of increasing tension before the act, and intense excitement immediately after it has been carried out.[138]

According to these diagnostic manuals an individual who suffers from pyromania may experience a state of dysphoria associated with rising tension and affective

136 DSM-IV-TR (n. 79) 671; ICD-10 (n. 81) 211; see also McElroy and P.E. Keck Jr, 'Habit and Impulse Control Disorders' (n. 97) 914, citing Lewis and Yarnell, *Pathological Firesetting (Pyromania)*, who note as a 'classic description' the following account provided by pathological fire-setters: 'mounting tension; ... restlessness; the urge for motion; ... conversion symptoms such as headaches, palpitations, ringing in the ears, and the gradual merging of their identity into a state of unreality'.

137 DSM-IV-TR (n. 79) 671.

138 ICD-10 (n. 81) 213.

arousal. There is certainly nothing in the diagnostic manuals to suggest that an accused's repeated acts of fire-setting are caused by an attempt to evade the unpleasant effects of the dysphoria. Indeed, there is no reason to doubt that such an accused engages in repeated acts of fire-setting because he or she has no choice but to start a fire, that is acts involuntarily, due to a state of mental disorder.

However, the fact that conduct is involuntary is not sufficient to establish the need for the provision of an independent volitional limb. In addition to involuntary conduct on the part of an individual, it must be also shown that such involuntariness arises independently of a relevant cognitive defect. The question of whether an individual suffering from pyromania knows both, the nature, quality and wrongness of his or her act will be considered next.

Lack of cognitive incapacity

As discussed in Chapter 3, severe conditions of mental disorder which are provided with an Axis I classification by the DSM-IV-TR are characterized by some form of severe psychological dysfunction.[139] In particular, instances of mental impairment will be characterized by a thought disorder such as, for example, psychosis. The DSM-IV-TR has accorded such psychotic disorders an 'Axis I' diagnostic category.[140] This may be seen in the case of a paradigmatic instance of psychotic disorder such as schizophrenia. The DSM-IV-TR defines the differential diagnosis of such a disorder as including psychotic symptoms. Psychosis 'refers to delusions, any prominent hallucinations, disorganized speech, or disorganized or catatonic behavior'.[141] According to the DSM-IV-TR, a delusion is defined as: 'a false belief based on incorrect inference about external reality … [in the face of] incontrovertible proof or evidence to the contrary'.[142] A hallucination is defined as 'a sensory perception that has the compelling sense of reality of a true perception but that occurs without external stimulation of the relevant sensory organ'.[143] How do the above characteristics of mental disorder relate to an individual who might suffer from a condition such as pyromania? In particular, does such an individual know the nature, quality and wrongness of his or her act as required by the criminal law?

Pyromania is considered to be an Axis 1 clinical disorder according to the DSM-IV-TR which, along with psychotic disorders, are characterized by mental or emotional symptoms of a more clinically significant nature.[144] As described in the diagnostic criteria, one particular criterion (E) used to establish the existence of pyromania stipulates that 'the fire starting is not done … in response to a delusion

139 DSM-IV (n. 79) 28.
140 Ibid.
141 Ibid. 821.
142 Ibid.
143 Ibid. 823.
144 Ibid. 327.

or hallucination, or as a result of impaired judgment'. As noted earlier criterion E (along with criterion F) clarifies the context in which pyromania may occur in order to ensure that fire-setting that occurs in association with other mental disorders is excluded from the clinical definition of pyromania. That is, an individual suffering from pyromania does not experience paradigmatic psychotic symptoms, such as delusions and hallucinations resulting in an incapacity on his or her part to engage reality. Consequently, an individual suffering from pyromania does not experience perceptual errors or draw 'false beliefs on the basis of incorrect inferences about reality' which are the hallmarks of delusional thinking. An individual who suffers from pyromania may be said to know both the nature and quality of the act of fire-setting. That is, such an individual appreciates both 'the physical thing he [or she] was doing and its consequences'.[145]

Is an individual suffering from pyromania incapable of thinking rationally about whether his or her act is morally wrong? It is not part of the diagnostic criteria of pyromania that an individual suffering from this disorder will be precluded from appreciating that his or her act would be morally condemned. That is, there is nothing to suggest that there is a failure of public agreement between such an individual's intra-subjective and inter-subjective meanings. In fact the capacity of fire-setters to avoid detection is indicative (though not conclusive) of the fact that they at least know that their act is legally, if not morally, wrong. However, this is only one aspect of this limb of the argument.

Another aspect concerning an individual's capacity to think rationally of the normative implications of his or her act concerns the consequent state of dysphoria associated with rising tension on the part of a person suffering from pyromania. A severe level of dysphoria resulting from a state of rising tension might lead an individual not to be able to think with a moderate degree of sense and composure about the reasons which make his or her act wrong.[146] That is, there is clearly a sense in which an individual may, through an intense state of dysphoria due to increasing tension or affective arousal, fail to think clearly about the moral consequences of his or her actions. In such a case, he or she may be said to lack the capacity to 'reason about the matter with a moderate degree of sense and composure' and therefore lack the capacity to know that his or her act is wrong.[147] Both the DSM-IV-TR and the ICD-10 acknowledge such a state of dysphoria as a criterion of pyromania.[148]

However, if the absence of a moderate degree of sense and composure on the part of an accused is taken literally as amounting to an excuse it would seem to be a condition which would be easy to satisfy. For example, on such an approach

---

145 *R v Porter* (1933) 55 CLR 182, 189 per Dixon J.

146 As formulated by Dixon J in *Porter* (1933) 55 CLR 182 approved *Stapleton* (1952) 86 CLR 358.

147 See *Criminal Code* (Cth) s 7.3(1)(b); *Crimes (Mental Impairment and Unfitness to be Tried) Act 1997* (Vic) s 20(1)(b).

148 DSM-IV-TR (n. 79) 671; ICD-10 (n. 81) 211.

an individual such as the defendant in *Sebalj's* case (explored in Chapter 4) would be excused without recourse to a drug-induced-psychosis argument.[149] Bronitt and McSherry remark that while there is no guidance in either the legislation or case law as to the meaning of the expression 'moderate degree of sense and composure', it would seem to accord with the 'defect of reason' requirement in the M'Naghten rules.[150] Nevertheless, certain observations may be made in respect of the proposed literal application of the expression. Taking the expression 'moderate degree of sense and composure' literally would result in excusing those mental conditions covered by the partial defence of diminished responsibility. However, the fact that the partial defence of diminished responsibility is not recognized in Victoria suggests that a literal interpretation of the expression 'moderate degree of sense and composure' is not one which would find favour with the courts.[151] Further, the relative narrowness of 'what is already a very restrictive defence' would suggest that courts have not interpreted the requirement of 'a moderate degree of sense and composure' literally.[152] Consequently, there is no reason to believe that a state of dysphoria associated with rising tension on the part of an individual suffering from pyromania would be interpreted as sufficient to preclude rational thought and thereby excuse.

Pyromania and disease of the mind

In Chapter 3, I argued for an account of disease of the mind which is informed by several factors: a judgment of responsibility, social-defence considerations and expert evidence.[153] In this section I will consider the potential effects that characterizing pyromania as a disease of the mind will have on the various aspects of the disease of the mind enquiry. I begin with the judgment of responsibility.

Judgment of responsibility The moral aspect of the judgment of responsibility holds that an accused who lacks the requisite capacities for responsible behaviour due to a mental disorder that is not attributable to his or her fault or nature should not be punished for engaging in criminal behaviour. A pre-condition of responsible behaviour is the capacity for voluntary conduct. Where there is an absence of

149 *R v Sebalj* [2003] VSC 181.

150 Bronitt and McSherry, *Principles of Criminal Law* (n. 37) 248.

151 See ibid. 315-21; the VLRC recommended against the introduction of the defence in Victoria in its most recent *Defences to Homicide: Final Report* Report No 94, (Melbourne, 2004), 243, 'Recommendation 45'.

152 Yeo, 'The Insanity Defence in the Criminal Laws of the Commonwealth of Nations' (n. 70) 248, citing G. Ferguson, 'The Insanity Defence in Canada, Malaysia and Singapore: A Tale of Two Codes' (1990) 17 *Journal of Malaysian and Comparative Law* 1, 12; see *R v Mills* [2005] NSW CCA 175, para [57]–[61].

153 See D. Greig, *Neither Mad nor Bad: The Competing Discourses of Psychiatry, Law and Politics* (London, 2002).

voluntariness that has not been brought about through an internal state due to the fault or nature of an accused, it would not be morally justified to punish him or her as he or she cannot guide his or her behaviour in accordance with the law. Hence, if it could be established that an individual suffering from pyromania has a clinically recognized disorder not attributable to his or her fault or nature that in fact causes him or her to act in an involuntary fashion, the moral aspect of the judgment of responsibility would be satisfied. In such an instance a state of involuntariness arising from pyromania will give rise to the responsibility judgment that holds an individual non-responsible for involuntary acts. The question of whether pyromania does in fact result in a lack of capacity on the part of an accused to act in a voluntary fashion has been discussed in the previous section. I have contended there that the best explanation of the conduct of an individual who suffers from pyromania is that such behaviour is involuntary. Consequently, on the best-explanation approach, the recognition of pyromania as a disease of the mind would not run counter to the judgment of responsibility aspect of the disease of the mind enquiry.

Expert evidence Clinical evidence will assist in determining both the meaning of 'disease of the mind' and whether in fact the evidence is capable of supporting an accused's claim. While not conclusive, clinical evidence will assist the court in determining whether a condition satisfies the disease of the mind enquiry by detailing the symptoms, nature and causes of the accused's condition. Further, expert evidence will provide an outline of the precise manifestations of various types of mental malfunctioning. In this way the clinical evidence will assist the trier of fact in establishing whether the accused's conduct at the time of the offence was attributable to such mental malfunctioning. Further, the clinical expertise with which diagnostic categories are applied to individuals is an aspect of psychiatry's therapeutic rationale. Such expertise allows expert evidence to be employed in order to diagnose an individual accused's treatability and evaluate his or her future risk to others. Such questions will be relevant to the issue of an accused's treatment and disposition.

In respect of the psychiatric evidence, the fact that pyromania is accorded an Axis 1 classification indicates that such a disorder is in keeping with paradigmatic instances of mental state malfunctioning. As a paradigmatic instance of mental-state disorder, pyromania represents an appropriate subject for clinical intervention.

Moreover, the treatability of an impulse-control disorder such as pyromania is an aspect that further supports therapeutic intervention. The prognosis for those experiencing pyromania is mostly favourable with 'about two-thirds of cases improv[ing] by the end of a year. Cases lasting more than a year usually run a fluctuating course, with periods of partial or complete remission lasting a few months to several years'.[154] The evidence indicates that a treatment regime accords

154 M. Gelder, D. Gath and R. Mayou, *The Oxford Textbook of Psychiatry* (2nd edn, Oxford, 1989) 198; see T.A. Gannon and A. Pina, 'Firesetting: Psychopathology, Theory

with the therapeutic rationale underpinning psychological medicine. Consequently, individuals suffering from pyromania may be considered to be appropriate targets of therapeutic intervention in a hospital setting. It would be both a humane and morally appropriate response for these individuals to be provided with such intervention rather than being punished, particularly as 'there is a real risk that generic prison interventions of the cognitive skills type may be missing the mark in terms of addressing the specific criminogenic needs of this population'.[155] Both the offender's and the community's interests would be served by the adoption of a therapeutic regime in a hospital setting: the former would be treated humanely while being kept in a secure facility in the light of social defence considerations.

Social defence In respect of the social-defence concerns underpinning the disease of the mind enquiry, it is clearly in the community's interest to safeguard against the potential danger of an individual's irresistible impulse to set fires. In this regard it is noteworthy that estimates of one-year prevalence of all impulse-control disorders in the general community vary from 0.1–2.3 per 1,000 with studies revealing a life-time prevalence of 2–3 per cent.[156] A series of long-term follow-up studies indicate that about 10 per cent of offenders were re-convicted for arson.[157] In respect of pyromania in particular, it has been suggested that when other causes of fire-setting are excluded, it is 'rare'.[158] These figures suggest that only a relatively small number of people in the community will be affected by pyromania. Nevertheless, the conditional nature of my argument is not reliant on the extent of the disorder. The fact remains that in the light of the damage an individual suffering from pyromania may cause, if there are individuals who satisfy the diagnostic criteria of pyromania in the world at large, a timely principled response to the issue of societal protection is required.

While the imprisonment of such individuals would alleviate any immediate social-defence concerns, such a solution forecloses any discussion of the responsibility of an individual who may suffer from pyromania. The acknowledgment of such an individual's non-responsibility necessitates that, as a matter of justice, it is clinical intervention rather than criminal punishment that is required. A recent review of the way fire-setters are treated across several jurisdictions, including 'treatment packages developed in secure hospitals in the

---

and Treatment' (2010) 15 *Aggression and Violent Behaviour* 224.

155 R. Doley and K. Fritzon, 'Assessment and Treatment of Fire-Setting Behaviour' in *Forensic Psychology and Criminology: An Australian Perspective*, ed. K. Fritzon and P. Wilson (North Ryde, NSW, 2008) 101, 102.

156 Gannon and Pina, 'Firesetting' (n. 154) 227.

157 Soothill, Ackerley and Francis, 'The Criminal Careers of Arsonists' (2004) 44 *Medical Science and Law* 27, cited in M. Gelder, P. Harrison and P. Cowen, *Shorter Oxford Textbook of Psychiatry* (5th edn, Oxford, 2006) 744.

158 Gelder, Harrison and Cowen, *Shorter Oxford Textbook of Psychiatry* (n. 104) 736.

UK' aimed at fire-setters, concludes with the observation that 'providing support for a more treatment and rehabilitative approach would prove ultimately more rewarding for the community at a variety of levels, rather than imprisonment without treatment, or with a generic programmatic approach to treatment'.[159] However, as discussed in Chapter 2 above, in order to ensure that individual justice is not subsumed under social-defence considerations, certain evidentiary and procedural safeguards must be implemented in mental-health legislation and cost burdens borne by the community in order to provide treatment facilities and services.

All of the above factors militate towards acknowledging pyromania as a disease of the mind. That is, recognizing pyromania as a disease of the mind would not run counter to the judgment of responsibility, social-defence considerations or psychiatric medicine's therapeutic rationale, all of which are aspects of the disease of the mind enquiry.

Conclusion: between principle and policy

I began by noting that pursuant to the general principle of voluntariness as a necessary condition of criminal liability an involuntary act should result in an outright acquittal. However, an accused whose act is involuntary due to a disease of the mind may not plead involuntariness but must plead insanity. A plea of insanity however generally leads only to a qualified rather than an outright acquittal. Such a result is necessitated by a policy concern with societal protection it being incumbent on the law to protect the community from dangerous people.

Moreover, even where an accused whose act is involuntary due to a disease of the mind raises the defence, he or she is forced to satisfy the traditional cognitive requirements of the M'Naghten rules. That is, he or she must show that the involuntariness arising from the disease of the mind was symptomatic of a defect of reason, which incapacitated him or her from knowing the nature or wrongness of his or her act. If he or she satisfies the knowledge requirement, he or she will receive a qualified acquittal. However, if he or she fails to satisfy the knowledge requirement, he or she will be criminally sanctioned.

While code jurisdictions recognize an independent volitional limb, the common law has been, in general, reluctant to do so. Two means by which the recognition of an independent volitional limb has failed to be implemented by courts is by a refusal on their part to characterize conditions giving rise to states of volitional impairment as diseases of the mind or, alternatively, by refusing to acknowledge states of volitional impairment arising from such conditions as a sufficiently incapacitating condition for the purposes of the insanity defence.

---

159 Doley and Fritzon, 'Assessment and Treatment of Fire-Setting Behaviour' (n. 155) 109.

This chapter has endeavoured to show why at common law involuntary conduct arising from mental disorder without cognitive impairment on the part of an accused should be acknowledged as an independent ground of the defence of insanity.

The chapter began by noting the contentious nature of the diagnostic category of pyromania. While some writers have doubted its existence,[160] others have more cautiously remarked that 'the validity of the diagnostic criteria is unsubstantiated'.[161] As noted above, the High Court cases of *Sodeman*[162] *and A-G (SA) v Brown*[163] make it clear that the common-law position avoids injustice only if cognitive (in)capacity tracks volitional (in)capacity. If in fact the common-law approach adopted by cases such as *Sodeman* and *Brown* is incorrect, and there are instances where an accused's cognitive (in)capacity does not track his or her volitional (in)capacity refusing to extend the defence to individuals suffering from pyromania may result in injustice. For it has been suggested above, that, if there are individuals who satisfy the diagnostic category of pyromania, they suffer from a mental disorder characterized by involuntary conduct without any cognitive impairment. Given that individuals who suffer from pyromania may reveal no cognitive defect it is only by extending the defence to states of involuntariness arising from mental disorder independent of a knowledge requirement that these individuals will be provided with a defence. A case such as *Doyle*[164] endeavours to expand the common-law defence by recognizing a state of mental disorder characterized by involuntary conduct independent of a cognitive impairment. The approach in *Doyle* is of interest only if it is established that the diagnostic category of pyromania is shown to correspond to an extant or verifiable mental disorder characterized by an accused experiencing involuntary conduct arising from mental disorder without any cognitive impairment.

In discussing the above cases, an important symmetry was noted between *Sodeman/Brown* and *Doyle*. In particular, it was noted that to the extent to which both the *Sodeman/Brown* and *Doyle* approaches were reliant on psychiatric evidence they both remain hostage to empirical evidence. While *Sodeman* and *Brown* argue that volition and cognition track one another, *Doyle* argues conversely that cognition may come apart from volition.

Nevertheless, there is an important asymmetry between the *Sodeman/Brown* and *Doyle* approaches. Under the *Sodeman/Brown* approach, if pyromania is in fact found to be a clinically established condition correlating with the diagnostic criteria there is a risk of injustice occurring. Under the *Doyle* approach however,

---

160 Geller, Erlen and Pinkus, 'A Historical Appraisal of America's Experience with "Pyromania"' (n. 125) 201 and references.

161 Gelder, Harrison and Cowen, *Shorter Oxford Textbook of Psychiatry* (n. 104) 744.

162 *Sodeman v R* (1936) 55 CLR 192, 214–15 per Dixon J.

163 [1960] AC 432 on appeal to PC.

164 *Doyle v Wicklow County Council* [1974] IR 55.

no harm will result if pyromania is found not to be a clinically established condition correlating with the diagnostic criteria. That is, if it is subsequently shown that the diagnostic category of pyromania does not in fact correspond to an extant or verifiable mental disorder no harm will be done by introducing an independent volitional limb, as the introduction of such a limb will merely prove to be redundant. For this reason this chapter has argued that the common law should play it safe and recognize an independent volitional limb giving rise to the defence of insanity alongside the M'Naghten rules.

This chapter has also noted the fact that an essential feature of pyromania according to diagnostic manuals is a repeated act of fire-setting without any obvious motive.[165] I have argued that the best explanation for repeated acts of fire-setting without an obvious and clear motivation on the part of the accused is that they amount to a state of involuntariness due to mental disorder. Where an individual acts involuntarily as a result of a state of mental disorder, he or she cannot be deterred by the threat of punishment. From the point of view of criminal responsibility it would serve no purpose to threaten such an individual with punishment. Such individuals are appropriate targets of therapeutic intervention and for this reason are best provided for by a treatment regime in a secure hospital setting where such is needed. In this way individuals who cannot control their conduct are provided with a humane response and social-defence considerations are appropriately addressed.

What the M'Naghthen rules provide is a criterion by which an accused's responsibility or non-responsibility may be evaluated. Criticism of the cognitive bias of the M'Naghten rules has led to calls for its abolition as a test of insanity and its replacement by various alternatives.[166] However, rather than seek alternatives to the M'Naghten rules, I have argued for the introduction of an independent volitional limb alongside the cognitive limbs of the defence. Such an approach I believe represents a viable solution to the demands of both principle and policy. As a matter of principle, an individual whose behaviour is involuntary should be fully acquitted. As a matter of policy, community protection necessitates placing an individual whose involuntary behaviour arose from an underlying pathological state of mind in a secure facility. The recognition of an independent volitional limb would ensure that such an individual receives the benefit of a qualified acquittal, thereby acknowledging his or her non-responsibility, while satisfying community anxiety about his or her possible dangerousness.

---

165 DSM-IV-TR (n. 79) 30; ICD-10 (n. 81) 31.

166 See M. Lagrone, 'Alternatives to the Insanity Defence' [1984] *Journal of Psychiatry and Law* 93.

Chapter 6
Involuntary Conduct: Defence of Impaired Consciousness

Introduction

It was noted in the previous chapter that the importance of voluntariness to criminal liability is recognized in both common law and code jurisdictions.[1] All criminal offences require proof of a physical element or *actus reus*. The physical element must be performed voluntarily. Conduct is only voluntary where it is the product of the will of the person performing the conduct.[2] A person is not criminally responsible for conduct which occurs independently of the exercise of his or her will.[3] The requirement that an accused's conduct be the result of the exercise of his or her will has been interpreted to be the same as the requirement that conduct be voluntary.[4] On the above analysis, the absence of voluntariness means that while the *actus reus* or physical element of the offence may be established (for example, the accused shot the victim), the accused may avoid criminal liability on the basis that he or she did not will the prohibited act (for example, the shooting was the result of a spasm or impaired consciousness).

Traditionally two varieties of states of involuntariness are distinguished: those which do not involve some form of impaired consciousness and those which do involve a state of impaired consciousness. Cases involving behaviour arising from a reflex response, bodily spasm and convulsions do not arise as a result of a state of impaired consciousness. However, some claims of involuntary conduct arise from causes involving a state of impaired consciousness. Such states include concussion caused from a blow to the head,[5] the consumption of alcohol or drugs,[6] hypoglycaemia[7] and epilepsy.[8] Further, the High Court in *R v Falconer*[9] has held

1 *Criminal Code* (ACT) s 15; *Criminal Code* (NT) s 31; *Criminal Code* (Qld) s 23; *Criminal Code* (Tas) s 13(1); *Criminal Code* (WA) s 23A; *Woolmington v DPP* [1935] AC 462; *Ryan v R* (1967) 121 CLR 205.

2 *Criminal Code* (Cth), s 4.2(2).

3 *Criminal Code* (Qld) s 23(1)(a); *Criminal Code* (WA) s 23A.

4 *R v Falconer* (1990) 171 CLR 30.

5 *Wakefield v R* (1957) 75 WN (NSW) 66; *Wogandt v R* (1988) 33 A Crim R 31.

6 *R v Cogdon* [1951] 5 *Res Judicata* 29.

7 *R v O'Connor* (1980) 146 CLR 64; *R v Meddings* [1966] VR 306.

8 *R v Sullivan* [1984] 1 AC 156; *R v Youssef* (1990) 50 A Crim R 1.

9 *R v Falconer* (1990) 171 CLR 30.

that an emotionally traumatic event (a 'psychological blow') may produce an extraordinary degree of stress so as to result in a state of dissociation.[10] A state of involuntary conduct arising from some form of impaired consciousness is referred to as automatism.[11]

A distinction is drawn between two varieties of automatism depending on whether the condition suffered by the accused is a form of mental disorder. Where the state of impaired consciousness resulting in involuntariness stems from some form of mental disorder such a state is referred to as 'insane automatism'. Where however, the state of impaired consciousness resulting in involuntariness does not arise from some form of mental disorder such a state is referred to as 'sane automatism'. This chapter will be concerned with states of sane automatism.

Arranged schematically the above taxonomy may be figured as follows:

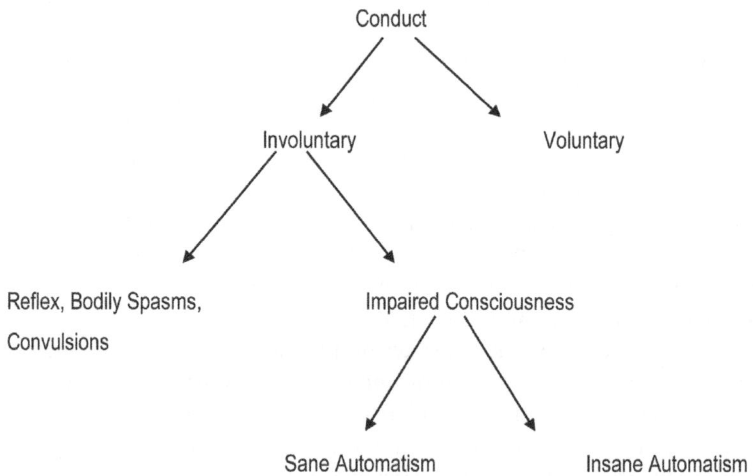

Figure 6.1 Traditional taxonomy of conduct

10 *R v Falconer* (1990) 171 CLR 30; *R v Tsigos* [1964–5] NSWR 1607; *R v Radford* (1985) 42 SASR 266. 'Psychological blow' or 'hysterical dissociation' is a clinical concept characterized by a state of depersonalization, derealization, identity confusion and identity alteration paradigmatically caused by a severe emotional shock (see J. McCaldon, 'Automatism' (1964) 91 *Canadian Medical Association Journal* 917; B. McSherry, 'Getting Away with Murder? Dissociative States and Criminal Responsibility' (1998) 21 *International Journal of Law and Psychiatry* 163, 168–9).

11 B. McSherry, 'Men Behaving Badly: Current Issues in Provocation, Automatism, Mental Impairment and Criminal Responsibility' (2005) 12 *Psychiatry, Psychology and Law* 15, 18.

As discussed in Chapter 2, different procedural and dispositional issues arise depending on whether a state of impaired consciousness is characterized as arising from a disease of the mind or not. In the context of conduct arising from a disease of the mind at common law, where such conduct is not voluntary, it will at best give rise to a defence of mental impairment: it will not result in an outright acquittal.[12] As discussed in Chapter 5, notwithstanding the involuntary nature of such conduct, social-defence considerations require an accused to plead the defence of mental impairment and receive the special verdict rather than obtain an outright acquittal. As a result, Chapter 5 argued for the recognition at common law of an independent volitional limb to the defence of mental impairment. While such a limb would continue to recognize social-defence considerations, it would dispense with the current requirement that an accused raise evidence that his or her volitional impairment is symptomatic of a cognitive defect. Where, however, an accused's involuntary behaviour does not arise from a disease of the mind, then an accused is entitled to an acquittal as a pre-condition of criminal responsibility, that is, voluntariness, is not satisfied.

Before proceeding it may be noted that the Criminal Codes of Queensland and Western Australia which are based on the Griffith Code take a fundamentally different approach to the common law. Unlike the common law, the Griffith Code does not conceptualise voluntariness as part of the physical element or *actus reus* of the offence. The concepts of *actus reus* and *mens rea* are not used in the Queensland and Western Australian Codes.[13] In Queensland and Western Australia a lack of will operates as a defence, it being found in the Queensland and Western Australian Codes in 'Chapter 5-Criminal Responsibility', and 'Chapter V-Criminal Responsibility' respectively, alongside other factors which operate to negate criminal responsibility such as mistake, emergency and duress. This chapter will not be concerned with these Code States but will focus on altering the common law approach to the question of voluntariness as an aspect of the physical element of an offence. A consequence of the change sought to be made will be to bring the common law approach more in line with the current Griffith Code approach to voluntariness as an excuse.

Behaviour arising from a reflex response, bodily spasm or convulsion has been viewed as being an uncontroversial instance of involuntariness.[14] In such situations, quite clearly, an accused's bodily movements are not the result of an exercise of

---

12 *Sodeman v R* (1936) 55 CLR 192. However, it is noted that the defence of mental impairment may on rare occasions give rise to the unconditional release of the accused, for example, under s 23(b) of the *Crimes (Mental Impairment and Unfitness to be Tried) Act 1997* (Vic).

13 See *Widgee Shire Council v Bonney* (1907) 4 CLR 977, 981 per Griffith CJ: 'under the criminal law of Queensland, as defined by the Criminal Code, it is never necessary to have recourse to the old doctrine of *mens rea*'. See *Criminal Code* (Qld); *Criminal Code* (WA).

14 *Ryan v R* [1969] 121 CLR 205, 215.

will on his or her part but are produced by some other agency. However, instances which are more problematic are those where the alleged lack of voluntariness stems from a mental state. In particular, the extension of the doctrine of sane automatism to cases of dissociation arising from psychological-blow automatism has been viewed as problematic in several respects.[15]

In order to meet the challenge posed by such problematic cases this chapter will argue for moving the voluntariness requirement for instances other than reflex, spasm and convulsion from the *actus reus* or physical element of an offence to a defence structure akin to that found in the Griffith Code. Hence, it will be argued that claims of involuntariness arising from a state of impaired consciousness which do not arise from a disease of the mind should be treated as excuses. That is, rather than being viewed as it currently is in the common law as relevant to the *actus reus*, or physical element of an offence, it will be argued that an instance of sane automatism is best viewed as operating as it does in the Griffith Code, as an excuse.

The chapter will begin with an outline of the operation of excuses, showing a necessary condition of such excuses and the degree to which certain criminal-law defences satisfy such a condition. This will be followed by an analysis of the voluntariness requirement in the criminal law. The analysis will distinguish between involuntary movements which are the result of bodily spasms and reflex actions and those states of volitional impairment which are the result of a state of impaired consciousness (sane automatism). It will then be indicated why claims of sane automatism should be viewed in terms of an excusatory defence rather than as an aspect of the *actus reus* of an offence. Succinctly stated, by viewing sane automatism as a defence, claims of volitional impairment arising from a state of impaired consciousness will be required to satisfy an objective condition as is demanded of other excuses in the criminal law. Before proceeding to formulate the proposed partial defence of impaired consciousness, this section will note and respond to the claim that removing sane automatism from the *actus reus* of the offence and viewing it as a defence would be unfair to an accused seeking an outright acquittal. Following on from this, the next section will formulate and describe the proposed partial defence of impaired consciousness. The defence of impaired consciousness aims to ensure that claims of volitional impairment are subject to the same restrictions as other excuse conditions in the criminal law. The final substantive matter which will be considered is a suggestion calling for the subsuming of states of involuntariness under a broad mental-disorder defence. It will be argued that such an approach should be rejected in favour of using the defence of impaired consciousness in order to distinguish between those varieties of impaired consciousness which arise from a disease of the mind and those which do not. The conclusion will provide an overview of the results of the analysis.

15 See McSherry, 'Getting Away with Murder? (n. 10); McSherry 'Men Behaving Badly' (n. 11); Victorian Law Reform Commission, *Defences to Homicide: Final Report*, Report No 94 (Melbourne, 2004) 5.160.

A working theory of excuses

This section will outline a working theory of excuses in the criminal law. In the first part of this section I will aim to show that criminal-law excuses share a structure that reveals a necessary condition that must be satisfied before an accused is able to raise such a defence. The second part of this section will use examples of extant criminal-law defences to show how this condition may be satisfied.

Structure of excusatory defences

Several distinctions may be drawn amongst the extant varieties of substantive, as distinct from procedural, criminal-law defences.[16] One distinction which may be drawn in the classification of criminal-law defences is that between 'justifications' and 'excuses'.[17] Justifications involve conduct which is morally warranted, that is, conduct which is not considered to be wrong.[18] A paradigmatic instance of justification is self-defence: the defence of self or other from unlawful attack being considered to be morally warranted conduct under all circumstances. An excuse represents a legal conclusion that the conduct is wrong, undesirable, ought not to be tolerated and should be avoided in the future, even in the same situation.[19] However, criminal liability is reduced in cases of excuse because while the conduct is wrong for one reason or another the accused's blameworthiness is mitigated. That is, excuses are applied to those instances where, while an accused's conduct is wrong, there is some reason for which he or she is not held fully responsible.

As will be outlined below, the reasons for which an accused's blameworthiness is reduced will differ from one excuse to another. It has been held that as there are no formal dispositional consequences arising from the distinction between justifications and excuses, the distinction is of little practical significance in Australian law.[20] However, the distinction between excuses and justifications remains important in terms of the analysis of complex moral situations.[21] References to criminal-law defences in this chapter will be taken to refer to excuses as the conduct engaged in by an accused wishing to raise evidence of involuntariness

16 Substantive defences refer to those defences, such as provocation, self-defence, duress or mistake of fact, which have developed as part of common law over time, and mental-condition defences such as insanity and automatism. Procedural defences include abuse of process, due diligence and the like. This chapter will only be concerned with substantive defences. For a detailed account of the operation of criminal law defences, see P.A. Fairall and S. Yeo, *Criminal Defences in Australia* (4th edn, Sydney, 2005).

17 Ibid. 1.

18 Ibid.

19 P. Allridge, 'The Coherence of Defences' [1983] *Criminal Law Review* 665.

20 Fairall and Yeo, *Criminal Defences in Australia* (n. 16) 2, citing *Zecevic* (1987) 162 CLR 645.

21 Fairall and Yeo, *Criminal Defences in Australia* (n. 16), 'Chapter 6: Necessity or Emergency'.

will not involve conduct which is morally warranted. If such conduct was justified there would be no need for an accused to raise evidence of involuntariness, as he or she could rely on an outright acquittal on the basis of a justificatory defence. My concern in this chapter is with the provision of excuses to those accused that because of a mental, emotional or physical condition experience a state of impaired consciousness resulting in volitionally impaired conduct.

An accused will be allowed to raise an excuse if and when it is judged that even someone well equipped with rational powers (of self-control, foresight and so on) would have behaved in a similar fashion in the circumstances. That is, in order to judge whether an accused is deserving of an excuse, the law introduces an objective standard into excuse formulations so as to allow an accused's behaviour to be assessed against such a standard. In principle, modern excuses hold an accused to some form of objective standard in judging his or her efforts. For example, in the context of the defence of duress, current excuse formulations require that an accused's capacity to resist be sufficiently impaired that he or she could not reasonably have been expected to have avoided the offence.[22] The law's willingness to excuse an accused under such conditions reflects a normative judgment in respect of the adequacy of his or her effort to resist. Several excuses have explicit objective standards as part of their criteria,[23] while others have broad criteria that invite a general normative assessment by the jury and, in this fashion, introduce what is essentially an objective standard.[24] The operation of this normative judgment, or objective standard, in respect of several defences will be considered below.

A further distinction which may be drawn amongst criminal-law defences is that between those defences which deny a necessary element of an offence, such as the physical (*actus reus*) or fault (*mens rea*) element ('failures of proof'), and those defences which operate subsequent to the establishment of the requisite elements of the offence ('excuses'). Failures of proof are raised in order to show that, as an element of the criminal offence has not been proved, there is no case for which the accused must answer. Technically, where an accused raises evidence that an element of the offence has not been established, he or she may avoid liability given that he or she has not committed the requisite elements of a criminal offence. Consequently, in such a situation, rather than raising a true defence, the accused claims that there is a failure of proof in respect of a necessary element of the offence. For example the failure of the prosecution to prove the

---

22 P. Robinson, *Structure and Function in Criminal Law* (Oxford, 1997) 89; see also E. Colvin, 'Ordinary and Reasonable People: The Design of Objective Tests of Criminal Responsibility' (2001) 27 *Monash University Law Review* 197, 226; *Criminal Code* (Cth) s 10.2.

23 Duress: *Criminal Code* (Cth) s 10.2; Provocation: *Stingel* (1990)171 CLR 312; *Masciantonio* (1995)183 CLR 58; *Green* (1997)191 CLR 334.

24 Diminished responsibility: *Crimes Act 1900* (NSW) s 23A; mental impairment: *Criminal Code* (Cth) s 7.3(2).

occurrence of voluntary conduct beyond reasonable doubt will result in an outright acquittal.[25] Similarly, mental disorder falling short of insanity may be used to show that the element of specific intention has not been established.[26] In the latter case, an accused will not be held liable for an offence which requires proof of specific intent.[27] Where however, the elements of the offence have been established, an accused may seek to mitigate his or her blameworthiness by raising an excuse. In such a case the accused will seek to show that he or she should be provided with an excuse in the light of mitigating factors. For example, the defence of duress operates subsequent to the prosecution having established that the accused voluntarily performed the relevant criminal conduct with the necessary intent albeit under constrained circumstances.[28]

One of the features distinguishing excuses from failures of proof is that the underlying normative element to excuses is lacking in pure failure of proof claims.[29] The ascription of praise or blame to an accused raising an excusatory defence will be determined according to whether his or her behaviour accords with the normative element, or objective standard, underlying the excuse. Such a normative element tells us when an accused's action is clearly inexcusable. There are some actions that are inexcusable under particular excuses and therefore should not be done. For example, in certain jurisdictions duress will not excuse an act of murder, and where such an act is committed the defence will not be allowed to be raised.[30] In contrast, as voluntariness is an aspect of the physical element of an offence, a denial of voluntariness will constitute a failure of proof. As a failure of proof the application of the voluntariness requirement to particular offences is not determined by a normative element.[31]

---

25 As discussed in Chapter 4, such a result will not ensue where the cause of an accused's involuntariness is found to be a state of mental disorder characterized as a disease of the mind.

26 *Hawkins v R* (1994) 179 CLR 500.

27 Though he or she may be liable for a lesser included offence which does not require proof of such intent, for example, manslaughter rather than murder (*Hawkins* (1994) 179 CLR 500).

28 *R v Palazoff* (1986) 43 SASR 99, 105 per Cox J.

29 J. Horder, *Excusing Crime* (Oxford, 2004) 58.

30 NSW: *Bassett and Steele* (SC NSW) (Unreported, Hunt CJ at CL, 29 Apr. 1994); South Australia: *Brown and Morley* [1968] SASR 467; *Criminal Code* (Qld) s 31; *Criminal Code* (WA) s 31(4), *Criminal Code* (Tas) s 20(1). In contrast to the above jurisdictions, in Victoria s 9AG of the *Crimes Act 1958* (Vic) permits the defence to be raised in the context of 'relevant offences' of which murder is one. Moreover, both the Commonwealth and ACT Criminal Codes have created a defence of duress of general application to all offences (*Criminal Code* (Cth) s 10.2; *Criminal Code* (ACT) s 40).

31 Horder *Excusing Crime* (n. 29) 8; see also J. Gardner, 'Criminal Law and the Uses of Theory: A Reply to Laing' (1994) 14 *Oxford Journal of Legal Studies* 217, 221.

Hence, a claim of lack of voluntariness will constitute a failure of proof in respect of all offences.[32]

The above section has detailed a particular condition which must be satisfied before an excusatory defence is recognized in the criminal law. As noted an excuse will be available to an accused who for some reason evinces a degree of impairment considered sufficient, when assessed against an objective standard, to reduce his or her blameworthiness. Unlike the case of a failure of proof defence, the application of an excusatory defence will be determined on the basis of an objective standard or, normative element. The normative element underlying the excuse will indicate those instances when an accused's action is inexcusable. I turn now to a consideration of the degree to which various criminal law defences comply with the above condition of excuses.

Substantive defences

This section will outline the operation of an objective standard in the context of several defences. The defences of duress and provocation will be considered as examples of defences which have explicit objective standards as part of their criteria. The partial defence of diminished responsibility will be used in order to show how the use of broad criteria in an excusatory defence may invite a general normative assessment by the jury and, in this fashion, introduce what is essentially an objective standard. In order to further refine the discussion of excusatory defences both the insanity defence and the doctrine of *doli incapax* will be presented by way of contrast as instances of a defence resulting in an accused being rendered *exempt* from criminal responsibility.

Duress The defence of duress excuses criminal behaviour where such behaviour arises in circumstances where the fear of violence induces the accused to commit the crime.[33] The defence has been defined as arising

> where the accused has been required to do the act charged against him (i) under a threat that death or grievous bodily harm will be inflicted unlawfully upon a human being if the accused fails to do the act and (ii) the circumstances were such that a person of ordinary firmness would have been likely to yield to the threat in the way the accused did and (iii) the threat was present and continuing, imminent and impending and (iv) the accused reasonably apprehended that the threat would be carried out and (v) he was induced thereby to commit the crime charged and (vi) that the crime was not murder, nor any other crime so heinous as to be excepted from the doctrine and (vii) the accused did not, by fault on his part when free from the duress, expose himself to its application and (viii) he

---

32 *Criminal Code* (Cth) s 4.2(1).

33 Fairall and S. Yeo, *Criminal Defences in Australia* (n. 16) 134; *DPP for Northern Ireland v Lynch* [1975] AC 653, 686 per Lord Simon; *Criminal Code* (Cth) s 10.2(2).

> had no means, with safety to himself, of preventing the execution of the threat, then the accused, in such circumstances at least, has a defence of duress.[34]

The defence is recognized as having three requirements: (1) there must have been a threat made by another against the accused if he or she does not perform the criminal offence (the nature of the threat requirement), (2) the threat must have induced the accused to commit the crime (the subjective test) and (3) the threat was such that it might have caused an ordinary person in the accused's position to also have committed the offence (the objective test).[35]

The fact that an accused was induced to commit a crime because of a threat does not negate either the physical element (*actus reus*) or the fault element (*mens rea*) of the offence. The defence implies that the accused has deliberately chosen to commit the criminal offence. Unlike physical compulsion which negates an accused's will the defence of duress does not deny the voluntariness of an accused's action.[36] Because of a threat, the accused is forced to engage in conduct, which he or she would not, under normal circumstances, engage in.

While many crimes are committed under various sorts of pressure, that which distinguishes duress as a defence is that the crime committed by the accused is a reasonable response to the threat in circumstances arising through no fault of his or hers. Hence, an accused individual must hold a well-grounded fear of death or grievous bodily harm arising from the conduct of the party making the threats.[37] Equally however the defence will arise only when it is judged that even someone well equipped with rational powers (of self-control, foresight and so on) might also have acted in that way under like circumstances. As stated by Hunt J in *Abusafiah*:

> The Crown must establish in relation to any such threat which may reasonably have been made that there is no reasonable possibility that such was its gravity that a person of ordinary firmness of mind and will as the accused, would have yielded to the threat in the way the accused did.[38]

To this end, the defence holds an actor to some form of objective standard in judging his or her efforts. An accused's capacity to resist must be sufficiently impaired so that he or she could not reasonably have been expected to have avoided the offence. That is, in order for the defence of duress to operate, the

---

34 *R v Hurley and Murray* [1967] VR 526, 543 per Smith J.

35 S. Bronitt and B. McSherry, *Principles of Criminal Law* (3rd edn, Pyrmont, NSW, 2010) 354–5; R. Murugason and L. McNamara, *Outline of Criminal Law* (Sydney, 1997) 241.

36 *R v Palazoff* (1986) 43 SASR 99, 105 per Cox J.

37 *R v Hurley and Murray* [1967] VR 526; *R v Howe* [1987] AC 417.

38 *R v Abusafiah* (1991) 24 NSWLR 531 per Hunt J (the NSW Court of Criminal Appeal opted for a more stringent test ('would') than that found in Victoria ('might or could')).

accused must have the firmness of mind reasonably to be expected of an ordinary person in like circumstances. The objective element requires that the threat posed is of such gravity as might cause an ordinary person in the accused's position to commit an offence.[39]

A modern statutory formulation is to be found in section 9AG of the Victorian Crimes Act the relevant parts of which read:

> 9AG Duress
> (2) A person carries out conduct under duress if and only if the person reasonably believes that –
> (a) subject to subsection (3), a threat has been made that will be carried out unless an offence is committed; and
> (b) carrying out the conduct is the only reasonable way that the threatened harm can be avoided; and
> (c) the conduct is a reasonable response to the threat.

It will be noted that the Victorian formulation stipulates as a requirement of the defence that the accused's belief in the threat is well-founded ('reasonably believes'), acting on the threat was 'the only reasonable way' of avoiding the threatened harm and that the conduct engaged in was a 'reasonable response'. Hence, the Victorian statute makes explicit the objective element against which an accused's conduct will be assessed by requiring that both the carrying out of the conduct and the nature of the accused's conduct were reasonable.

Provocation Another defence revealing an explicit use of an objective standard is the defence of provocation.[40] As a substantive partial defence, the successful operation of the defence of provocation reduces an accused's liability for murder to that of manslaughter. There are several elements to the substantive defence which must be satisfied before an accused will be partially excused: first, the accused must have killed the victim in circumstances recognized as provocative at law; secondly, the accused must because of the provocative circumstances have lost self-control; thirdly, that the provocation was sufficient to render an ordinary person to have lost control and form an intention to cause serious harm or death; and fourthly, while in such a state, the accused must have used retaliatory force

---

39 *R v Palazoff* (1986) 43 SASR 99, 108 per Cox J.

40 In South Australia, the defence is governed by the common law; in Queensland the common-law interpretation has been held to apply under s 304 of the *Criminal Code* (Qld) which sets out provocation as a partial defence to murder; in the Australian Capital Territory, New South Wales and the Northern Territory, there are statutory provisions (*Crimes Act 1900* (ACT) s 13; *Crimes Act 1900* (NSW) s 23(2); *Criminal Code* (NT) s 34); in Tasmania, Victoria and Western Australia, the defence has been abolished.

before regaining control.[41] In order to establish whether an ordinary person would have lost control under similar circumstances two questions are posed: (1) what is the gravity of the provocation faced by the agent? and (2) could provocation of that gravity cause an ordinary person to lose self-control and react as the agent did? However, while both questions are concerned with an objective standard, all of the characteristics of the defendant are relevant only to the first question.[42] The only characteristic of the defendant relevant to the second question is his or her age.[43]

Jeremy Horder has noted that the ordinary-person aspect of the defence is founded on what is termed the 'objective-capacity' theory of evaluating an accused's blameworthiness.[44] On the objective-capacity theory, an accused's blameworthiness will be determined according to whether or not his or her conduct met a 'morally salient standard'.[45] Such a standard will be altered only to the degree to which it adequately reflects the age of the accused.[46] The requirement under the substantive defence that an ordinary person would have lost self-control was a historical development which resulted in the defence moving from being a partial justification to a partial excuse.[47] On the loss of self-control model the provoked response by an accused was no longer viewed as a rational response to being wronged by another. Rather, an accused's blameworthiness was mitigated on the basis that the loss of self-control he or she experienced might also have occurred to an ordinary person in such circumstances.[48] While the above account describes the conventional rationalization of the defence there are, however, other models which have been proposed.

More recent formulations of the defence have suggested that provocation should be viewed in terms of an accused's justified sense of being wronged.[49] In

---

41 *Masciantonio v R* (1995) 183 CLR 58, 66; *R v R* (1981) 28 SASR 321, 321–2 per King CJ.

42 *DPP v Camplin* [1978] AC 705; *Stingel v R* (1990) 171 CLR 312.

43 *Masciantonio v R* (1995) 183 CLR 58.

44 Horder, *Excusing Crime* (n. 29) 123.

45 Ibid. 125.

46 Ibid.

47 J. Horder, *Provocation and Responsibility* (Oxford, 1992) 5–59; see Law Reform Commission of Ireland, *Consultation Paper on Homicide: The Plea of Provocation*, LRC CP-27 (Dublin, 2003) 2.02.

48 The objective capacity theory has been criticized by courts and commentators who argue that it should be the actual ability of the particular accused, given his or her circumstances and background or his or her subjective capacity, which should determine his or her blameworthiness (*Moffa v R* (1977) 138 CLR 601 per Murphy J; Victorian Law Reform Commission, *Provocation and Diminished Responsibility as Defences to Murder*, Report No 12 (Melbourne, 1982)).

49 A. Freiberg and F. Stewart, *Provocation in Sentencing: Research Paper* (Melbourne, 2008); A. Freiberg and F. Stewart, 'Provocation in Sentencing: A Culpability-Based Framework' (2008) 19 *Current Issues in Criminal Justice* 283; United Kingdom Law

this latter formulation, in place of a requirement that an accused lose his or her self-control in circumstances in which an ordinary person might, the moral basis for mitigating the accused's offence arises where 'the defendant acts in response to gross provocation in the sense of words or conduct (or a combination) giving the defendant a justified sense of being severely wronged'.[50] As the United Kingdom Law Commission noted:

> The preferred moral basis for recognizing the partial defence of provocation is that the defendant had legitimate ground to feel strongly aggrieved at the conduct of the person at whom his/her response was aimed, to the extent that it would be harsh to regard their moral culpability for reacting as they did in the same way as if it had been an unprovoked killing.[51]

On this proposed rationale for the defence, the issue of loss of self-control no longer plays a major role as an element of the defence.[52] Rather, it is the gravity of the victim's conduct and the accused's justifiable sense of being wronged which will determine whether the offence should be mitigated from murder to manslaughter.

Similarly, the notion that provocation reduced an accused's culpability given his or her loss of self-control was ultimately rejected by the VLRC, which recommended the abolition of the defence.[53] In its place the VLRC called for provocation along with other circumstances to be taken into account at sentencing. The VLRC argued that in order to determine an accused's culpability in the context of provocation for sentencing purposes it was important to consider the reasons why a person killed. In this respect the commission noted that contemporary community standards demanded that individuals control their anger notwithstanding a degree of provocation.[54] Moreover, the VLRC cited empirical evidence indicating that the defence was applied in a gender-biased way with men

---

Commission, *Partial Defences to Murder: Final Report*, Law Com No 290 (London, 2004); United Kingdom Law Commission, *Murder, Manslaughter and Infanticide*, Law Com No 304 (London, 2006).

50 United Kingdom Law Commission, *Partial Defences to Murder* (n. 49) 3.63.

51 Ibid. 3.68.

52 Though note that, notwithstanding the views expressed by the Law Commission for England and Wales, the approach currently adopted in England and Wales is to hold that loss of self-control remains a central element of the defence: *Coroners and Justice Act 2009* (England and Wales) s 54 'Partial Defence to Murder: loss of self-control'.

53 Victorian Law Reform Commission, *Defences to Homicide: Final Report* (n. 15) 58, 'Recommendation 1'. This recommendation was later put into force through the *Crimes (Homicide) Act 2005* (Vic); cp. Model Criminal Code Officers Committee, *Model Criminal Code – Chapter 5: Fatal Offences Against the Person: Discussion Paper* (Canberra, 1998) 105.

54 Victorian Law Reform Commission, *Defences to Homicide: Final Report* (n. 15) 2.95–7.

raising the defence in the context of the deterioration of intimate relationships.[55] Graeme Coss has remarked that the use of the defence occurs in situations where 'the real "loss of control" is that men have lost control of their women'.[56] The VLRC argued in their report that:

> Emotion is not an uncontrollable irrational force. Instead our emotions embody judgments and ways of seeing the world for which we can and should be held to account. If we accept that emotions can be objectively assessed and judged, then arguably it is also possible to assess culpability based on people's reasons for behaving (and the emotions underlying those reasons).[57]

On a reasons-based approach to the question of an accused's culpability, the reasons why a person killed may be analysed and evaluated. Such an approach focuses on the wrongfulness of the victim's conduct and the justifiable nature of the accused's retaliatory response. The act of the accused will be mitigated when the reasons for the accused's anger are found to be good reasons even though the act of the accused in using lethal retaliatory force is not warranted.[58]

The VLRC recommendations were ultimately accepted by the legislature and the partial defence subsequently abolished in Victoria.[59] Nevertheless, both the traditional interpretation of the substantive defence and the more recent rationalizations of the defence and its relationship to culpability involve an explicit acknowledgment of the objective aspect of the excusatory defence. The former, traditional approach emphasises the requirement that an accused's loss of self-control be such that an ordinary person in like circumstances would react in a similar fashion. The latter rationale highlights the fact that the reasons for which an accused is justified in feeling aggrieved must be good reasons. The reasons for which an accused will be justified in feeling aggrieved will be good reasons, when the victim's actions and/or words cause the accused to have 'a justifiable sense of being seriously wronged'.[60] For the purpose of establishing the gravity of a victim's provocative conduct and the justifiability of an accused's aggrievement,

55 Ibid. 2.22–3.

56 G. Coss, 'The Defence of Provocation: An Acrimonious Divorce from Reality' (2007) 18 *Current Issues in Criminal Justice* 51, 52; see also comments by the Law Commission for England and Wales in United Kingdom Law Commission, *Partial Defences to Murder: Final Report* (n. 48) 3.28.

57 Victorian Law Reform Commission, *Defences to Homicide: Options Paper* (Melbourne, 2003) 7.24–5 (citations omitted).

58 Ibid. 7.37.

59 *Crimes (Homicide) Act 2005* (Vic) s 3. The defence has also been abolished in Tasmania: *Criminal Code Amendment (Abolition of Defence of Provocation) Act 2003* (Tas), and Western Australia: *Criminal Law Amendment (Homicide) Act 2008* (WA).

60 United Kingdom Law Commission, *Murder, Manslaughter and Infanticide* (n. 49) 3.68.

a jury will be required to evaluate these issues against an objective morally salient standard.

Diminished responsibility The defence of diminished responsibility is a partial defence to murder which reduces the offence to a lesser form of culpable homicide. The rationale for the defence emanated from the view that certain states of cognitive or volitional impairment which were not recognized by the common-law defence of insanity were deserving of recognition in reducing an accused's criminal responsibility. Further, the defence arose in response to the provision of mandatory death sentences for the crime of murder, which came to be viewed as unduly harsh. Diminished responsibility ameliorated the strictures of the law in what were felt to be deserving cases by recognizing a degree of cognitive or volitional impairment as mitigating an accused's culpability and providing the accused with an alternative verdict of manslaughter.[61]

The defence was originally developed by the Scottish courts and found statutory expression in section 2(1) of the United Kingdom's *Homicide Act 1957*: [62]

> Where a person kills or is a party to a killing of another, he shall not be convicted of murder if he was suffering from such abnormality of mind (whether arising from a condition of arrested or retarded development of mind or any inherent causes or induced by disease or injury) as substantially impaired his mental responsibility for the acts or omissions in doing or being a party to the killing.

The defence of diminished responsibility is only available in the Australian Capital Territory, New South Wales, the Northern Territory and Queensland.[63] A modern restatement of the partial defence is to be found in section 23A of the New South Wales *Crimes Act*,[64] the relevant parts of which read:

> A person who would otherwise be guilty of murder is not to be convicted of murder if:
> (a) at the time of the acts or omissions causing the death concerned, the person's capacity to understand events, or to judge whether the person's actions were right or wrong, or to control himself or herself, was substantially impaired by an abnormality of mind arising from an underlying condition, and

---

61 Though the recognition of both a volitional limb to the insanity defence and the abolition of mandatory death (and life) sentences in most jurisdictions have rendered the defence superfluous (see Victorian Law Reform Commission, *Homicide*, Report No 40 (Melbourne, 1991).

62 *Homicide Act 1957* (UK).

63 *Criminal Code* (ACT) s 14; *Crimes Act 1900* (NSW) s 23A; *Criminal Code* (NT) s 37; *Criminal Code* (Qld) s 304A.

64 *Crimes Act 1900* (NSW).

(b) the impairment was so substantial as to warrant liability for murder being reduced to manslaughter.

The statutory definitions incorporate three elements all of which must be proved in order for the defence to succeed:

1. The accused must have been suffering from an 'abnormality of mind' at the time of the offence;

2. The 'abnormality of mind' must result from one of the prescribed causes;

3. The 'abnormality of mind' must have substantially impaired the accused's mental responsibility for the act or omission resulting in death.[65]

The issue of whether the above elements have been proved on the balance of probabilities is a question for the jury. The defence reflects the view that the abnormality of mind experienced by the accused had such an effect on the accused's capacity as to reduce his moral culpability and thereby diminish his legal liability.[66]

The expression 'abnormality of mind' has been defined as 'a state of mind so different from that of ordinary human beings that the reasonable man would term it abnormal'.[67] It is not a requirement that the abnormality of mind is caused by a mental illness, though a mental illness will suffice for the operation of the defence.[68] Conditions such as anxiety and depression[69] and neurotic personality[70] will suffice for the purposes of the defence. The three prescribed causes which must be operative and result in an abnormality of mind are an arrested or retarded development of the mind, inherent causes or where the result is induced by disease or injury. Courts will distinguish between those causes which are due to external factors and prescribed causes thereby ensuring that an abnormality of mind due to transient drug use, hate or jealousy are excluded from the ambit of the defence.[71] Due to problems experienced in practice with the defence as originally outlined certain statutory revisions to the United Kingdom formulation were recommended and subsequently implemented in the New South Wales *Crimes Act*.[72] Amongst

---

65 *Advocate v Savage* (1923) SLT 659, 660–1 per Lord Alness.

66 E. Griew, 'The Future of Diminished Responsibility' [1988] *Criminal Law Review* 75.

67 *R v Byrne* [1960] 2 QB 396, 403 per Lord Parker CJ.

68 *Rose v R* [1961] AC 496 (PC).

69 *Hinze v R* (1986) 24 A Crim R 185.

70 *Biess v R* [1967] Qd R 470.

71 *R v Fenton* (1975) 61 Cr App R 261; *Whitworth v R* [1989] 1 Qd R 437.

72 The formulation adopted in New South Wales was the result of the New South Wales Law Reform Commission's review of the operation of the defence in that state

such changes was the introduction of the expression 'underlying condition' in place of the description found in the United Kingdom Act of the conditions which may give rise to an abnormality of mind.[73]

The final element of the defence is the requirement that the abnormality of mind must have 'substantially impaired [the accused's] mental responsibility'. Both the defence of insanity and diminished responsibility arise as a result of an accused's mental abnormality. However, an important difference between the two defences is in respect of the degree of impairment required before an accused's responsibility for the offence will be affected. While insanity requires a total loss of capacity as a result of mental illness, diminished responsibility will only partially reduce the accused's capacity leaving him or her partially responsible for his or her acts or omissions. As expressed in *R v Byrne*:[74]

> The expression 'mental responsibility for acts' points to a consideration of the extent to which the accused's mind is answerable for his physical acts which must include a consideration of the extent of his ability to exercise willpower to control his physical acts…was the abnormality such as substantially impaired his mental responsibility for his acts in doing or being a party to the killing? This is a question of degree and essentially one for the jury.[75]

The mental responsibility, which must be substantially impaired in order for the defence to be established, refers to both the accused's ability to control his or her acts and to his or her degree of awareness of the nature and wrongness of the acts which he or she commits. The question for the jury in such a case is whether the accused had sufficient capacity to resist doing the act leading to the death and whether he or she had sufficient awareness of the nature and wrongness of this act.[76] Such a question will require a jury to undertake an evaluation of the degree of impairment in order to determine whether it may be called substantial and thereby warrant the reduction of the offence from murder to manslaughter. As expressed in *R v Trotter*:[77]

> Expert medical evidence is not really of great assistance in determining this crucial question of whether the impairment is substantial... [W]hether that impairment to the accused's mental responsibility for his actions may 'properly'

(New South Wales Law Reform Commission, *Partial Defences to Murder: The Defence of Diminished Responsibility*, Report No 82 (Sydney, 1997)).

73 *Crimes Amendment (Diminished Responsibility) Act 1997* (NSW); see, S. Yeo, 'Reformulating Diminished Responsibility: Learning from the New South Wales Experience' (1999) 20 *Singapore Law Review* 159.

74 [1960] 2 QB 396.

75 Ibid. 403–4.

76 *R v Miers* [1985] 2 Qd R 138, 143 per Campbell J.

77 (1993) 35 NSWLR 428.

> be called substantial (in the sense of being such as to warrant the reduction of the crime from murder to manslaughter) is *not* a matter within the expertise of the medical profession. This is a task for the tribunal of fact, which must approach the task in a broad commonsense way...It involves a value judgment by the jury representing the community (or by a judge where there is no jury), not a finding of medical fact.[78]

I noted above that an excuse will be available to an accused who for some reason evinces a degree of impairment considered sufficient when assessed against an objective standard to reduce his or her blameworthiness. In the context of an excusatory defence such as diminished responsibility the use of a broad criterion invites a general normative assessment by the jury. In particular, in determining whether an accused's requisite capacities are substantially impaired, a jury will be required to evaluate the accused's culpability when judged against community standards. By means of such a value judgment the jury will decide whether the degree of impairment warrants a reduction of the accused's culpability to be acknowledged by holding him or her liable for manslaughter rather than murder.

Mental impairment For an accused to raise the defence of insanity, or mental impairment as it is known in certain jurisdictions,[79] he or she must not only show that he or she is mentally ill, but also that, as a result of such mental illness, he or she has a mental malfunction which renders him or her not a fit subject of the criminal law. The defence is an exception to the operation of most excuses which rely for their operation on the accused meeting a normative standard before he or she may be excused. In contrast, where successfully pleaded, the defence of insanity establishes that the accused in failing to meet an objective standard is not a fit subject of the criminal law. The defence will be distinguished later in the chapter from the proposed defence of impaired consciousness.

As previously outlined, pursuant to the M'Naghten rules, the relevant mental malfunction will consist of either a lack of knowledge of the nature and quality of the act or a lack of knowledge that what he or she was doing was wrong.[80] As noted in Chapter 2, situations where an accused's mind is so disturbed that he or she does not know the nature or quality of his or her act are rarely encountered in practice. In most instances where the defence is raised, the issue will turn on whether the

78 Ibid. 431 per Hunt CJ at CL; cp. *R v Simcox* [1964] Crim LR 402, 403.

79 *Crimes (Mental Impairment and Unfitness to be Tried) Act 1997* (Vic) s 20; *Criminal Code* (ACT) s 28; *Criminal Code* (NT) s 43C; *Criminal Code* (Cth) s 7.3(1), 'Defence of Mental Impairment'.

80 *M'Naghten v R* (1843) 10 Cl and Fin 200, 210 per Tindal CJ.

accused knew he or she was doing wrong.[81] Australian courts have interpreted 'wrong' to mean 'morally' rather than 'legally' wrong.[82]

Commentary on this particular limb of the M'Naghten rules was provided by Dixon J in the following direction in *R v Porter*:[83]

> The question is whether he was able to appreciate the wrongness of the particular act he was doing at the particular time. Could this man be said to know in this sense whether his act was wrong if through a disease or defect of the mind he could not think rationally of the reasons which to ordinary people make that act right or wrong. If through the disordered condition of the mind he could not reason about the matter with a moderate degree of sense and composure it may be said that he could not know that what he was doing was wrong.[84]

This formulation has been adopted and paraphrased by the Commonwealth Criminal Code, Australian Capital Territory Code, Northern Territory Code, and, the Victorian statutory formulation of the defence.[85] The relevant part of the Victorian statute reads

> 20 Defence of Mental Impairment
> (1) The defence of mental impairment is established for a person charged with an offence if …
> (b) he or she did not know that the conduct was wrong (that is, he or she could not reason with a moderate degree of sense and composure about whether the conduct, as perceived by reasonable people was wrong).[86]

Similarly, the Queensland Code formulation provides that the defence will be established where the accused was deprived of 'the capacity to know that the person ought not to do the act or make the omission'.[87] This has been interpreted as meaning that the question to be asked is whether the accused knew that such conduct 'was wrong according to the ordinary standards adopted by reasonable men'.[88] Pursuant to the jury direction from *Porter* above for an accused to 'know that what he was doing was wrong' is for him or her to 'appreciate the wrongness

---

81 Bronitt and McSherry, *Principles of Criminal Law* (n. 35) 246; Murugason and McNamara, *Outline of Criminal Law* (n. 35) 14.18.

82 *R v Porter* (1933) 55 CLR 182, 189 per Dixon J; *Stapleton v R* (1952) 86 CLR 358 per Dixon CJ, Webb, Kitto JJ.

83 *R v Porter* (1933) 55 CLR 182.

84 Ibid. 189–90.

85 *Criminal Code* (Cth) s 7.3(1)(b); *Criminal Code* (ACT) s 28(2); *Criminal Code* (NT) s 43C(b); *Crimes (Mental Impairment and Unfitness to be Tried) Act 1997* (Vic) s 20.

86 *Crimes (Mental Impairment and Unfitness to be Tried) Act 1997* (Vic) s 20 (1) (b).

87 *Criminal Code* (Qld) s 27.

88 *Stapleton v R* (1952) 86 CLR 358, 375 per Dixon CJ, Webb, Kitto JJ.

of the particular act he [or she] was doing'. To 'appreciate' is to 'think rationally' which is further defined as to 'reason with a moderate degree of sense and composure'. That which the accused must be capable of reasoning about with such a degree of sense and composure are the 'reasons which to ordinary people make that act right or wrong'. An individual who knows that ordinary people consider his or her act to be wrong will be taken to know that it is wrong, notwithstanding his or her personal view of the matter. The direction indicates that someone who is not able to 'reason about the matter with a moderate degree of sense and composure' is to be taken as not knowing that his or her act is wrong. This follows from the observation that someone who is not able to 'reason about the matter with a moderate degree of sense and composure' will not be able to know how others might judge whether his or her conduct is wrong. Hence, the issue in respect of this particular limb concerns whether, at the time of the offence, the accused was able to reason about right and wrong in the same manner as do ordinary people rather than as he or she might given the nature of his or her individual beliefs.

This is a test which requires a general normative assessment to be made by the jury on the basis of an objective standard.[89] By inviting the jury to engage in such a normative assessment the defence introduces what is essentially an objective standard. However, unlike the excusatory defences discussed above the insanity defence is an exemption. Where an accused cannot reason about the matter as ordinary people do, he or she will fail to meet the standard expected of ordinary people. Failure to meet such a standard means it would be unfair to treat him or her as subject to the sanctions imposed by the criminal law.

In this respect the insanity defence is comparable to the common-law doctrine of *doli incapax* (incapable of crime), which provides that a child under the age of 7 is incapable of being found guilty of a crime.[90] The rationale for this irrebuttable presumption is that, as a result of the immaturity of the child, he or she is incapable of comprehending the consequences of his or her act. As a result of such immaturity, he or she is not able to understand and distinguish between right and wrong. The common-law doctrine has been enacted in all jurisdictions with the minimum age raised to 10 years.[91] The doctrine of *doli incapax* also provides a rebuttable presumption that a child between the ages of 7 and 14 may be held criminally responsible where he or she is shown to have both the relevant fault

89 Contrast the South Australian formulation which is wholly subjective and stipulates 'the accused did not know the conduct was wrong' (*Criminal Law Consolidation Act 1935* (SA) s 269C).

90 *M (A Minor)* [1977] 16 SASR 589, 590 per Bray CJ; *C (A Minor) v DPP* [1996] AC 1; see, in general, T. Crofts, *The Criminal Responsibility of Children and Young Persons in Germany and England* (Aldershot, 2002).

91 *Criminal Code* (Cth) s 7.1; *Criminal Code* (NT) s 38(1); *Children (Criminal Proceedings) Act 1987* (NSW) s 5; *Criminal Code* (Qld) s 29(1); *Young Offenders Act 1993* (SA) s 5; *Criminal Code* (Tas) s 18(1); *Children and Young Persons Act 1989* (Vic) s 127; *Criminal Code* (WA) s 29; *Criminal Code* (ACT) s 25.

element and know that the act was seriously wrong.[92] The rebuttable presumption in respect of a child under the age of 14 has also been statutorily enacted in several jurisdictions.[93] The rationale for the presumption is that a child under the age of 14 may be criminally responsible only where he or she is able to distinguish between right and wrong to the same degree as an individual of 14 years of age and over. For the purposes of the criminal law it is only a child of 14 years of age and above that will be considered sufficiently mature to distinguish between right and wrong.[94] The presumption relies on a child's lack of 'knowledge that he or she was, according to the principles of ordinary people, wrong'.[95] While at common law, the presumption requires a child to lack actual knowledge, several jurisdictions require a child to lack the capacity to know right from wrong.[96] However, the central issue in the code jurisdictions, as with the common law, remains whether the individual in question knew that the act was wrong pursuant to the 'ordinary principles of a reasonable man'.[97] Hence, at both common law and in jurisdictions which have enacted the presumption, a child may not avoid criminal responsibility for criminal conduct where he or she knows that his or her conduct is wrong.[98] The presumption of *doli incapax* does not permit an assumption to be made that because a normal child of the accused's age would have known that the crime was wrong the particular child also knows it. This would be to reverse the *doli incapax* presumption.[99]

This section has outlined the operation of the objective standard in the context of several defences. The defences of duress and provocation were shown to involve explicit objective standards as part of their criteria. The modern formulation of the defence of duress requires that both the carrying out and nature of the accused's conduct in the face of constraining circumstances were reasonable. Both current and traditional rationalizations of the defence of provocation made reference to an objective aspect. On the traditional approach the substantive defence required an accused's loss of self-control to be such as

92 *M (A Minor)* [1977] 16 SASR 589, 590 per Bray CJ; *Field and South Australia v Gent* (1996) 87 A Crim R 225; *C (A Minor) v DPP* [1996] AC 1.

93 *Criminal Code* (Cth) s 7.2; *Criminal Code* (Tas) s 18; *Criminal Code* (WA) s 29; *Criminal Code* (ACT) s 26.

94 T. Crofts, 'Rebutting the Presumption of Doli Incapax' [1998] *Journal of Criminal Law* 185, 189.

95 *Field and South Australia v Gent* (1996) 87 A Crim R 225, 230 per Mullighan J, citing *M (A Minor)* [1977] 16 SASR 589 and *C (A Minor)* v DPP [1996] AC 1.

96 *Criminal Code* (NT) s 38(2); *Criminal Code* (Qld) s 29(2); *Criminal Code* (WA) s 29. It has been suggested that a test of capacity is less stringent then a test of actual knowledge (*JMF; Ex Parte A-G* (1998) CA 20/98 (Unreported, SC Qld, 19 May 1998)).

97 *F (A Child)* (1998) 101 A Crim R 113, 116 per Davies JA, citing *M (A Minor)* [1977] 16 SASR 589, 591.

98 Crofts, 'Rebutting the Presumption of Doli Incapax' (n. 94) 191.

99 Ibid. 189.

an ordinary person in like circumstances could have experienced. More recent formulations require that an accused have good reasons for feeling seriously wronged because of the victim's words and/or actions. Establishing whether the reasons for which the victim's actions and/or words cause the accused to feel justifiably aggrieved are good reasons require the jury to evaluate these reasons against an objective morally salient standard. The partial defence of diminished responsibility in turn was shown to involve the use of a broad criterion (substantial impairment) inviting a general normative assessment by the jury. By requiring the jury to undertake an evaluation of the degree of impairment experienced by the accused sufficient to mitigate his or her mental responsibility, the defence introduced an objective standard. Finally, by way of contrast, both the insanity defence and the doctrine of *doli incapax* were presented as instances where an accused's failure to meet an objective standard renders him or her exempt from criminal responsibility.

The following section will distinguish between what have been traditionally considered to be two varieties of involuntary conduct. It will be argued that it would be more in keeping with the nature of cases involving instances of impaired consciousness if such states were viewed as instances of volitional impairment rather than as being akin to spasms, convulsions or reflex actions.

Impaired consciousness and voluntariness

I noted above that, as conventionally understood, two varieties of involuntary conduct may be distinguished: conduct which involves a state of impaired consciousness and conduct which does not arise from a state of impaired consciousness, such as behaviour arising from a reflex response or bodily spasm. A further distinction may be drawn between those states of impaired consciousness which are the result of a disease of the mind (insane automatism) and those states of impaired consciousness which are not the result of a disease of the mind (sane automatism). I will argue in this section that only those instances of behaviour which arise from a reflex response or bodily spasm should for the purposes of the criminal law be treated as involuntary. In contrast, for reasons to be discussed below, it will be argued that cases of sane automatism are better viewed as instances of volitional impairment rather than as instances of involuntariness. As a corollary to this view, it will be argued that rather than being viewed as an aspect of the physical element of an offence, claims of sane automatism should be treated as falling within the criminal law's system of excuses.

It has been remarked that it is the natural connection between voluntariness and action which explains why voluntariness is conventionally understood as an aspect of the physical element of an offence.[100] However, states of voluntariness

---

100 See D. Lanham, 'Involuntary Acts and the Actus Reus' (1993) 17 *Criminal Law Journal* 97.

may be viewed as situated along a continuum with involuntary conduct positioned at the extreme end of such a continuum.[101] As will be argued below, a paradigmatic instance of fully voluntary conduct is exemplified by conscious action on the part of an accused motivated by his or her pursuit of a goal. In contrast, a state of involuntariness is characterized by a lack of control and is exemplified by behaviour accompanying reflex responses, bodily spasms and convulsions. In this respect, reflex responses, spasms and bodily convulsions may be said to occupy the other extreme end of the voluntariness continuum and are readily recognized as involving conduct which is not willed.[102]

While such conduct amounts to an act on the part of the accused, such an individual has not acted voluntarily.[103] The recognition of both reflex responses and bodily spasms in terms of involuntary conduct is not problematic given the characteristic loss of control accompanying behaviour due to a reflex response or bodily spasm. In contrast to cases involving reflex actions and bodily spasms, conduct arising from a state of impaired consciousness often appears to be purposeful and goal-directed. Warren Brookbanks has observed:

> Unlike other cases based on the notion of irresistible force, however, where the offender is a mere instrument under the control of a more powerful force or agency and automatism is claimed, the person may appear to perform deliberate, voluntary actions at the time of the offence.[104]

However, it has been questioned whether actions arising from a state of impaired consciousness that are purposeful and goal-directed will provide a basis for a claim of involuntariness.[105] Moreover, some experts have gone so far as to interpret such behaviour as voluntary arguing that 'any complex, directed and purposeful action is difficult to conceive as being carried out by someone whose mind is

---

101 See J. Feinberg, *Harm to Self* (New York, 1986) 117, remarking on voluntariness as 'a variable concept, determined by higher and lower cut-off points depending on the nature of the circumstances, the interests at stake, and the moral or legal purposes to be served'.

102 *Criminal Code* (Cth) s 4.2(3)(a); *Ryan* (1967) 121 CLR 205; *Williams* (1990) 50 A Crim R 213; *Hughes* (1989) 42 A Crim R 270.

103 Unlike the case where A takes B's hand and strikes C. In this context, B is said not to have acted as he or she has been used as an instrument (see I. Leader-Elliott, *The Commonwealth Criminal Code: A Guide for Practitioners* (Canberra, 2002) 33).

104 W. Brookbanks, 'Insanity' in *Psychiatry and Law: Clinical and Legal Issues*, ed. W. Brookbanks and S. Simpson (Wellington, 2007) 123, 144.

105 See Victorian Law Reform Commission, *Defences to Homicide: Final Report* (n. 15) 5.143; see *R v Leonboyer* [2001] VSCA 149, para 49, for a similar view expressed by expert witness, Professor Mullen; cp *Burr v R* [1969] NZLR 736, 744–5, where it was held that, while sane automatism does not require a total loss of consciousness, a sufficient condition for satisfying the definition will be a state where all the deliberative functions of the mind are absent.

so disorganized that they cannot will their actions'.[106] Indeed, E Michael Coles remarked:

> On the basis of the available knowledge of human behaviour, it may be suggested that many of the crimes that the courts have decided were committed in an automatistic state – that is, in the absence of conscious, volitional control, or while the mind was a total blank – actually may have occurred in a state of diminished consciousness, with the diminished consciousness resulting in the diminished conscious control of behaviour. In other words, the individual becomes disinhibited, and behaviour that the individual would otherwise be able to control gains expression.[107]

The fact that certain states of sane automatism involve co-ordinated, goal-directed conduct which an accused may have reason to perform for his or her own purposes, is at least suggestive of such states not having been performed 'in the absence of conscious, volitional control'.[108] In this respect, such states are closer to instances of provocation, where the loss of self-control is partial rather than total.[109] The self-control experienced by a defendant raising provocation is substantially impaired rather than totally lost and for this reason results in a partial defence.[110] Provocation is a partial rather than a total defence as the accused is blamed for not refraining from proscribed conduct by exercising the degree of control which he or she nevertheless retains. By contrast, where a total loss of self-control occurs an accused will be totally acquitted, as he or she cannot be blamed for acting involuntarily.

Nevertheless, it may be objected that the fact that conduct performed by an individual in a state of impaired consciousness is goal-directed does not necessarily imply that such conduct is performed voluntarily. That is, it might be argued that the fact that an accused exercises certain capacities should not be taken to imply that he or she is acting voluntarily. Someone arguing in this fashion

106 *R v Leonboyer* [2001] VSCA 149, para 18 per Phillips CJ, summarizing evidence given by two psychiatrists for the prosecution; see also E.M. Coles and S. Armstrong, 'Hughlings Jackson on Automatism as Disinhibition' (1998) 6 *Journal of Law and Medicine* 73; J.A. Bargh and T.L. Chartrand, 'The Unbearable Automaticty of Being' (1999) 54 *American Psychologist* 462.

107 E.M. Coles, 'Scientific Support for the Legal Concept of Automatism' (2000) 7 *Psychiatry, Psychology and Law* 33, 37.

108 See B. McSherry, 'Automatism in Australia since Falconer's Case' (1996) 6 *International Bulletin of Law and Mental Health* 3; McSherry 'Getting Away with Murder?' (n. 10) 163; B. McSherry, 'Mental Impairment and Criminal Responsibility: Recent Australian Legislative Reforms' (1999) 23 *Criminal Law Journal* 135.

109 See *Phillips v R* [1969] 2 AC 130, 137 per Lord Diplock, the defence of provocation applies at 'an intermediate stage between icy detachment and going berserk'.

110 S. Odgers, 'Contemporary Provocation Law: Is Substantially Impaired Self-Control Enough?' in *Partial Excuses to Murder*, ed. S. Yeo (Sydney, 1991) 103.

may put forward the following example in order to show that an individual may act involuntarily even though his or her actions are goal-directed. The example might begin with the assumption that an individual's mind has been taken over by someone who has devised a method by which to control such an individual's behaviour from a distance. The experiment is intended to show that while the individual in question might as a result of the control exercised by the other person behave in a goal-directed fashion we would not, assumedly, call his or her conduct voluntary. Consequently, by analogy, an individual may act in a goal-directed fashion while in a state of impaired consciousness and yet still be said to be acting involuntarily.

However, the above view and accompanying example designed to show that goal-directed behaviour may be performed involuntarily fail to comprehend what is entailed by the claim that an individual's acts are voluntary. It is not sufficient in order to show that goal-directed behaviour may be performed involuntarily that one person may act according to the desires of another person. All that is shown by the above experiment is that one person's bodily movements may be used in order to bring about another person's goal-directed design. However, this will not be sufficient to establish the claim which the example is designed to support, namely, that goal-directed behaviour may be performed involuntarily. The problem with the argument and the supporting example is that it mistakes the nature of the claim which it attempts to meet. In particular, the argument mistakenly believes that the claim against which it is arguing merely amounts to the proposition that an individual's goal-directed behaviour alone will be sufficient in order to establish his or her voluntariness. However, this is to ignore that it is an individual's actions when exercised for his or her own goals which will determine the voluntariness of these actions.[111]

This claim may be brought out by considering the analysis undertaken in Chapter 5 of the (lack of) motivation characterizing states of pyromania. As noted in the context of Chapter 5, the best explanation for acts of repeated fire-setting by an individual suffering from pyromania, is a state of mental disorder. The reason why this explanation was adopted was that, in the absence of any characteristic motivating reason for such complex behaviour, there was no other cogent reason to explain, or rationalize, why an individual would engage in repeated acts of fire-setting. While the acts of an individual suffering from pyromania are goal-

111 See J.M. Fischer and M. Ravizza, *Responsibility and Control: A Theory of Moral Responsibility* (Cambridge, 1998),'Chapter 8: Taking Responsibility', 230: 'In certain cases involving direct manipulation of the brain (and similar influences), it is natural to say that the mechanism [of practical reason] leading to the action is not, in an important sense, the agent's own … ahistorical, purely structural accounts cannot adequately treat such cases. An ahistorical theory must focus solely on current time-slice features of an agent (such as a certain sort of "harmony" – or lack thereof – in the internal psychological economy). What is left out, then, is attention to the process that leads to those current time-slice features being in place and their leading to the action.'

directed, this in itself is not sufficient to establish that these acts are performed voluntarily. What would be required in order to establish that an individual's own goal-directed behaviour may be performed involuntarily is an example showing that an individual's exercise of his or her own purposes or goals may be performed involuntarily. However, this would require an example showing that an individual may act pursuant to a motivating reason and yet not be acting in a voluntary fashion. The example above does not show this.

In this context it is noteworthy that in most instances where a state of impaired consciousness has been raised in order to establish involuntariness,

> it is very difficult (if not impossible) to verify a person's claim that they were acting in such a state. The claim is made in circumstances where the person has been extremely upset or traumatised because of something which has been done by the person they subsequently kill, that is they generally have a very clear motive for the killing.[112]

As a result, the question of whether conduct arising from a state of impaired consciousness which reveals co-ordinated goal-directed behaviour performed for an accused's own purposes should be viewed as involuntary is at least controversial.[113] In the light of such controversy it is contended that the presence of a motive accompanying goal-directed behaviour should be sufficient to establish a rebuttable presumption that the acts of the accused were fully voluntary. If the accused chooses to rebut such a presumption on the basis that he or she was acting in a state of impaired consciousness, he or she should be required to satisfy the conditions attached to an excusatory defence. The formulation of such an excuse (the defence of impaired consciousness) will be discussed in the following section.

In the following section, it will be argued that claims of volitional impairment arising from a state of impaired consciousness should be viewed as an excuse rather than as an aspect of the physical element or *actus reus* of an offence. The final part of the section will respond to the charge that requiring instances of sane automatism to satisfy the necessary condition of excuses rather than be treated as an aspect of the physical element or *actus reus* of an offence may result in an accused being unfairly treated.

---

112 Victorian Law Reform Commission, *Defences to Homicide: Final Report* (n. 15) 5.144, citing *Falconer* (1990) 171 CLR 30; *Leonboyer* [2001] VSCA 149; *Hawkins* (1994) 179 CLR 500.

113 See *R v Leonboyer* [2001] VSCA 149, for an instance of differing expert opinion in respect of the voluntariness of the defendant's behaviour.

Sane automatism as excuse

A question which this section will seek to answer is: why should conduct arising from a state of impaired consciousness which is not caused by a disease of the mind be treated as grounding a defence rather than a denial of the physical element of the offence? There are four aspects to the answer to this question which may be stated succinctly as follows. First, states of voluntariness are positioned along a continuum ranging from fully voluntary conduct to involuntary behaviour. Second, certain cases of sane automatism, such as, for example, those involving states of dissociation accompanying a psychological blow, give rise to conduct which, it will be seen, is better characterized as 'volitionally impaired' rather than involuntary. Third, a state of volitional impairment rather than total involuntariness should result in a partial rather than total excuse. Finally, an excuse will be provided to an accused where his or her conduct is found to satisfy a normative standard. Each of these aspects will be addressed in this section.

Voluntariness continuum

It was noted in the previous section that states of voluntariness may be viewed as situated along a continuum with involuntariness situated at one extreme of this. At one end of the continuum may be found those behaviours characterized by a lack of control, such as reflex responses, bodily spasms and convulsions. Such behaviour is characterized by a lack of control and is readily recognized as involuntary. At the other end of the continuum are the acts of individuals performed consciously in a purposive, goal-directed and motivated fashion. These acts may be characterized as fully voluntary conduct. While such behaviours are readily recognized as instances of both voluntary and involuntary conduct, there are a range of other states which fall somewhere between these two extremes. These will be referred to as instances of 'volitional impairment'. Instances of volitional impairment are situated along various parts of the involuntariness continuum. The correct characterization of conduct arising from a state of volitional impairment proves problematic where it is performed in a state of impaired consciousness while reflecting both purposive and motivated behaviour. Such conduct is neither fully voluntary nor fully involuntary. As a result, there is no reason to believe that instances of volitional impairment should be treated as instances of involuntary conduct resulting in a denial of the physical element of an offence. Equally, there is no reason to believe, given the accused's state of impaired consciousness, that his or her conduct is fully voluntary and the accused in full control. As a result, in acknowledgment of the continuum along which states of volitional impairment occur, and the difficulty of characterization which such states present, it would be more transparent if claims of volitional impairment were treated as an excuse. By treating claims of volitional impairment as excuses an accused will be required to meet an excusatory objective standard before his or her conduct will be treated as not fully voluntary.

Volitional impairment

However, a question which arises is whether an accused is placed at a disadvantage by conceptualizing behaviour arising from a state of impaired consciousness as an excuse and requiring him or her to satisfy the objective aspect of an excusatory defence. In particular, given that it is controversial whether an individual claiming sane automatism does in fact act in a voluntary fashion, should not he or she be given the benefit of the doubt, and be allowed to raise sane automatism without being required to satisfy an objective standard?

Contrast the more liberal approach adopted in Chapter 5. Chapter 5 argued for the recognition of an independent volitional limb in the light of the controversial nature of the psychiatric evidence in respect of pyromania. Given such controversy, it was argued that an independent volitional limb should be made available to an accused as a matter of justice. Motivating this view was the belief that if in fact the veracity of the diagnostic category of pyromania was established and an accused was found to be suffering from such a condition in the world at large, then the law should be prepared for such a contingency and be prepared to provide such an accused with a defence. It could be argued that, in keeping with the ecumenical approach adopted in Chapter 5, a similar approach should be adopted in the instance of sane automatism. That is, given the controversial nature of the evidence surrounding states of sane automatism the law should be equally prepared to allow an accused to simply raise involuntariness in order to deny the physical element of the offence rather than being required to satisfy the objective element of a defence.

However, it could be argued in response that there is an important asymmetry in respect of the nature of the accused's conduct in Chapters 5 and 6. In Chapter 5, there were doubts associated with the acts of the accused, in particular, whether in keeping with the diagnostic category of pyromania such acts were instances of irresistible impulse which could not be controlled. In such a case it was felt that there were both cogent and principled reasons for providing an accused with a defence in recognition of the possibility of such states being extant in the world. In particular, pursuant to the diagnostic criterion the absence of a discernible motivation for the repeated acts of fire-setting suggested that the best explanation of such an individual's behaviour was that it was the product of a state of mental disorder which resulted in his or her inability to control conduct. In this chapter, however, it has been argued that unlike instances of both reflex responses and bodily spasms, conduct arising from a state of impaired consciousness not due to the effects of a disease of the mind is characterized by purposive, goal-directed behaviour undertaken for the accused's own purpose. While such behaviour may be accompanied by a degree of volitional impairment, it is qualitatively different from the type of involuntary movement caused by reflex responses, spasms, and bodily convulsions.

In keeping with criminal-law principles an accused claiming volitional impairment due to a state of impaired consciousness will only be required to satisfy the evidential burden in respect of the elements of the defence. As will be seen below, this will require an accused to raise evidence from which it may be inferred that he or she experienced a similar degree of difficulty to that which an ordinary person in like circumstances would have faced in controlling his or her conduct. In Australian jurisdictions it would then be incumbent on the prosecution to rebut such evidence.[114] By placing the additional element of an objective standard on the defence, we are in fact creating an additional requirement which the accused must satisfy. However, the onerousness of such a requirement is more than counterbalanced by the problematic nature of the evidence and the desirability of ensuring that unjust acquittals do not eventuate.

Partial excuse

As discussed in the context of mental impairment in Chapter 2, total exculpation from responsibility will require a total impairment of an accused's capacity for control or knowledge. Where there is a partial impairment this should only lead to a partial excuse rather than an acquittal. It was contended above that a rebuttable presumption of voluntariness be recognized for instances of motivated goal-directed behaviour. Where the accused raises the defence which the prosecution then fails to rebut the accused's blameworthiness should be mitigated. As the accused has acted in a purposive goal-directed fashion his or her conduct reveals a degree of control. In the light of such a degree of control being extant he or she will not be acquitted but will be held responsible, albeit for a lesser offence.

Standard of impairment

When voluntariness is viewed as an aspect of the *actus reus* of an offence, a denial of voluntariness will amount to a failure of proof and result in the outright acquittal of an accused whose conduct is found to be involuntary. In contrast to a failure of proof leading to the outright denial of an element of the offence an excuse will require an inquiry to be undertaken into whether the degree of impairment is sufficient to mitigate an accused's blameworthiness. This will call for an examination of the accused's situation and a comparison to be made of his or her conduct with that of an explicitly or implicitly expressed objective standard.[115] As an aspect of the physical element of an offence there is no need to establish that an accused's conduct satisfies such a standard. By treating conduct arising from a

114 In contrast, the Canadian Supreme Court has reversed the onus in such cases and held that it is for the defence to prove involuntariness, albeit on the balance of probabilities *R v Stone* (1999) 134 CCC (3d) 353. This view has been criticized by several commentators, see B. McSherry, 'Case Commentary: *R v Stone*' (2000) 7 *Psychiatry, Psychology and Law* 279, citing R.J. Delisle, 'Stone: Judicial Activism Gone Awry to Presume Guilt' (1999) 24 *Criminal Reports* (5th) 91; D. Paciocco, 'Death by Stone-ing: The Demise of Simple Automatism' (1999) 26 *Criminal Reports* (5th) 273.

115 Colvin, 'Ordinary and Reasonable People' (n. 22) 226.

state of impaired consciousness as raising an excuse before an accused is excused for having acted in a volitionally impaired state due to impaired consciousness, his or her conduct will be assessed against an objective standard. An accused wishing to raise the defence will need to satisfy the evidentiary burden of the defence by raising a reasonable possibility of the elements of the defence being established. Where the elements of the excuse have been raised a failure by the prosecution to rebut the defence will result in the excuse being established.

Evaluating conduct

In Chapter 2, the case of *R v Singh*[116] was used to illustrate some of the difficulties associated with claims of involuntariness arising from instances of dissociation. An acrimonious separation led to domestic violence orders against the defendant. During an arranged child-visiting time an altercation arose between the defendant and his former wife leading to the defendant removing a rifle from his vehicle and shooting her dead with four shots fired at close range. At his first trial the defendant was found guilty of murder. After a successful appeal on the grounds of misdirection as to the burden of proof, at his second trial the defence raised automatism (dissociative amnesia) caused by external stress resulting in a state of involuntariness. Notwithstanding evidence of prior acrimony and purposive, goal-directed behaviour on the part of the defendant, the jury acquitted Singh by majority verdict.

A case such as *Singh* is problematic as it raises once again the gender-biased concerns mentioned in the context of the use of the substantive defence of provocation. As with the provocation defence, the defence of automatism was raised in the context of the deterioration of an intimate relationship. Moreover, the loss of control was experienced, as in the paradigmatic case found in provocation, by a man in respect of the killing of his estranged wife. The case of *Singh* is only one of several cases where claims of sane automatism, particularly states of dissociation due to psychological blow, have been raised.[117] The attractiveness of securing an outright acquittal coupled with the difficulty faced by the prosecution of rebutting involuntariness beyond reasonable doubt renders a plea of sane automatism an attractive alternative for defendants. However, given the possibility that acquittals which are not deserved may result, a principled response to this issue is rendered a matter of importance.

There are other reasons militating in favour of treating sane automatism as an excuse and requiring the accused to raise a defence. For example, requiring an accused to raise the elements of a defence is in keeping with the reasons-based

116 (2003) 86 SASR 473 (SC SA); see McSherry 'Men Behaving Badly' (n. 11) 17–19.

117 *Falconer* (1990) 171 CLR 30; *R v Parks* (1992) 75 CCC (3d) 287; *R v Leonboyer* [2001] VSCA 149 and cases referred to in McSherry, 'Automatism in Australia since Falconer's Case' (n. 108); McSherry, 'Getting Away with Murder?' (n. 10) 163.

approach of recent law-reform proposals.[118] Once claims of volitional impairment that arise from a state of impaired consciousness are viewed as excuses, such claims become implicitly subject to critical moral evaluation. Such a moral evaluation will focus on the reasons for which an accused committed the wrongdoing. In the absence of such an evaluative process appeals to, for example, a heightened state of emotional responsiveness may be viewed as sufficient to ground a claim of involuntariness. However, such an approach runs the risk of developing into 'an evaluative free-for-all'.[119] The evaluation of an accused's action will consider the reasons for which the action occurred before such reasons are permitted to mitigate the offence.[120] Further, the normative requirement, or objective standard, which I have argued is a necessary condition of excuses, will indicate when the conduct of an accused should be viewed as inexcusable. Certain situations may arise where a claim of volitional impairment on the part of an accused should not be recognized as alleviating his or her criminal responsibility. For example, claims of reactive depression by, paradigmatically, accused men who kill their partner after being told that their partner is leaving require close scrutiny.[121] There may be cogent reasons for denying an excusatory defence in such instances notwithstanding claims of volitional impairment.

In this section, I have argued that in order to ensure that unjust acquittals do not eventuate, claims of volitional impairment arising from a state of impaired consciousness should be treated as giving rise to an excusatory defence. In order to apply the necessary condition of excusatory defences to claims of volitional impairment arising from states of impaired consciousness, the next section will propose the formulation of a defence of impaired consciousness.

Reform: a defence of impaired consciousness

This section will begin with a concise statement of the proposed defence of impaired consciousness and its various elements. This will be followed by the presentation of an objection which questions the need for a distinct defence of impaired consciousness. This objection calls for subsuming states of impaired consciousness under a broad category of mental disorder. In response it will be argued that such a view should be rejected and it is indicated why a distinct defence of impaired consciousness should be implemented.

118 Victorian Law Reform Commission, *Defences to Homicide: Final Report* (n. 15) 7.24–5.

119 J. Gardner and T. Macklem, 'Compassion without Respect? Nine Fallacies in *R v Smith*' [2001] *Criminal Law Review* 623, 635.

120 See D.M. Kahan and M.C. Nussbaum, 'Two Conceptions of Emotion in Criminal Law' (1996) 96 *Columbia Law Review* 269; S.H. Pillsbury, 'Emotional Justice: Moralising the Passions of Criminal Punishment' (1989) 74 *Cornell Law Review* 655.

121 Victorian Law Reform Commission, *Defences to Homicide: Final Report* (n. 15).

The defence

An accused's claim of volitional impairment may arise from a state of impaired consciousness caused by, for example, severe emotional trauma. In such a case a similar inquiry as that undertaken in respect of excusatory defences should apply to an accused's claim of having experienced difficulty in controlling his or her conduct. In particular, such an inquiry should highlight the nature of an accused's mitigating mental state, address the issue of the sufficiency of the resulting impairment and pay heed to any underlying normative considerations that would preclude the raising of such an excusatory defence. The proposed defence of impaired consciousness is to be used in those instances in which an accused claims to have experienced a state of volitional impairment due to a state of impaired consciousness leading to the killing of another person. Such a defence may be defined as follows:[122]

> Impaired Consciousness: A person who would otherwise be convicted of murder may be convicted of manslaughter if, as a result of a condition not recognized as forming the basis for another defence, he or she at the time of the killing suffered from a state of impaired consciousness which caused him or her to experience substantial difficulty in controlling his or her conduct and such difficulty would have been experienced by an ordinary person in like circumstances.

It is a requirement of excusatory defences that the accused's personal mitigating factor be the cause of a particular result. The notion of 'result' highlights the nature of the relationship between an accused's personal mitigating factor ('condition') and the state of volitional impairment which excuses. In the instant case, an accused's state of impaired consciousness must be the cause of his or her difficulty in controlling the conduct constituting the offence. It is not the personal mitigating factor, or condition, itself which gives rise to the defence. For the defence to be established, it is the accused's difficulty in controlling his or her conduct, where such difficulty is comparable to that which would be experienced by an ordinary person in like circumstances, which gives rise to the defence. The requirement of a condition ensures that the accused's conduct is the product of a verifiable condition. That is, there must be factual support for the conclusion that the accused's conduct occurred in a state of volitional impairment as a result of a particular condition. The existence of such an identifiable condition will lend evidentiary support to the claim that a state of volitional impairment does in fact exist.[123]

---

122 For similar formulations, see P. Robinson, *Structure and Function in Criminal Law* (n. 22) 168 n. 32; J.C. Smith and B. Hogan, *Smith and Hogan: Criminal Law* (9th edn, London, 1999) 213.

123 Victorian Law Reform Commission, *Defences to Homicide: Final Report* (n. 15) 5.140.

A further requirement of the proposed defence is that the condition producing the state of volitional impairment is one which is 'not recognized as forming the basis for another excusing condition'. This aspect of the defence seeks to ensure that the defence of impaired consciousness is not used as an alternative to a defence of insanity or used as an alternative plea to the defence of diminished responsibility. In particular, the defence of impaired consciousness is not to be understood as collapsing the distinction between cases of volitional impairment characterized as sane automatism and those instances of volitional impairment characterized as insane automatism. As will be argued below, while superficially attractive, the subsuming of instances of volitional impairment under an umbrella concept such as mental disorder should be avoided given that such an approach fails to pay due regard to the precise nature of the respective defences. Both the insanity defence and the defence of diminished responsibility are reliant for their operation on an accused suffering from a mental illness or abnormality of mind respectively.[124] Where an accused's mental state condition is understood as falling within the range of states characterized as mental illness, the defence of impaired consciousness is not applicable. In such a case the accused's only defence should be, depending on both the nature of the impairment and availability of the defence, either insanity or diminished responsibility.

The distinction between insanity and diminished responsibility relates to the degree of impairment experienced by an accused. As outlined above, depending on the jurisdiction, insanity requires a total deprivation of the ability or capacity of an accused to either control or know the nature, quality or wrongness of his or her act.[125] For this reason an accused successfully pleading insanity is exempted from responsibility, as he or she cannot reach the standard expected of an ordinary person. Diminished responsibility requires a substantial impairment of an accused's capacities to a degree sufficient to reduce rather than exclude his or her criminal responsibility.

As with diminished responsibility, the defence of impaired consciousness is proposed as a partial defence reducing, rather than excluding, an accused's criminal responsibility. However, there is an important difference between the two defences. Unlike diminished responsibility, the partial defence of impaired consciousness does not rely on the existence of an underlying pathological state which would take it beyond the experience of an ordinary person. The partial defence of impaired consciousness will operate where an accused's difficulty in

---

124 The defence of diminished responsibility is operative in the ACT: *Crimes Act 1900* (ACT) s 14; the Northern Territory: *Criminal Code* (NT) s 37; and Queensland: *Criminal Code* (Qld) s 304A. New South Wales reformed its diminished responsibility defence in 1997: *Crimes Amendment (Diminished Responsibility) Act 1997* s 23A. The defence is now known as the defence of 'substantially impaired capacity': *Crimes Act 1900* (NSW) s 23A.

125 S. Yeo, 'The Insanity Defence in the Criminal Laws of the Commonwealth of Nations' [2008] *Singapore Journal of Legal Studies* 241, 248–9.

controlling his or her conduct is such as would be experienced by an ordinary person in like circumstances. The defence is partial, as, while the accused's difficulty in controlling his or her conduct may be an ordinary event, his or her decision to go on and kill the victim is inexcusable given his or her degree of control.

The notion of 'substantial' difficulty captures the degree of impairment which an accused must experience in respect of his or her ability to control his or her conduct before the excusatory defence will operate. In contrast to the total incapacity required by the insanity defence, it will be sufficient to establish the defence of impaired consciousness, if it is shown that the difficulty experienced by an accused in controlling his or her conduct is 'substantial' and comparable to that experienced by an ordinary person in like circumstances. Such a view follows from the claim made above that involuntary conduct does not arise from a state of impaired consciousness but is circumscribed to those movements accompanying convulsive bodily spasms, reflex responses and the like. Additionally, the requirement that the difficulty be 'substantial' rather than total is designed to take the edge off the argument that there is no objectively verifiable means by which to determine whether an accused did not or could not control his or her conduct.[126] Conditions which are particularly problematic to verify are those states of dissociation triggered by conditions of extreme stress (psychological blow). Such instances are problematic as there is no reliable way of determining whether the emotional stress was sufficient to cause the difficulty experienced by an accused in controlling his or her conduct or whether the accused was in fact suffering from such a difficulty prior to his or her exposure to the stress.[127] However, where a condition of the defence requires that an accused experience substantial difficulty rather than incapacity to control his or her conduct, the need to establish whether he or she did not or could not control such conduct becomes less pressing. It will be sufficient in such cases that the accused experienced a degree of difficulty in controlling his or her conduct comparable to that which 'would have been experienced by an ordinary person in like circumstances'.

Whether an accused's difficulty in controlling his or her conduct is similar to that experienced by an ordinary person will require a normative inquiry assessing such an accused's lack of control against the objective standard of an ordinary person in like circumstances. Such a normative inquiry, or objective test, will require a distinction to be drawn between those matters which relate to whether an accused has experienced difficulty in controlling his or her conduct and those matters which relate to whether an ordinary person in like circumstances

---

126 Fairall and Yeo, *Criminal Defences in Australia* (n. 16) 260. In respect of the argument in Chapter 5, the objection to establishing incapacity on the part of an accused in the absence of an objective test distinguishing those accused who did not from those who could not is further blunted by noting that where there is evidence of motivation the diagnostic category of pyromania as volitional insanity is not established.

127 Ibid.

'would' have experienced a similar degree of difficulty. The relevant test which the standard must satisfy is: 'would' an ordinary person have experienced such difficulty as was experienced by the accused?[128] The standard designated by the term 'would' is a higher standard than that which would be designated by the use of the terms 'could' or 'possibly'. The higher standard is meant to further restrict the operation of the defence by insisting that only those accused whose level of difficulty is comparable to that which would be experienced by an ordinary person should be offered the excuse.

As noted by three justices of the High Court in *Falconer*, the ordinary person 'is assumed to be a person of normal temperament and control'.[129] Hence, in assessing an accused's volitional impairment against an objective standard, the proposed defence of impaired consciousness ensures that the defence is restricted in its scope to instances of volitional impairment which may be experienced by an individual who does not lack sufficient self-control and who is not suffering from a mental illness. Hence, those accused who either lack sufficient self-control or are mentally ill will fail to satisfy the objective limb of the defence and will not be provided with an excusatory defence. However, an accused who fails to satisfy the defence due to a clinical condition which causes him or her to experience a degree of difficulty which would not be experienced by an ordinary person may nevertheless raise a defence of insanity.[130]

Nevertheless, certain courts and commentators have held that evidence of a state of impaired consciousness should not be allowed to ground an excusatory defence leading to the mitigation of an accused's blameworthiness. In particular, it has been suggested that claims arising from a state of impaired consciousness should be subsumed under the umbrella of a broader mental impairment defence.[131] On this approach, rather than being treated as an instance of volitional impairment, a state of impaired consciousness would be viewed as an instance of mental disorder resulting in appropriate dispositional outcomes in the light of social defence concerns. In the following sections I will consider the merit of one such argument and show why this approach should be rejected and a defence of impaired consciousness implemented.

Impaired consciousness as mental disorder

Certain commentators have argued that states of impaired consciousness should be treated as a category of mental impairment. For example, Bernadette McSherry

128 Cp. *R v Falconer* (1990) 171 CLR 30, 55 per Mason CJ, Brennan, McHugh JJ.

129 Ibid. 58 per Mason CJ, Brennan, McHugh JJ.

130 *R v Radford* (1987) 11 Crim LJ 231, 276.

131 B. McSherry, 'Voluntariness, Intention and the Defence of Mental Disorder: Toward a Rational Approach' (2003) 21 *Behavioural Sciences and Law* 581; for a similar proposal see E. Lederman, 'Non-Insane and Insane Automatism: Reducing the Significance of a Problematic Distinction' (1985) 34 *International Criminal Law Quarterly* 819.

has argued that, by broadening the definition of 'mental disorder' so as to include a condition of severely impaired consciousness, conduct arising from a state of impaired consciousness could be subsumed within a new defence of mental disorder.[132] Such a defence would incorporate both states of volitional impairment in addition to any 'evidence of mental disorder used in order to negate intention'.[133] According to McSherry, as 'the fundamental principle of criminal law is that individuals must only be punished if they are able to reason for criminal actions that are "willed" in some way', the focus of the mental disorder defence will be on an accused's inability to reason.[134] On the proposed defence of mental disorder, the focus of expert evidence will be limited to whether or not the accused was suffering from a mental disorder at the time of the offence.[135] On the broadened defence of mental disorder, conditions of impaired consciousness, no matter how they arose, would be viewed as potentially affecting reasoning processes in a similar way to states of severe mental illness. Consequently, the ultimate issue for the jury to decide would be what effect, if any, the mental disorder had on an accused's ability to reason at the time of the offence.[136] The significance of such a formulation will be that courts would not 'have to rely on unworkable and artificial tests of what are conditions stemming from internal or external causes'.[137] That is, courts would not have to apply tests in order to distinguish between those states which are the result of a state of mental impairment giving rise to insanity and those states which go to voluntariness.

The VLRC in its final report on defences to the offence of homicide decided against adopting McSherry's proposed defence of mental disorder.[138] In particular, the commission noted that, while the distinction between those states of involuntariness arising from a state of mental impairment giving rise to insanity and those which do not arise from a state of mental impairment giving rise to insanity was difficult to draw, 'it is nevertheless an important conceptual and legal distinction which should be maintained'.[139] Ultimately, the commission

132 McSherry 'Voluntariness, Intention and the Defence of Mental Disorder' (n. 131) 597; see also McSherry 'Getting Away with Murder?' (n. 10) 163, where the author argues for a revised defence of mental impairment incorporating a broad definition of 'mental impairment' including states of 'mental illness, severe intellectual disability or a condition of severe impaired consciousness'.

133 McSherry, 'Voluntariness, Intention and the Defence of Mental Disorder' (n. 131) 610.

134 Ibid. 598.

135 Ibid.

136 Ibid.; see also Victorian Law Reform Commission, *Defences to Homicide: Final Report* (n. 15) 5.21.

137 McSherry, 'Voluntariness, Intention and the Defence of Mental Disorder' (n. 131) 598.

138 Victorian Law Reform Commission, *Defences to Homicide: Final Report* (n. 15) 5.155.

139 Ibid. 5.156.

recommended that the distinction between those states of involuntariness arising from mental impairment and those which do not arise from mental impairment should be retained.[140] According to the commission, the question of whether an accused's involuntariness arose from a state of mental impairment or from some other cause is a question for the jury to decide on the basis of the evidence.

Nevertheless, by refusing to subsume the distinction between the varieties of automatism under a broader mental state defence ensures that problems associated with distinguishing between these states remains. This is the problem of distinguishing between those states of impaired consciousness which are the result of a state of mental impairment and those states which go to involuntariness.

The defence of impaired consciousness addresses those states of volitional impairment that do not arise from a disease of the mind, yet which are sufficient to mitigate an accused's blameworthiness. On the basis of the defence any 'condition not recognized as forming the basis for another defence' will be sufficient provided the accused experienced a degree of difficulty in controlling his or her conduct comparable to that which an 'ordinary person in like circumstances' would have experienced. Whether the condition has an impact on the degree of difficulty experienced by an accused in controlling his or her conduct is a question to be answered in the light of expert evidence.

However, there are instances where the cause of a state of impaired consciousness may be in dispute. For example, it may be open to question whether an accused's state of dissociation is to be characterized as volitional impairment or insanity. Assuming that a proper foundation has been raised in each instance both may be raised together.[141] A judge will determine and explain the legal significance of evidence which is admissible and that which is capable of raising a reasonable doubt in respect of a particular issue. Unless there is evidence in support of an accused's claim that he or she was acting in a state of volitional impairment at the time of the offence, a trial judge should not direct a jury in respect of the legal significance of such impairment.[142] Where there is sufficient evidence to raise a reasonable doubt as to the accused's capacity to control his or her conduct, the prosecution must remove such doubt by rebutting the defence. The expert evidence will assist the jury in determining whether the accused did in fact experience such difficulty in the instant case. Whether the accused does in fact satisfy this standard will require a normative inquiry to be undertaken assessing his or her conduct against the objective standard of an ordinary person in like circumstances. If the condition giving rise to the difficulty is seen as something that would cause an ordinary person to experience a similar degree of difficulty then the accused's behaviour will be viewed as deserving of excuse. If however, the condition giving rise to the accused's difficulty in controlling his or her conduct is such that an

140 Ibid. 5.160.

141 *Falconer* (1990) 171 CLR 30; *Radford* (1985) 42 SASR 266.

142 *O'Connor* (1980) 146 CLR 64, 87 per Barwick CJ; *McLeod* (1991) 56 A Crim R 320; *Boyd* (CCA 20 of 1985, 11 December 1987, unreported).

ordinary person in like circumstances would not have experienced the accused will not be able to raise the defence. For the purposes of the defence, the 'ordinary person' 'is assumed to be a person of normal temperament and control'.[143]

Conclusion

I concluded Chapter 2 with the observation that cases such as *R v Singh*[144] highlight the danger of bogus claims associated with pleas of involuntariness being raised by accused individuals and accepted by juries. Such cases reveal both the evidentiary and conceptual difficulties involved in distinguishing those states of involuntariness triggered by a sufficient degree of physical or psychological trauma and those states of involuntariness indicative of an accused's state of mental impairment. The defining line between these states reveals 'overlaps and blurred boundaries'.[145] In Chapter 5, I argued that an accused whose claim of involuntariness is the result of a state of mental impairment sufficient to ground a defence of insanity may have recourse to the defence of volitional insanity. In this chapter I have endeavoured to formulate a defence of impaired consciousness in order to address claims of volitional impairment arising from a state of impaired consciousness falling short of insanity.

By raising the defence of impaired consciousness, an accused's claim of volitional impairment may be restricted within a normatively structured framework. Where involuntariness is extant a denial of responsibility follows as an accused's behaviour does not satisfy the physical element of the offence. That is, the accused has not satisfied the conduct requirement of a criminal offence. However, not all instances of volitional impairment arising from a state of impaired consciousness may be said to amount to involuntariness. In fact, voluntariness is best understood as operating along a continuum with only the most extreme instances giving rise to a denial of responsibility on the part of the accused. Yet, even where understood as not amounting to involuntariness, states of volitional impairment arising from a state of impaired consciousness are not subject to a necessary condition imposed on substantive excusatory defences: the requirement that such impairment satisfies the normative standard of the ordinary person. To this end, I have proposed a defence of impaired consciousness to be formulated in order to ensure that not all claims of volitional impairment will give rise to a denial of responsibility. The provision of such a defence will ensure that claims of volitional impairment arising from a state of impaired consciousness satisfy the necessary condition demanded of other excuses in the criminal law. In framing the defence in terms of a comparable degree of difficulty as would be experienced by an ordinary person

143 *R v Falconer* (1990) 171 CLR 30, 58 per Mason CJ, Brennan, McHugh JJ.

144 (2003) 86 SASR 473 (SC SA).

145 Lederman, 'Non-Insane and Insane Automatism' (n. 131) 820.

in like circumstances, I have sought to bring out the normative underpinnings of the enquiry.

The final substantive section addressed a contrasting view that hoped to subsume all instances of severe impaired consciousness under the umbrella of mental disorder. Supporters of such a view argue that by doing so troublesome distinctions between a state of impaired consciousness which gives rise to insanity, on the one hand, or involuntariness, on the other, could be dispensed with. I noted that, according to the VLRC, such an approach relies on a failure to acknowledge the conceptual distinction between states of insanity and states of involuntariness. However, by refusing to collapse states of involuntariness into a mental disorder defence, the proposed defence of impaired consciousness was left with a potential difficulty: how were instances of volitional impairment leading to a mitigation of blame to be distinguished from those instances arising from mental illness? In this context I noticed that by applying an objective test a jury may decide whether the results of the accused's clinical condition is such as might be experienced by an ordinary person. Where the accused experienced a degree of difficulty greater than that which would be experienced by an ordinary person, he or she may be a fit subject of a therapeutic regime. Where however, the accused experiences a degree of difficulty comparable to that which would be experienced by an ordinary person in like circumstances then the partial defence should mitigate his or her criminal responsibility.

Chapter 7
Conclusion:
Reform Proposals, Looking Forward

Introduction

By way of conclusion this final chapter will seek to tie together the themes of the book and suggest avenues for future research. To this end, this chapter will indicate how the reform proposals discussed in Chapters 4, 5 and 6, are guided by the various competing 'options for reform' noted in Chapter 1. Additionally, this chapter will indicate how the analysis in Chapter 3 of the various factors constituting the concept 'disease of the mind', inform these same reform proposals. Finally, this chapter will suggest how by focusing on some of the doctrinal, evidentiary, and substantive problems which the reform proposals raise further research might take the work forward.

As discussed in Chapter 1 there are various 'options for reform' which must be taken into account by any reform program which seeks to develop a principled approach to determining the boundaries of the defence of insanity and the doctrine of automatism. Succinctly stated the relevant 'options for reform' include ensuring that the scope of the defence of insanity and automatism is not drawn too broadly so as to exempt from responsibility individuals who choose to engage in criminal activity while being able to both distinguish between right and wrong and control their conduct. This matter is taken up in the context of Chapter 4. Another factor to be considered when formulating a reform proposal involves ensuring that those conditions which are recognized as exempting an individual from responsibility are not overly restrictive in their range. This option is acknowledged in Chapter 5. The final option for reform is the requirement that there exist a consistent set of rules which will allow triers of fact to determine the appropriate verdict for an individual. The proposal put forward in Chapter 6 seeks to implement this option.

While Chapter 1 considered the various 'options for reform' which any reform proposal should consider Chapter 3 explored the various factors which assist the court in determining whether a 'disease of the mind' has been established. These factors include a judgment of responsibility, clinical evidence, and community interest. The judgment of responsibility articulates the intuition that it is unjust to punish an individual who lacks the ability to distinguish right from wrong or control his or her conduct. The judgment of responsibility was used in Chapter 4 to determine a defendant's liability for states of 'drug-induced psychosis' arising from the voluntary use of illicit drugs.

The clinical evidence aspect of the enquiry allows a diagnosis of an accused's condition to be made in the light of recognised diagnostic categories and an assessment made of the likelihood of such a condition recurring if he or she is released into the community. Chapter 5 made use of a clinically recognised diagnostic category to argue for the recognition of an independent volitional limb at common law.

The community interest aspect of the 'disease of the mind' enquiry is concerned with considerations of societal protection in the light of the likelihood that an individual's mental impairment might recur. To this end the correct characterization of an individual's state of mind is of relevance to the community interest aspect of the enquiry. This aspect of the 'disease of the mind' enquiry was utilised in Chapter 6 in order to formulate a new defence of 'Impaired Consciousness'.

The remainder of this chapter will consider how the above reform options and relevant factors constituting a 'disease of the mind' both inform the reform proposals in Chapters 4, 5 and 6, and might guide further research.

I begin with a discussion of the reform proposal canvassed in Chapter 4 determining the criminal liability of an individual who has experienced a state of drug-induced psychosis through the voluntary consumption of illicit drugs.

Drug-Induced psychosis

Reform proposal

Chapter 4 utilized the judgment of responsibility aspect of the 'disease of the mind' enquiry discussed in Chapter 3 to provide a principled response to several questions posed by the voluntary use of illicit drugs resulting in a state of non-responsibility. Motivating the discussion was a desire to ensure that the scope of the defence of insanity was not overly broad so as to result in the exculpation from responsibility of individuals who choose to engage in criminal activity while being able to both distinguish between right and wrong and control their conduct.

The chapter began by drawing a distinction between two varieties of question, one clinical the other normative. For the purposes of Chapter 4, only the normative question was of concern, asking whether an individual who has voluntarily consumed drugs that have led to a state of psychosis ('drug-induced psychosis') should be allowed to raise the defence of insanity.

Ultimately, the chapter endorsed one particular explanatory approach, Meta-Responsibility, in order to address the issue of an accused's responsibility while in a state of 'drug-induced psychosis'.

It was argued that Meta-Responsibility is an intuitively attractive option for assessing an individual's responsibility for bringing about a state of non-responsibility for a number of reasons. First, it articulates the idea that, in keeping with the 'judgment of responsibility' aspect of the 'disease of the mind' enquiry, responsibility is a historical phenomenon. That is, whether an accused will be held responsible while in a state of psychosis will depend in part on how such a state arose, in particular, whether such a state has been brought about through the accused's 'fault or nature'.

A further reason for the intuitive appeal of Meta-Responsibility is that it is in keeping with one of the 'options for reform' determining the boundaries of the insanity defence. In particular, it ensures that the scope of the defence of non-responsibility is not drawn too broadly. Meta-Responsibility restricts the defence by ensuring that an individual who has acted in a rational autonomous fashion in bringing about a state of non-responsibility should not be allowed to benefit from his or her state of non-responsibility. Hence, according to Meta-Responsibility an accused will be held responsible for conduct performed in a state he or she brings about in a conscious and voluntary fashion even if as a result of such a state he or she is rendered incapacitated.

On the basis of the analysis undertaken, Chapter 4 proposed that the following question be asked in order to determine the responsibility of an individual who has brought about a state of 'drug induced psychosis' through the voluntary consumption of drugs:

> Did the accused intend or foresee or ought to have foreseen that he or she would enter a psychotic state and commit the offence?

Where it is established that the accused has performed the act voluntarily and knew, or ought to have known, that by so doing he or she thereby risked becoming psychotic and committing the offence, he or she will be held morally responsible.

In contrast to the above approach, the Victorian Law Reform Commission (VLRC) in its *Defences to Homicide Report*[1] adopted the view that the causal antecedents of an accused's state of mind should be treated as irrelevant to his or her responsibility. The VLRC was critical of what it felt was an overly narrow approach adopted by the common law as exemplified in the case of *Sebalj*.[2] In respect of *Sebalj* the VLRC argued that the fact that the accused was psychotic at the time of the offence should have been sufficient for him to be held non-responsible.

The reform proposal suggested in Chapter 4 was applied to the case of *Sebalj* in an attempt to understand the ruling in that case. Ultimately, it was acknowledged that as Sebalj's psychosis was the result of his withdrawal from drugs, a straightforward application of the proposed reform formulation would be problematic.

In particular, our intuitions flounder in respect of the subject defendant's criminal responsibility as he was endeavouring to wean himself from drugs at the time of the offence and may for that reason be considered less blameworthy.

1 Victorian Law Reform Commission, *Defences to Homicide, Final Report*, Report No 94 (Melbourne, 2004).

2 *R v Sebalj* [2004] VSC 212.

As noted in Chapter 3 the judgment of responsibility holds that a responsible agent is an agent who is considered to be a fit subject of our responsibility practices. A particular aspect of this practice is encompassed by the normative exercise undertaken by the criminal law in according categories of liability to the rational and autonomous conduct of individuals. Consequently, it would be in keeping with the judgment of responsibility if an accused's criminal responsibility correlated with his or her moral culpability. In the instant case, however, as the accused's moral culpability was reduced, given that he had attempted to wean himself off drugs, holding him fully criminally responsible would be incongruent with his moral culpability.

Nevertheless, it should not be thought that while a correct interpretation of *Sebalj* is problematic, this in any way undermines the validity and utility of the application of the proposed reform formulation.

Looking forward

The doctrinal problem which the reform proposal in Chapter 4 raises and which further research may alleviate involves the doctrinal issue of determining the precise nature of our responsibility practices when considering the criminal responsibility of an accused experiencing 'drug-induced psychosis'.

One possible means of moving towards a resolution of this issue is to focus on the twin attractions presented by Meta-Responsibility. In particular, and in keeping with the judgment of responsibility aspect of the enquiry, given that responsibility is a historical phenomenon it could be argued that a defendant should be held responsible where an evidentiary test of relevance is satisfied. Applying such a test to the case of *Sebalj* it might be argued that the defendant is liable given that his psychosis has been brought about, albeit indirectly, by means of his initial act of drug taking.

Where this approach will prove problematic however is in determining the nature of the requisite fault the accused must have possessed at that particular point in time: must the accused have foreseen that he would suffer from a state of psychosis at the time at which he attempted to withdraw from drug-taking, or will it be sufficient if he foresaw such psychosis ensuing upon the voluntary use of drugs?

Unless we are prepared to create an offence of strict liability for such an offence the above approach will need to clearly indicate the nature of the requisite fault element the accused must have possessed at the time of the initial drug-taking.

Alternatively, it could be argued that a case such as *Sebalj* is best resolved on the basis of the relevant 'option for reform' motivating this discussion, namely, the desire to restrict the scope of the defence. As noted in Chapter 4 this was the reasoning employed by the Supreme Court in the instant case. In his judgment to the instant case Justice Smith held that unless the defence is delimited in this fashion vast numbers of the accused people could seek to rely on and be made subject to the statutory regime.[3]

That is, it would be to 'open the floodgates' to provide a defence of non-responsibility to accused who have voluntarily used illicit drugs which have resulted in a state of 'drug-induced psychosis'. On the basis of this reasoning the fact that the accused in *Sebalj* has used drugs which have resulted, albeit indirectly, in a state of psychosis should be sufficient to deny him the defence.

However, the attractiveness of this proposal is counter-balanced by a genuine concern in respect of the degree to which policy-driven reasoning should be permitted to trump criminal law principle. For the question still remains: what must the accused have foreseen in order for him or her to be held responsible. Consequentialist formulations cannot answer this question.

Nevertheless, we would be mistaken to believe that merely because a clear answer is not readily available we should not proceed with this line of enquiry.

These are difficult questions, not because they raise complex, indeterminate substantive, doctrinal, or evidentiary issues, but because by their nature they bring into sharp relief the nature of our responsibility practices. The temptation to bypass such difficulties by focusing on overly narrow time frames, or by abandoning fundamental legal principles, or by suggesting that these are empirically verifiable propositions, should be resisted. It is the difficulty of the enterprise, and the goal to be achieved, which makes it worth our while to consider these questions in as clear a light as possible.

I now turn to consider the reform proposal in Chapter 5 calling for the recognition of an independent volitional limb to the insanity defence at common law.

Volitional insanity

Reform proposal

Unlike the Code jurisdictions the common law in Victoria does not recognize an independent volitional limb to the insanity defence. Chapter 5 has argued for the recognition of an independent volitional limb to operate alongside the cognitive limbs of the M'Naghten Rules. Such a limb would acknowledge as an independent ground of the insanity defence involuntary conduct arising from mental disorder without cognitive impairment.

The relevant 'disease of the mind' factor informing the reform proposal outlined in Chapter 5 is what was described in Chapter 3 as 'clinical evidence'. The clinical evidence aspect of the 'disease of the mind' enquiry will allow the trier of fact to determine whether an individual's behavior accords with a relevant

3 *R v Sebalj* [2003] VSC 181 (Unreported, SC Vic, Smith J, 5 June 2003), para 10.

diagnostic category. Additionally, the clinical evidence aspect of the enquiry will be of relevance to the court in determining whether evidence of the symptoms, nature and causes of an accused's condition is capable of constituting a 'disease of the mind'.

In keeping with the 'options for reform' detailed in Chapter 1 motivating this discussion is the desire to ensure that those conditions which are recognized as exempting an individual from responsibility are not overly restrictive in their range.

Chapter 5 began by noting as a general principle that, as voluntariness is a necessary condition of criminal liability, involuntary acts by an accused should result in an outright acquittal. Yet, under the common law and in Victoria, where an accused pleads involuntariness as a result of a 'disease of the mind' his or her plea will not result in an outright acquittal but in the 'special verdict'. Moreover, in order for the 'special verdict' to be established it will be necessary for such an accused to show, pursuant to the M'Naghten Rules, that his or her involuntariness was symptomatic of a recognized cognitive defect.

Chapter 5 then employed the diagnostic category of Pyromania as an, albeit controversial, example of a clinically recognised instance of volitional disorder without any associated cognitive impairment. It was noted that a diagnostic feature of Pyromania is repeated acts of fire-setting without any obvious motive.

In the light of this clinical evidence, it was argued that it was open to a trier of fact to characterize repeated acts of fire-setting without a motive as falling within the diagnostic category of Pyromania.

It was suggested that the 'best explanation' of such acts of fire-setting without an obvious and clear motive on the part of the accused is that they amount to a state of involuntariness due to mental disorder.

On this basis, Chapter 5 concluded that in the light of the clinical evidence of the symptom, nature and causes of Pyromania it was open to a court to characterize an individual suffering from such a condition as suffering from a 'disease of the mind' which should be recognized as giving rise to a defence of non-responsibility.

Nevertheless, given the contentious nature of the clinical evidence in respect of the diagnostic category of Pyromania, it was considered necessary to explain why the law should extend a volitional limb to an accused if in fact there are no such individuals in the world who would satisfy the diagnostic criteria associated with this category.

By way of justification it was argued that if there are instances of volitional impairment arising from a 'disease of the mind' which do not track cognitive defects refusing to extend a defence to an individual suffering from such volitional impairment may result in injustice. If however, it is found that there are no individuals whose volitional impairment does not track a cognitive defect then the provision of a volitional limb would be rendered merely redundant.

In the light of this contingency, and in keeping with the 'option of reform' ensuring that exempting conditions are not overly restrictive, Chapter 5 argued that it is incumbent on the criminal law to 'play it safe' by providing a defence of volitional impairment to these individuals.

Looking forward

Chapter 5 raises an evidentiary issue in respect of the validity of the diagnostic criteria used to establish the diagnostic category of Pyromania. As this category was used, by way of example in calling for the introduction of an independent volitional limb, the contentious nature of these criteria warrant further examination.

Chapter 5 readily acknowledged the various evidentiary concerns associated with the diagnostic features of Pyromania. In particular, the chapter openly remarked on the contentious nature of the validity of the diagnostic criteria used to verify this diagnostic category. Nevertheless, it was argued that this has less to do with any inherent 'diagnostic vagueness' associated with this particular condition than with there being a paucity of extant systematic reports in respect of this group of fire-starters. Moreover, it was noted that of the reports which are available most suffer from both definitional and methodological bias.

The validity of the diagnostic category is clearly a matter for expert evidence. However, as previously noted, clinical evidence of this category would assist the trier of fact to determine whether an accused's behavior is congruent with such a disorder. Equally, evidence of this category would assist the court in determining whether such a condition is capable of being characterized as a 'disease of the mind'. For this reason it would best serve the purposes of the criminal law if large scale epidemiological studies are undertaken in order to determine the validity of the diagnostic criteria associated with this category.

Moreover, there is a doctrinal issue which stands to be resolved on the basis of this enquiry. In particular, the resolution of the question concerning the validity of this diagnostic category will assist the law in attaining a desirable degree of parsimoniousness, there being no need for laws which are not required. Conversely, having a law which is in fact required will assist the law by ensuring both its relevance and consequent observance. That is, where the formulation of the relevant substantive law accords with clinical reality and is not overly restrictive in its scope, it may be expected that such a law will be applied where needed.

At present current formulations of the insanity defence represent

> means whereby juries work rough justice in a difficult area of law and morality.[4]

As outlined the proposed reform of the insanity defence incorporating an independent volitional limb represents an attempt to secure a more just outcome for accused.

---

4 N. Morris, '"Wrong" in the M'Naghten Rules' (1953) 16 *Modern Law Review* 435, 437.

In order to secure such an outcome endeavours to move the discussion forward should seek to better accommodate the reform proposal within the body of criminal law defences by validating the clinical evidence which renders such reform necessary.

The next section will turn to consider the formulation of the partial defence of 'Impaired Consciousness' introduced in Chapter 6 in response to various concerns associated with the plea of sane automatism.

Impaired consciousness

Reform proposal

It is the 'community interest' aspect of the 'disease of the mind' enquiry which informs the reform proposal put forward in Chapter 6. As noted in Chapter 3, the community interest aspect of the 'disease of the mind' enquiry is concerned with societal protection in the light of the likelihood that an individual's mental impairment might recur. To this end the correct characterization of an individual's state of mind is of relevance to the community interest aspect of the enquiry. The reform proposed by the defence of 'Impaired Consciousness' formulated in Chapter 6 was motivated by that aspect of the 'options for reform' which seeks to ensure that there exist a consistent set of rules so that a proper verdict may be reached by triers of fact.

Chapter 6 began by noting that as voluntariness is a necessary condition of criminal liability, states of involuntariness will result in an outright acquittal. However, as voluntariness occurs along a continuum, not all instances of volitional impairment will necessarily amount to a state of involuntariness.

In recognition of this it was contended that only instances of reflex action, bodily spasms and convulsions should be acknowledged as instances of involuntariness. As a corollary to this suggestion, it was argued that claims of sane automatism, in contrast to instances of reflex action, spasms, and convulsions, should be treated as falling short of involuntariness. As instances of volitional impairment rather than involuntariness such states should not be allowed to give rise to an outright acquittal but should, where appropriate, be allowed to partially excuse an individual's liability.

However, as Chapter 6 noted, in order to establish at which point of the voluntariness continuum an accused's claim of volitional impairment will be located, and whether it should be allowed to partially excuse his or her wrongdoing, there needs to be a standard against which such a claim may be assessed.

Yet, given that, as currently understood, voluntariness is not conceptualized as an excuse claims of volitional impairment bypass the usual normative requirement of a standard found operative in most excusing conditions. However, without recourse to a specified standard as a baseline, even those states of volitional impairment which amount to something less than involuntariness may result in the outright acquittal of an accused.

In order to remedy this Chapter 6 proposed the formulation of a new partial excuse of 'Impaired Consciousness' to be applied in cases of 'sane automatism':

> Impaired Consciousness: A person who would otherwise be convicted of murder may be convicted of manslaughter if, as a result of a condition not recognized as forming the basis for another defence, he or she at the time of the killing suffered from a state of impaired consciousness which caused him or her to experience substantial difficulty in controlling his or her conduct and such difficulty would have been experienced by an ordinary person in like circumstances.

The defence would apply in those instances where an accused claims that due to an external factor he or she has experienced a degree of difficulty in controlling his or her conduct comparable to that which would be experienced by an ordinary person in similar circumstances. Where the degree of difficulty experienced by the accused is comparable to this normative standard the defence provides a partial excuse. The provision of a partial excuse implicitly acknowledges that while the accused's degree of control was impaired it was not lost and, as a result, he or she should be held partly responsible for the offending conduct.

In keeping with the 'option for reform' guiding this discussion the proposed defence offers a substantive formulation which aids consistency of application and thereby ensures that the trier of fact will be well placed to reach a proper verdict.

Moreover, the proposed defence facilitates the community interest aspect of the enquiry by ensuring the correct characterization of an accused's state of mind. In particular, the defence permits a distinction to be drawn between two types of accused. On the one hand is the accused that experiences a 'psychological blow' resulting in a state of impaired consciousness that is

> the reaction of a sound mind to external stimuli, including stress producing factors.[5]

On the other hand is the accused whose state of impaired consciousness arising from a 'psychological blow' represents

> the reaction of an unsound mind to its own delusions or to external stimuli.[6]

In keeping with the analysis of the High Court in Falconer a 'sound mind' is one which corresponds with the standard of mental strength to be expected of an ordinary person.[7] In contrast, where an accused's strength of mind is below the

5 *R v Radford* (1985) 42 SASR 266, 276 per King CJ.

6 Ibid.

7 *R v Falconer* (1990) 171 CLR 30, 55 per Mason CJ, Brennan and McHugh JJ.

standard of the ordinary person it shall be characterized as 'unsound' and will, in the language of the proposed defence, be 'recognized as forming the basis for another defence'.

Where an accused of sound mind satisfies the requisite normative standard he or she will be provided with the partial defence of 'Impaired Consciousness'. As the condition of an accused of unsound mind distinguishes him or her from an ordinary person, he or she will not be permitted to raise the defence of 'Impaired Consciousness' but will be required to raise the defence of insanity or diminished responsibility.

Looking forward

The defence of 'Impaired Consciousness' introduced in Chapter 6 raises substantive issues in respect of the conditions under which various elements of the defence will be satisfied. Further research should provide a clear indication of these conditions in order to ensure the proper operation of the defence.

In particular, two related aspects of the proposed defence warrant further consideration. The first aspect warranting consideration will require determining the type of behavior which will allow the defence to be raised. The second aspect of the defence warranting further examination will require determining the degree of trauma which will satisfy the objective standard of the defence.

In respect of the first aspect, and as noted in Chapter 6, the ascription of praise or blame to an accused raising an excusatory defence will be determined according to whether his or her behavior satisfies the normative element, or objective standard, underlying the excuse. This normative element allows us to determine when an accused's behavior is inexcusable under certain excuses and for this reason should not be done.

When voluntariness is conceived of as an excuse the reasons for which an individual acts become subject to critical analysis. Such an analysis requires a consideration of the reasons for which the relevant conduct is undertaken. Where such reasons are found not to be 'good reasons', as, for example, in the instance of possessive partners who kill, the defence should not be permitted to be raised.

As a key aspect of the proposed excusatory defence of 'Impaired Consciousness' the clarification of those instances where an accused's behavior precludes the raising of the defence warrants further research. Moreover, and in the light of the 'reasons-based' approach to the proposed defence, further examination of those reasons which will be recognized as partially excusing an individual's criminal responsibility may prove of interest.

In respect of the second aspect of the defence warranting examination, as formulated the defence requires a 'condition', or 'psychological blow', to bring about a state of impaired consciousness leading to an individual's volitional impairment. It nevertheless remains an open question as what degree of, paradigmatically, physical or sexual abuse will be sufficient to result in a 'psychological blow' leading to such a state of impaired consciousness.

Hence, further research may be warranted in order to determine the degree of trauma an ordinary person would not be likely to have withstood in order to satisfy the objective standard as required by the defence. That is, what is called for is an analysis of those extraordinary events which may cause an accused of sound mind to react and bring about a state of dissociation resulting in 'substantial difficulty' in controlling his or her conduct.

The analysis of this question will run in tandem with the normative enquiry at the heart of the 'reason-centred' account of the reasons why an individual acted in the way he or she did. In both cases it will be incumbent on the law to ensure that heightened emotional responses to ordinary events, such as the breakdown of a relationship, are not sufficient without more to constitute a psychological blow, in order to

> firmly repress any tendency for people harbouring…dark emotions to give in to them by way of murderous violence.[8]

Conclusion

Overall, this book has been concerned with exploring the appropriate boundaries for the defence of insanity and the doctrine of automatism. By drawing on an analysis of the various factors which inform the concept of 'disease of the mind' as outlined in Chapter 3 this book has sought to provide a consistent and principled approach to the reform of the insanity defence and the doctrine of automatism. In particular, it has been argued that by using a refined notion of 'Meta-Responsibility' in relation to drug-associated psychosis, by including a volitional limb in the common law defence of insanity, and by introducing a new defence of Impaired Consciousness, a more consistent and principled approach to mental state defences can be developed.

8 *R v Radford* (No 2) (1987)11 Crim LJ 231, 232 per King CJ.

Bibliography

American Law Institute, *Model Penal Code*, Proposed Official Draft 1962 (Philadelphia: American Law Institute, 1985).

American Psychiatric Association, *Diagnostic and Statistical Manual of Mental Disorders* (4th edn, text revision, Washington, DC: APA, 2000).

Allridge, P., 'The Coherence of Defences' [1983] *Criminal Law Review* 665.

Ashworth, Andrew, 'The Doctrine of Provocation' (1976) 35 *Cambridge Law Journal* 292.

Bargh, J.A., and T.L. Chartrand, 'The Unbearable Automaticity of Being' (1999) 54 *American Psychologist* 462.

Bowers, M.B., and M.E. Swigar, 'Vulnerability to Psychosis Associated with Hallucinogen Use' (1983) 9 *Psychiatry Research* 91.

Brady, K., et al., 'Cocaine Abuse among Schizophrenic Patients' (1990) 147 *American Journal of Psychiatry* 1164.

Bronitt, Simon, and Bernadette McSherry, *Principles of Criminal Law* (Sydney: LBC, 2001; 2nd edn, Pyrmont, NSW: Thomsons Reuter, 2005; 3rd edn, Pyrmont, NSW: LBC, 2010).

Brookbanks, W., 'Insanity' in *Psychiatry and the Law: Clinical and Legal Issues*, ed. W. Brookbanks and S. Simpson (Wellington: Brooker's 2007).

Brookbanks, W., and S. Simpson (ed.), *Psychiatry and the Law: Clinical and Legal Issues* (Wellington: Brooker's, 2007).

Brookbanks, W., and J. Skipworth, 'Fitness to Plead' in *Psychiatry and the Law: Clinical and Legal Issues*, ed. W. Brookbanks and S. Simpson (Wellington: Brooker's, 2007).

Campbell, Ian G., *Mental Disorder and Criminal Law in Australia and New Zealand* (Sydney: Butterworths, 1988).

Cane, Peter,—— 'Fleeting Mental States' (2000) 59 *Cambridge Law Journal* 273.

—— *Responsibility in Law and Morality* (Oxford: Hart, 2002).

Carroll, A., et al., 'Drug-Associated Psychoses and Criminal Responsibility' (2008) 26 *Behavioural Sciences and the Law* 633.

Coles, E.M., 'Scientific Support for the Legal Concept of Automatism' (2000) 7 *Psychiatry, Psychology and Law* 33.

Coles, E.M., and S. Armstrong, 'Hughlings Jackson on Automatism as Disinhibition' (1998) 6 *Journal of Law and Medicine* 73.

Colvin, E. 'Ordinary and Reasonable People: The Design of Objective Tests of Criminal Responsibility' (2001) 27 *Monash University Law Review* 197.

Colvin, E., and J. McKechnie, *Criminal Law in Queensland and Western Australia* (5th edn, Chatswood, NSW: Butterworths, 2008).

Committee on Mentally Abnormal Offenders (Butler Committee), *Report of the Committee on Mentally Abnormal Offenders* (London: HMSO, 1975).

Community Development Committee of the Parliament of Victoria, *Inquiry into Persons Detained at the Governor's Pleasure*, Report No 57 (Melbourne: CDCP, 1994).

Criminal Law Officer's Committee, *Model Criminal Code – Chapter 2: General Principles of Criminal Responsibility: Final Report* (Canberra: Attorney-General's Office, 1992).

Crofts, T., *The Criminal Responsibility of Children and Young Persons in Germany and England* (Aldershot: Ashgate, 2002).

—— 'Rebutting the Presumption of Doli Incapax' [1998] *Journal of Criminal Law* 185.

Crofts, T., and K. Burton, *The Criminal Codes: Commentary and Materials* (6th edn, Pyrmont, NSW: LBC, 2009).

Delisle, R.J., 'Stone: Judicial Activism Gone Awry to Presume Guilt' (1999) 24 *Criminal Reports* (5th) 91.

Dixon, O, 'A Legacy of Hadfield, McNaghten and Maclean' (1957) 31 *Australian Law Journal* 255.

Diesfeld, K., and S. Sjostrom, 'Interpretive Flexibility: Why Doesn't Insight Incite Controversy in Mental Health Law?' (2007) 25 *Behavioural Sciences and the Law* 85.

Doley, R., 'Pyromania: Fact or Fiction?' (2003) 43 *The British Journal of Criminology* 797.

Doley, R., and K. Fritzon, 'Assessment and Treatment of Fire-Setting Behaviour' in *Forensic Psychology and Criminology: An Australian Perspective*, ed. K. Fritzon and P. Wilson (North Ryde, NSW: ACI, 2008).

Duff, Antony R., (ed.), *Philosophy and the Criminal Law: Principle and Critique* (Cambridge: Cambridge University Press, 1998).

Eastman, N., 'Psychiatric, Psychological and Legal Models of Man' (1992) 15 *International Journal of Law and Psychiatry* 157.

Elliot, Ian D., 'Responsibility for Involuntary Acts: *Ryan v The Queen*' (1968) 41 *Australian Law Journal* 497.

Evans, J.St.B.T., D.E. Over and K.I. Manktelow, 'Reasoning, Decision-Making and Rationality' (1993) 49 *Cognition* 165.

Fabian, J.M., 'Metamphetamine Motivated Murder: Forensic Psychological/Psychiatric and Legal Applications in Criminal Contexts' (2007) 35 *Journal of Psychiatry and Law* 443.

Fairall, Paul A., 'Voluntariness, Automatism and Insanity: Reflections on *Falconer*' (1993) 17 *Criminal Law Journal* 81.

Fairall, Paul A., and Stanley M.H. Yeo, *Criminal Defences in Australia* (4th edn, Chatswood, NSW: LexisNexis Butterworths, 2005).

Farrell, B.A., 'Mental Illness: A Conceptual Analysis' (1979) 9 *Psychological Medicine* 21.

Feinberg, Joel, *Harm to Self* (New York: Oxford University Press, 1986).

Ferguson, G., 'A Critique of Proposals to Reform the Insanity Defence' (1989) 14 *Queen's Law Journal* 135 .

—— 'The Insanity Defence in Canada, Malaysia and Singapore: A Tale of Two Codes' (1990) 17 *Journal of Malaysian and Comparative Law* 12.

Fingarette, Herbert, *The Meaning of Criminal Insanity* (Berkeley: University of California Press, 1972).

Fischer, John Martin, and Mark Ravizza, *Responsibility and Control: A Theory of Moral Responsibility* (Cambridge: Cambridge University Press, 1998).

Fisse, Brent, *Howard's Criminal Law* (5th edn, Sydney: LBC, 1990).

Fitzjames Stephen, J., *A History of the Criminal Law of England* (London: Richard Clay and Sons,1883).

Foust, L.L., 'The Legal Significance of Clinical Formulations of Fire-setting Behaviour' (1979) 2 *International Journal of Law and Psychiatry* 371.

Freckelton, I., 'Decision-Making about Involuntary Psychiatric Treatment' (1998) 5 *Psychiatry, Psychology and Law* 249.

Frieberg, A., 'The Disposition of Mentally Disordered Offenders in Australia: "Out of Mind, Out of Sight" Revisited' (1994) 1 *Psychiatry, Psychology and Law* 97.

Freiberg, A., and F. Stewart, 'Provocation in Sentencing: A Culpability-Based Framework' (2008) 19 *Current Issues in Criminal Justice* 283.

—— and —— *Provocation in Sentencing: Research Paper* (Melbourne: AIC, 2008).

Fritzon, K. and P. Wilson (ed.), *Forensic Psychology and Criminology: An Australian Perspective* (North Ryde, NSW: ACI, 2008).

Fulford, K.W.M., 'Value, Action, Mental Illness and the Law' in *Action And Value in Criminal Law*, ed. Stephen Shute, John Gardner and Jeremy Horder (Oxford: Clarendon Press, 1993) 279.

Gabbard, G.O. (ed.), *Gabbard's Treatment of Psychiatric Disorders* (4th edn., Washington D.C.: APA, 2007).

Gannon, T.A. and A. Pina., 'Firesetting: Psychopathology, Theory and Treatment' (2010) 15 *Aggression and Violent Behaviour* 224.

Gardner, John, and Timothy Macklem, 'Compassion without Respect? Nine Fallacies in *R v Smith*' [2001] *Criminal Law Review* 623.

Gelder, M., D. Gath and R. Mayou, *Oxford Textbook of Psychiatry* (2nd edn, Oxford: Oxford University Press, 1995).

Gelder, M., P. Harrison and D. Cowen, *Shorter Oxford Textbook of Psychiatry* (5th edn, Oxford: Oxford University Press, 2006).

Gelder, M, N.C.Andreason, J.J. Lopez-Ibor, J.R. Geddes (eds) *New Oxford Textbook of Psychiatry* (2nd edn, Oxford: Oxford University Press, 2009).

Geller, J.L., J. Erlen and P.J. Pinkus, 'A Historical Appraisal of America's Experience with "Pyromania": A Diagnosis in Search of a Disorder' (1986) 9 *International Journal of Law and Psychiatry* 212.

Glazebrook, S., 'Risky Business: Predicting Recidivism' (2010) 17 *Psychiatry, Psychology and Law* 97.

Goldstein, A.S., *The Insanity Defence* (New Haven: Yale University Press, 1967).
Goode, M., 'On Subjectivity and Objectivity in Denial of Criminal Responsibility' (1987) 11 *Criminal Law Journal* 131.
Gough, Stephen, 'Taking the Heat out of Provocation' (1999) 19 *Oxford Journal of Legal Studies* 481.
Greenawalt, Kent, 'The Perplexing Borders of Justification and Excuse' (1984) 84 *Columbia Law Review* 1897.
Greig, D., *Neither Bad nor Mad: The Competing Discourses of Psychiatry, Law and Politics* (London: Jessica Kingsley, 2002).
Griew, E. 'The Future of Diminished Responsibility' [1988] *Criminal Law Review* 75.
Hafner, H., and W. Boker, *Crimes of Violence by Mentally Abnormal Offenders* (Cambridge: Cambridge University Press, 1982).
Hall, Jerome, 'Mental Disease and Crime' (1945) 45 *Columbia Law Review* 677.
—— 'Mental Disease and Criminal Responsibility' (1958) 33 *Indiana Law Journal* 212.
Hannan, B., 'Depression, Responsibility and Criminal Defences' (2005) 28 *International Journal of Law and Psychiatry* 321.
Hart, H.L.A., *Punishment and Responsibility* (Oxford: Clarendon Press, 1968).
Horder, Jeremy, *Excusing Crime* (Oxford: Oxford University Press, 2004).
—— *Provocation and Responsibility* (Oxford: Clarendon Press, 1992).
Insurance Council of Australia, *Research into Insurance Fraud: Member Survey 1996/1997* (Sydney: ICA, 1998).
Johnson-Laird, P.N., and E. Shafir, 'The Interaction between Reasoning and Decision-Making: An Introduction' (1993) 49 *Cognition* 1.
Jones, T.H., 'Insanity, Automatism and the Burden of Proof on the Accused' (1995) 111 *Law Quarterly Review* 475.
Kadish, Sandford, 'Excusing Crime' (1987) 75 *California Law Review* 257.
Kahan, D M., and Martha C. Nussbaum, 'Two Conceptions of Emotion in Criminal Law' (1996) 96 *Columbia Law Review* 269.
Kendell, R.E., 'The Concept of Disease and its Implications for Psychiatry' (1975) 127 *British Journal of Psychiatry* 305.
Lacey, Nicola, 'A Clear Conception of Intention: Elusive or Illusory?' (1993) 56 *Modern Law Review* 621.
—— 'Contingency, Coherence, and Conceptualism' in *Philosophy and the Criminal Law*, ed. A. Duff (Cambridge: Cambridge University Press, 1998) 9.
—— 'In Search of the Responsible Subject: History, Philosophy and Criminal Law Theory' (2001) 64 *Modern Law Review* 350.
—— 'Responsibility and Modernity in Criminal Law' (2001) 9 *Journal of Political Philosophy* 249.
Lagrone, M., 'Alternatives to the Insanity Defence' (1984) 12 *Journal of Psychiatry and Law* 93.
Laing, R.D., *The Self and Others* (Harmondsworth: Penguin, 1969).

Lanham, David, 'Involuntary Acts and the *Actus Reus*' (1993) 17 *Criminal Law Journal* 97.

Law Reform Commission of Ireland, *Consultation Paper on Homicide: The Plea of Provocation*, LRC CP-27 (Dublin: LRCI, 2003).

Leader-Elliott, Ian D., 'Criminal Cases in the High Court: *Falconer*' (1991) 15 *Criminal Law Journal* 205.

—— *The Commonwealth Criminal Code: A Guide for Practitioners* (Canberra: Attorney-General's Office, 2002).

—— 'Insanity, Involuntariness and the Mental Element in Crime: *Hawkins v The Queen*' (1994) 18 *Criminal Law Journal* 347.

Lederman, E., 'Non-Insane and Insane Automatism: Reducing the Significance of a Problematic Distinction' (1985) 34 *International Criminal Law Quarterly* 819 .

Lewis, A., 'Health as a Social Concept' (1953) 4 *British Journal of Sociology* 109.

Lewis, N.D.C., and H. Yarnell, *Pathological Firesetting (Pyromania)*, Nervous and Mental Disease Monograph 82 (New York: Coolidge Foundation, 1951).

Leyoux, M., M. McLoughlin and J. Ades, 'Pyromania' in *Clinical Manual of Impulse Control Disorders*, ed. E. Hollander and D.J. Stein (Arlington, VA: APP, 2006) 229.

Lightfoot, J., 'Striking the Balance: The Abolition of the Victorian Governor's Pleasure System' (1998) 5 *Psychiatry, Psychology and Law* 265.

McAuley, F., *Insanity, Psychiatry and Responsibility* (Dublin: Round Hall Press Sweet and Maxwell, 1993).

McAuley, Finbarr, and John Paul McCutcheon, *Criminal Liability: A Grammar* (Dublin: Round Hall Press Sweet and Maxwell, 2000).

McCaldon, J., 'Automatism' (1964) 91 *Canadian Medical Association Journal* 914.

McElroy, S.L., and P.E. Keck Jr, 'Habit and Impulse Control Disorders' in *New Oxford Textbook of Psychiatry*, ed. M.G. Gelder et al. (2nd edn, Oxford: Oxford University Press, 2009) 911.

—— and —— 'Impulse Control Disorders' in *Gabbard's Treatments of Psychiatric Disorders*, ed. G.O. Gabbard (4th edn, Washington D.C.: APA, 2007).

Mackay, Ronald D., *Mental Condition Defences in the Criminal Law* (Oxford: OUP , 1995).

—— 'Non-Organic Automatism-Some Recent Developments' [1980] *Criminal Law Review* 350.

McLellan, A.T., G.E. Woody and C.P. O'Brien, 'Development of Psychiatric Illness in Drug Abusers' (1979) 301 *New England Journal of Medicine* 1310.

McSherry, Bernadette, 'Automatism in Australia since Falconer's Case' (1996) 6 *International Bulletin of Law and Mental Health* 73.

—— 'Casenote: *Falconer*' (1993) 17 *Criminal Law Journal* 81.

—— 'Criminal Detention of those with Mental Impairment' (1999) 6 *Journal of Law and Medicine* 216.

—— 'Criminal Responsibility, "Fleeting Mental States" of Mental Impairment, and the Power of Self-Control' (2004) 27 *International Journal of Law and Psychiatry* 445.

—— 'Defining What is a "Disease of the Mind": The Untenability of Current Legal Interpretations' (1993) 1 *Journal of Law and Medicine* 76.

—— 'Getting Away with Murder? Dissociative States and Criminal Responsibility' (1998) 21 *International Journal of Law and Psychiatry* 163.

—— 'Men Behaving Badly: Current Issues in Provocation, Automatism, Mental Impairment and Criminal Responsibility' (2005) 12 *Psychiatry, Psychology and Law* 15.

—— 'Mental Impairment and Criminal Responsibility: Recent Australian Legislative Reforms' (1999) 23 *Criminal Law Journal* 135.

—— 'Voluntariness, Intention and the Defence of Mental Disorder: Toward a Rational Approach' (2003) 21 *Behavioural Sciences and Law* 581.

Margolis, Joseph, 'The Concept of Disease' (1976) 1 *Journal of Medicine and Philosophy* 238.

Meloy, J. Reid, 'Voluntary Intoxication and the Insanity Defence' (1992) 22 *Journal of Psychiatry and Law* 439.

Miller, R.D., 'Hidden Agendas at the Law–Psychiatry Interface' (1990) 20 *Journal of Psychiatry and Law* 35.

Mitchell, E., 'Culpability for Inducing Mental States: The Insanity Defence of Dr Jekyll' (2004) 32 *The Journal of the American Academy of Psychiatry and the Law* 63.

—— 'Meta-Responsibility and Mental Disorder: Causing the Conditions of One's Own Insanity Plea' (1999) 10 *Journal of Forensic Psychiatry* 597.

—— *Self-Made Madness: Re-Thinking Illness and Criminal Responsibility* (Aldershot: Ashgate, 2004).

Model Criminal Code Officers Committee, *Model Criminal Code – Chapter 5: Non-Fatal Offences Against the Person, Discussion Paper* (Canberra: Attorney-General's Office, 1998).

Morris, Norval, 'Somnambulistic Homicide: Ghosts, Spiders and North Koreans' (1951) 5 *Res Judicatae* 29.

—— '"Wrong" in the M'Naghten Rules' (1953) 16 *Modern Law Review* 435.

Morse, Stephen, 'Craziness and Criminal Responsibility' (1999) 17 *Behavioural Sciences and Law* 147.

—— 'Diminished Capacity' in *Action And Value in Criminal Law*, ed. Stephen Shute, John Gardner and Jeremy Horder (Oxford: Clarendon Press, 1993) 239.

Moore, Michael, *Law and Psychiatry: Rethinking the Relationship* (Cambridge: Cambridge University Press, 1985).

Mullen, P.E., 'The Dangerousness of the Mentally Ill and the Clinical Assessment of Risk' in *Psychiatry and Law: Clinical and Legal Issues*, ed. W. Brookbanks (Wellington: Brooker's, 1996) 93.

____ 'Mental Disorder and Dangerousness' (1984) 18 *Australian and New Zealand Journal of Psychiatry* 8.

—— 'A Reassessment of the Link Between Mental Disorder and Violent Behaviour, and its Implications for Clinical Practices' (1997) 31 *Australian and New Zealand Journal of Psychiatry* 3.

—— 'Schizophrenia and Violence: From Correlations to Preventative Strategies' (2006) 12 *Advances in Psychiatric Treatment* 239.

—— 'Schizophrenic Syndrome, Violent and Other Antisocial Behaviours' in *Psychiatry and the Law: Clinical and Legal Issues*, ed. W. Brookbanks and S. Simpson (Wellington: Brooker's 2007) 293.

Mullen, P.E., and J. Ogloff, 'Assessing and Managing the Risks of Violence Towards Others' in *New Oxford Textbook of Psychiatry*, ed. M. Gelder et al. (2nd edn, Oxford: Oxford University Press, 2009) 1991.

Murugason, R., and L. McNamara, *Outline of Criminal Law* (Sydney: Butterworths, 1997).

New South Wales Law Reform Commission, *People with Cognitive and Mental Health Impairments in the Criminal Justice System: Criminal Responsibility and Consequences*, Consultation Paper 6 (Sydney: NSWLRC, 2010).

—— *Partial Defences to Murder: Diminished Responsibility*, Report No 82 (Sydney: Government Printer, 1997).

Norrie, Alan, *Crime, Reason and History* (2nd edn, London: Butterworths, 2001).

—— 'Simulacra of Morality? Beyond the Ideal/Actual Antinomies of Criminal Justice' in *Philosophy and the Criminal Law*, ed. A. Duff (Cambridge: Cambridge University Press, 1998), 101.

Odgers, S., 'Contemporary Provocation Law: Is Substantially Impaired Self-Control Enough?' in *Partial Excuses to Murder*, ed. Stanley M.H. Yeo (Sydney: LexisNexis, 1991) 103.

Paciocco, D. 'Death by Stone-ing: The Demise of Simple Automatism' (1999) 26 *Criminal Reports* (5th) 273.

Pathé, Michael T., and Paul E. Mullen, 'The Dangerousness of the DSM-III- R' (1983) 1 *Journal of Law and Medicine* 47.

Pattenden, R., 'Conflicting Approaches to Psychiatric Evidence in Criminal Trials: England, Canada and Australia' [1986] *Criminal Law Review* 92.

Pillsbury, S.H., 'Emotional Justice: Moralising the Passions of Criminal Punishment' (1989) 74 *Cornell University Press* 655.

Pols, Jan, 'Mental Illness and Rationality: A Critique' (1989) 12 *International Journal of Law and Psychiatry* 71.

Radden, Jennifer, *Madness and Reason* (London: George Allen & Unwin, 1985).

Reilly, A., 'Loss of Self-Control in Provocation' (1997) 21 *Criminal Law Journal* 320.

Rider, A.O., 'The Firesetter: A Psychological Profile' (1980) 49 *FBI Law Enforcement Bulletin* 7.

Robinson, Paul H., 'Causing the Conditions of One's Own Defence' (1985) 71 *Virginia Law Review* 1.

—— *Structure and Function in Criminal Law* (Oxford: OUP, 1997).

Roth, Michael, 'Schizophrenia and the Theories of Thomas Szasz' (1976) 129 *British Journal of Psychology* 317.

Satel, S., and W. Edell, 'Cocaine-Induced Paranoia and Psychosis Proneness' (1991) 148 *American Journal of Psychiatry* 1708.

Schopp, Robert F., *Automatism, Insanity and Criminal Responsibility* (Cambridge: Cambridge University Press, 1991).

—— 'Depression, the Insanity Defence and Civil Commitment: Foundations in Autonomy and Responsibility' (1989) 12 *International Journal of Law and Psychiatry* 81.

Scott, R., and W. Kingswell, 'Amphetamines, Psychosis and the Insanity Defence: Disturbing Trends in Queensland' (2003) 23 *Queensland Lawyer* 151.

Shute, Stephen, John Gardner and Jeremy Horder (eds), *Action And Value in Criminal Law* (Oxford: Clarendon Press, 1993).

Slodow, M.D., 'Criminal Responsibility and the Noncompliant Psychiatric Offender: Risking Madness' (1989) 40 *Case Western Reserve Law Review*, Comment, 271.

Smith, John C., and Brian Hogan, *Smith and Hogan: Criminal Law* (9th edn, London: Butterworths, 1996).

Soothill, K., E. Ackerley and B. Francis, 'The Criminal Careers of Arsonists' (2004) 44 *Medicine, Science and the Law* 27.

Steadman, H.J., 'From Dangerousness to Risk Assessment of Community Violence: Taking Stock at the Turn of the Century' (2000) 28 *Journal of the American Academy of Psychiatry and Law* 265.

Steinberg, M., *Handbook for the Assessment of Dissociation: A Clinical Guide* (Washington, DC: APA, 1995).

Stephen, James F., *History of the Criminal Law of England*, vol. 2 (London: Richard Clay & Sons, 1883).

Szasz, Thomas, *Ideology and Insanity* (Hammersmith: Penguin, 1970).

—— *Insanity: The Idea and its Consequences* (New York: Pan Books, 1997).

—— *Law, Liberty and Psychiatry* (New York: Pan Books, 1963).

—— *The Myth of Mental Illness* (London: Paladin, 1962).

Tadros, Victor, 'The Characters of Excuse' (2001) 21 *Oxford Journal of Legal Studies* 495.

—— *Criminal Responsibility* (Oxford: Oxford University Press, 2005).

Tsuang, M., J. Simpson and Z. Kronfol, 'Subtypes of Drug Use with Psychosis: Demographic Characteristics, Clinical Features, and Family History' (1982) 39 *Archives of General Psychiatry* 141.

Tollefson, E.A., and B. Starkman, *Mental Disorder in Criminal Proceedings* (Toronto: CPA 1993).

United Kingdom Law Commission, *A Criminal Code for England and Wales*, Law Com No 177, vol. 1: *Report and Draft Criminal Code Bill* (London: HMSO, 1989).

—— *Murder, Manslaughter and Infanticide*, Law Com No 304 (London: HMSO, 2006).

—— *Partial Defences to Murder*, Law Com No 290 (London: Law Commission, 2004).

Volkow, N.D., 'Drug Abuse and Mental Illness: Progress in Understanding Co-Morbidity' (2001) 158 *American Journal of Psychiatry* 1181.

Victorian Law Reform Commission, *Defences to Homicide: Final Report*, Report No 94 (Melbourne: Government Printer, 2004).

—— *Defences to Homicide: Options Paper* (Melbourne: Government Printer, 2003).

—— *Homicide*, Report No 40 (Melbourne: VLRC, 1991).

—— *Mental Malfunction and Criminal Responsibility*, Paper 14 (Melbourne: Government Printer, 1982).

—— *Provocation and Diminished Responsibility as Defences to Murder*, Report No 12 (Melbourne: VLRC, 1982).

Walker, N., 'Book Review: Mitchell, EW (2003) *Self-Made Madness: Rethinking Illness and Criminal Responsibility*' (2005) 16 *Journal of Forensic Psychiatry and Psychology* 612.

Wartofsky, Marx W., 'The Dialectics of Rationality: The Historicity of Norms in Psychiatry and the Law' (1980) 3 *International Journal of Law and Psychiatry* 279.

Western Australian Law Reform Commission, *The Criminal Process and Persons Suffering from Mental Disorder*, Discussion Paper (Fremantle: WALRC, 1987).

Williams, C.R., 'Development and Change in Insanity and Related Defences' (2000) 24 *Melbourne University Law Review* 711.

—— 'Psychopathy, Mental Illness and Preventive Detention: Issues Arising from the *David* Case' (1990) 16 *Monash University Law Review* 161.

Williams, Glanville, *Criminal Law: The General Part* (2nd edn, London: Stevens, 1961).

—— *Textbook of Criminal Law* (2nd edn, London: Stevens & Sons, 1983).

Wilson, W., 'The Structure of Criminal Law Defences' [2005] *Criminal Law Review* 108.

World Health Organisation, *The ICD-10 Classification of Mental and Behavioural Disorders: Clinical Descriptions and Diagnostic Guidelines* (Geneva: WHO, 1992).

Yannoulidis, Steven, 'Causation in the Law of Negligence' (2001) 27 *Monash University Law Review* 319.

—— 'Drug Use and the Defence of Mental Impairment: Some Conceptual and Explanatory Issues' (2006) 18 *Bond Law Review* 165.

—— 'Excusing Fleeting Mental States: Provocation, Involuntariness and Normative Practice' (2005) 12 *Psychiatry, Psychology and Law* 23.

—— 'Mental Illness, Rationality and Criminal Responsibility' (2003) 25 *Sydney Law Review* 189.

—— 'Negotiating "Dangerousness": Charting a Course Between Psychiatry and Law' (2002) 9 *Psychiatry, Psychology and Law* 151.

Yeo, Stanley M.H., 'Clarifying Automatism' (2002) 25 *International Journal of Law and Psychiatry* 445.
—— 'Commonwealth and International Perspectives on the Insanity Defence' (2008) 32 *Criminal Law Journal* 11.
—— 'The Insanity Defence in the Criminal Laws of the Commonwealth of Nations' [2008] *Singapore Journal of Legal Studies* 241.
—— (ed.), *Partial Excuses to Murder* (Sydney: Federation Press, 1991).
—— 'Reformulating Diminished Responsibility: Learning from the New South Wales Experience' (1999) 20 *Singapore Law Review* 159.
Zdenkowske, G., 'Community Protection through Imprisonment without Conviction: Pragmatism versus Justice' (1997) 3 *Australian Journal of Human Rights* 8.

Index

For Product Safety Concerns and Information please contact our EU representative GPSR@taylorandfrancis.com Taylor & Francis Verlag GmbH, Kaufingerstraße 24, 80331 München, Germany